Sport as History

Published to mark the career of one of sports history's pioneers, this book traces the evolution of sport across three continents. It brings together some of sports history's leading scholars to investigate not only the history of sport but also how that history is written.

This *Festschrift* marks the retirement of Professor Wray Vamplew – an internationally-renowned leader in the field of sports history. His 1976 book *The Turf* was one of the very first academic histories of sport and he has been a prolific writer, scholar and teacher for almost forty years. No-one has played such an important role in the field of sports history across North America, Europe and Australia. President of the Australian, Australian Society of Sports History (ASSH), the British Society of Sports History (BSSH), the European Committee for the History of Sport (CESH) and the International Society for the History of Physical Education and Sport (ISHPES), Vamplew is currently editor of the North American Society for Sports History's (NASSH) journal, the *Journal of Sport History*.

This collection reflects his interests and his appeal across the three continents: essays deal with sport in America, Australia, Britain and Ireland and focus on the themes of national and regional identity, gender, trade unionism in sport and historiographical debates. It is essential reading for anyone who wants to understand the history of sport and how it is studied today.

This book was published as a special issue of *Sport in History*.

Tony Collins is Professor of the Social History of Sport at Leeds Metropolitan University, UK. As well as writing a trilogy on the history of rugby - *Rugby's Great Split, Rugby League in Twentieth Century Britain* and *A Social History of English Rugby Union* - he has also worked with Wray Vamplew on the *Encyclopedia of Traditional Rural Sports* (all published by Routledge) and *Mud, Sweat and Beers: A Cultural History of Sport and Alcohol.*

Sport as History

Essays in Honour of Wray Vamplew

Edited by Tony Collins

Routledge
Taylor & Francis Group
LONDON AND NEW YORK

First published 2011
by Routledge
2 Park Square, Milton Park, Abingdon, Oxon, OX14 4RN

Simultaneously published in the USA and Canada
by Routledge
711 Third Avenue, New York, NY 10017

Routledge is an imprint of the Taylor & Francis Group, an informa business

First issued in paperback 2013

This book is a reproduction of *Sport in History*, vol. 29, issue 3. The Publisher requests to those authors who may be citing this book to state, also, the bibliographical details of the special issue on which the book was based

Typeset in Minion by Value Chain, India

British Library Cataloguing in Publication Data
A catalogue record for this book is available from the British Library

ISBN13: 978-0-415-57500-3 (hbk)
ISBN13: 978-0-415-85081-0 (pbk)

Contents

Abstracts

'An Excellent Means of Combining Fresh Air, Exercise and Society': Females on the Fairways, 1890–1914

Jane George

This paper attempts to give some focus to what the game of golf offered to women in a period which saw an expansion of leisure pursuits for the health and well-being of the middle class. With the establishment of a national body to develop the game in the interests of British women and the leadership of a few pioneers, consideration is given to what it was like for the 'fair sex' to participate in the male dominated world of golf.

Still Going After All These Years: Text, Truth and the *Racing Calendar*

Joyce Kay

The *Racing Calendar*, the 'bible' of the British turf, is one of the longest continuous series of sporting records in the world. Yet it is unlikely to receive the widespread recognition it deserves as a sporting text because it reflects a relatively minor sport in twenty-first century terms. This article will briefly outline its history, analyse its contents and attempt to evaluate its worth to historians of sport. Its reliability as a source will be scrutinised in the light of current debate, and the information it can supply with regard to gender and racing abroad will be assessed.

The Proto-globalisation of Horseracing 1730–1900: Anglo-American Interconnections

Mike Huggins

This study explores racing's global interconnectedness through an analysis of the ways in which English racing was represented, exploited and engaged by the American horseracing and thoroughbred breeding groups from c.1730 to 1900. It examines the American importation of British bloodstock; the formation of jockey clubs and rules and regulations of racing on the English model; the emigration to America of English jockeys and grooms; visits of English racing men; and media coverage of English racing. Finally it briefly examines the ways whereby American racing began in its turn to impinge upon England as American-bred horses began to compete on the English turf from the 1850s onward.

What Went Wrong with Counting? Thinking about Sport and Class in Britain and Ireland

Mike Cronin

This paper argues that the methodologies employed in much of Wray Vamplew's work, that of a 'traditional' economic historian, have great relevance in current studies of sports history. The issue of class, and in particular, the middle classes, have been a central theme in much recent sports history work, yet the work presented to date has not been underpinned by the kind of empirical work which Vamplew excelled at. The paper concludes that without a double approach — both empirical and cultural — our understanding of class and other key questions in sports history will be weakened.

Australian Sport History: From the Founding Years to Today

Daryl Adair

The academic study of sport history in Australia is a relatively recent initiative, dating back to the 1970s. It was inspired by a handful of enterprising scholars, each of whom is now retired. The following paper has two aims. First, it reflects on the efforts of early sport historians to carve out a research niche within the Australian academy. In keeping with the festschrift theme, it also dwells upon the profound influence of Wray Vamplew — a Yorkshireman who had the temerity to help pioneer sport history in an Antipodean setting. Second, the main body of the paper goes on to identify three key areas of research developed over the past thirty years by scholars of Australian sport history, then concludes with recommendations for further research.

The Tyranny of Deference: Anglo–Australian Relations and Rugby Union before World War II

Tony Collins

Historians have traditionally viewed sport in Australia as a vehicle for nationalist sentiment. This paper explores the history of Australian rugby union and its relationship with Britain in the first half of the twentieth century to argue against that assumption that sporting rivalry automatically means national rivalry at a cultural or political level. It suggests that the reality is much more complex and that, for rugby union at least, Australians were far more deferential to Britain than has hitherto been believed.

Boxers United: Trade Unionism in British Boxing in the 1930s

Matthew Taylor

Historians have been slow to follow the lead provided by Wray Vamplew's pioneering work on trade unionism in the British sports industry. The attention paid to permanent unions in sports such as golf and football has led to a neglect of those bodies which failed to make a lasting impact. This paper focuses on the history of one of those forgotten organisations, the National Union of Boxers (NUB). It argues that, despite organisational and financial difficulties, the NUB became an influential voice in the politics of British professional boxing during the 1930s.

Deeply Honoured: The Rise and Significance of the British Sporting Award, 1945–c.1970

Dave Russel

Focusing on four awards, the Sporting Record/Daily Express 'Sportsman/Sportswoman of the Year', the 'Footballer of the Year', the Sportswriters's 'Sportsman/Sportswoman of the Year' and the BBC's 'Sports Personality of the Year', this study examines the general factors impacting upon the establishment of a sporting 'honours system' in the 1940s and the specific commercial and political reasons behind the foundation of these individual awards. It argues that while such awards can have an 'objective' value in helping us identify contemporary sporting pantheons, they are best seen as cultural rituals designed to elevate particular models of sporting behaviour, encourage a belief in the expert status of sports journalists, and to allow sporting stars and the sports media to show themselves to the public in the kindest possible light.

'In a Yorkshire Like Way': Cricket and the Construction of Regional Identity in Nineteenth-century Yorkshire

Rob Light

This paper examines how by 1900 cricket had come to be seen as an important representation of Yorkshire identity. It places the start of this process in the game's popular pre-modern context, as professional-centred, competitive, commercial cricket dominated its formative development across the region. The way these values led to local rivalries which became focused on the concept of a representative team building Yorkshire's status within the national context of cricket is then explored. Finally these events are set against the formation of the 'Gentleman Amateur' controlled county club in 1863, to show how a distinctive concept of county cricket developed in Yorkshire which offers a different perspective on the English county game during its formative decade and beyond.

Egg and Chips with the Connellys: Remembering 1966

Dilwyn Porter

More than 40 years have passed since England beat West Germany to win FIFA's World Cup in 1966 yet this singular historical event remains with us, securely embedded in English popular culture and revisited by the media whenever occasion justifies. References to it are so frequent and so ubiquitous that they have become banal yet powerful signifiers of English national identity. It is argued here that the folk memory of 1966 is also shaped by the way in which the story of England's triumph dovetails with other narratives through which the English try to make sense of the world they live in and the history they have lived through.

Introduction

Tony Collins

There are many Wray Vamplews. The economic historian. The historian of British sport. The Australian sports historian. The pro-vice chancellor. The pioneer. The teacher. The fan.

This festschrift aims to reflect just a part of that many-faceted career, by engaging with his work, building on his contributions to history, and reflecting some of his enthusiasms. The contributors are those who have worked with Wray, those who have been his research assistants and PhD students, and some who have merely been inspired by his work. Given more time, this could have been a multi-volumed work, such was the appreciation of Wray's career in Europe, Australia and North America.

Just to glance at the bibliography compiled here by Richard Cox is to appreciate the sheer volume of Wray's scholarly output. Few historians range so confidently across so many fields, and even fewer can claim the authority gained by such extensive archival research. His work has encompassed the entire lifetime of the history of sport as a distinct discipline. *The Turf: A Social and Economic History of Horse Racing* published in 1976 was the first serious historical monograph to be published on sport in Britain. It was followed by numerous other works, perhaps most notably the 1982 *Economic History Review* (EHR) article on 'The Economics of a Sports Industry: Scottish Gate Money Football, 1890–1914', which even today remains one of the *EHR*'s few excursions into the history of sport.

The culmination of this pioneering period of Wray's work was *Pay Up and Play the Game*, ostensibly a study of the rise of professional sport in Britain between 1875 and 1914 but in fact an economic history of sport from the

Tony Collins, Institute of Northern Studies, Leeds Metropolitan University.

mid-eighteenth century. Needless to say, it was equally at ease discussing theories of profit maximisation alongside descriptions of the daily tribulations of the nineteenth-century cricket professional. For me, and I suspect many others, the publication in 1988 of *Pay Up and Play the Game* – and of Tony Mason's 1981 *Association Football and English Society, 1863–1915* – finally settled the argument about the value of studying the history of sport. Moreover, they provided the tools with which to investigate it.

But research and publication are merely a fraction of Wray's overall contribution to history. There are dozens, perhaps hundreds, of students and scholars at all levels who have benefited personally from his advice and guidance, including myself. Open, inclusive and democratic with everyone he encountered, he is a man who has led and inspired by example.

As Daryl Adair's article makes clear, Wray also played a pivotal role in Australia in establishing sport as a legitimate field for historians. This was not simply due to his extensive research and publications on the history of Australian sport. Wray's egalitarian ethos also heavily influenced the culture of the field down under, especially in the culture of the Australian Society of Sports History (ASSH). When ASSH held a roundtable discussion to celebrate its thirtieth anniversary in 2007, the three speakers – founders of ASSH Richard Cashman, Braham Dabscheck and John O'Hara – all paid tribute to the crucial role played by Wray in the organisation's history. It is also safe to say that without Wray's contribution at so many levels, sports history in Britain would be immeasurably poorer.

The great Yorkshire and England batsman Herbert Sutcliffe is reputed to have once told a reporter 'I'm only setting these records so Hutton can break them'. Perhaps unconsciously Wray echoed his fellow Yorkshireman in the preface to *Pay Up and Play the Game*, when he wrote that 'nothing would please me more than that all my chapters be rendered obsolete within the next decade, for it would signal that substantial research had been undertaken in the subject'. It is a challenge that still stands.

'An Excellent Means of Combining Fresh Air, Exercise and Society': Females on the Fairways, 1890–1914

Jane George

This paper attempts to give some focus to what the game of golf offered to women in a period which saw an expansion of leisure pursuits for the health and well-being of the middle class. With the establishment of a national body to develop the game in the interests of British women and the leadership of a few pioneers, consideration is given to what it was like for the 'fair sex' to participate in the male dominated world of golf.

> Golf is a perfect game for women; here they can walk at their own pace, in fresh air. At golf they may 'drive' as they like, no harm results. Their lungs are filled with fresh air, their shoulders expanded. They tread lightly the verdant pasture land. Nothing in the way of healthful exercise, incited by an object in view, is to compare with golf. [1]

In recent years Wray Vamplew's work in golf history has highlighted the extent of professionals within the sport both as players and as club servants. He has also given consideration to the humble caddies as well as the other employees of private clubs focusing on their involvement in the game from the early part of the nineteenth century to the start of World War I. Some of this material has been presented as conference papers as well as being published in academic journals. But as yet there are relatively few articles which focus on those who pioneered women's golf and their endeavour to involve more women in the game not only at a social level but as competitive participants. This article offers some consideration of

Jane George, University of Stirling.

what it was like for British women to participate in the male dominated world of golf.

Whether viewed as purely recreational or played in a competitive manner, the game of golf offered middle-class women the opportunity to engage in a healthy outdoor pursuit with opportunities to improve their sporting skills. While not attempting to defy the conventions imposed on women by fashionable society, their enthusiasm and motivation to participate was undertaken in a positive spirit. In banding together to form their own clubs as well as instituting a national union to represent their interests, the nature of these pioneering women in their endeavour to be recognised and accepted as valid participants in their own right, requires to be considered and celebrated.

Domestic goddesses

Although occupying a significant social space in the twentieth century, it is generally agreed that women have been largely excluded from the sporting revolution of the late nineteenth and early twentieth centuries and that British sport has traditionally been regarded as a male preserve. [2] This leads one to believe that women were only on the periphery of sport and not part of it. As argued by Tranter, what was partly responsible for their limited involvement was the 'ideology of domesticity' something which 'was sufficient to restrict women to a subordinate, minor and persistently derided role'. [3] Hargreaves, in her analysis of the social constructs of gender in the relationship of sport and social class to women, suggests that the complexities surrounding the ideological 'domesticity' issue of middle-class women in the latter part of the nineteenth century prevented many women from involvement in 'vigorous and diverse forms of physical activities'. [4] She points to constraints emanating from the social position of women who were expected to adopt 'appropriate' behaviour which reflected their class as well as their gender. As Holt indicates, those women who did become involved in sport had to strike 'a delicate balance between physical emancipation and social respectability' which could be one of the reasons why only a minority of middle-class women became active participants in sports during the late Victorian and Edwardian period. [5]

If middle-class women did indulge in sport they were considered to be entering a masculine world. Women could be regarded as legitimate participants by men and accepted as such if they played to their own strengths and abilities and retained their 'womanliness'. An aggressive, reckless, muscular type of woman was not the feminine ideal; therefore the more attention sportswomen paid to the requisites of ideal womanhood, the more social acceptance they found. The stereotypical images of women as the 'weaker sex' and 'fair sex' accentuated their supposed lack of ability and seriousness of purpose. If women participated then they had to do so within the bounds of the middle-class understanding of 'ladylike' behaviour. The sporting activities that women undertook reflected a leisurely outlook with much emphasis on maintaining femininity in whatever was undertaken. As far as their health was concerned the underlying notion was that sport could be beneficial to women but as Ada Ballin declared, 'moderation in all things should be the motto of the Sportswoman'. [6] As a professional journalist and the editor of *Womanhood*, a monthly magazine which featured articles on health, hygiene, beauty and sport, Ballin considered 'rational physical training' important in women's lives. [7] Middle-class women tended towards feminine-appropriate sports such as tennis and golf which offered opportunities for social contact and moderate exercise. More significantly these sports were deemed acceptable in middle-class society and women could emphasise their femininity by the way they adopted a playing style which reflected their gender difference.

While issues reflecting femininity, class and accessibility were important in the Victorian period, on the golf course fashion as well as showing femininity in playing style emphasised the gender difference. In the 1890s, the majority of women golfers complied with what was expected and appeared in clothing which hampered to some degree their style of play. They realised that if they did not fit the social construct of femininity at this time, they could become the subject of derision and individuals could be singled out because of their flamboyant nature in approach and dress sense. Mrs Louie Mackern, a well-known player at Blackheath, advised lady golfers not to step beyond the bounds of their position by drawing unwarranted attention to themselves. She was scornful of those who advocated 'hunting ties, shapeless red coats and the narrowest of bicycling skirts' as, in her opinion, they were doing no service to the image of the lady golfer. Moreover, she disapproved of the bicycling skirt with its side pockets which encouraged ladies to ape the mannerisms of men if they 'rammed both hands into the pockets'. [8] Miss May Hezlet, from a Irish family of golfers, was another who was never short of advice and cautioned that anything that made the wearer conspicuous was out of place on the links and would be judged negatively by non-golfers. Some cartoonists were beginning to challenge traditional ideas of female frailty and poke fun at the robustness of the sporting 'New Woman' especially in the case of golfers and any divergence from the norm was immediately seized upon and lampooned. [9]

Out of sight, out of mind

To begin with, women remained in passive mode as onlookers, bystanders and supporters of their golfer husbands, fathers and brothers. But they soon realised the pleasure of being outdoors and the benefits to health which a round on the links offered. While some held back, meekly accepting their subservient role, others ignored the restrictions imposed by clubs and social convention and were unwilling to be excluded as participants. If golf was no more than a diverting pastime for some, for more serious sportswomen it offered competition and the opportunity to participate at club, county and even national level. It has to be recognised that the way women were perceived as participants in golf is complex and issues of social acceptance deterred as well as determined the extent of their involvement in Britain. [10] Surprisingly a demographic divide was evident as John Kerr, the nineteenth-century Scottish clergyman and golf historian opined that, 'English ladies had so to speak, a fair start . . . North of the Tweed the ladies were handicapped by a past'. [11] This implies that Englishmen were more liberal than their Scottish counterparts when it came to accepting ladies on the links, although it has to be said not all male golfers stood aside and gave way. [12] There did appear however to be something of a tradition of inviting a lady to hit the first ball when a new club or course was opened in Scotland as in Biggar in June 1895, when Miss Thomson of Huntfield, daughter of founder member, A.J. Thomson, duly drove off the first ball. She was presented with a silver mounted clock as a memento of the occasion. [13] A decade later on the opening of a new course at Ballater in 1906, the honour of hitting the first ball went to Mrs Anderson, wife of club president Mr H.G. Anderson who disclosed a prior acquaintance with the game as her 'well hit shot' was greeted with 'a hearty cheer'. [14]

Nevertheless men were unenthusiastic about women as golfers and felt they should know their place as implied in the line from George Fullerton Carnegie's classic poem, 'The Golfiad'; '. . . Men play the game . . . and lovely woman give the prize away'. [15] Lord Wellwood, formerly Henry James Moncrieff, a Scottish High Court judge and a member of North Berwick Golf Club, considered women an intrusion and voiced a typical reactionary Victorian response to women golfers in 1890 questioning their right to play the 'long round' with or without male companions. He queried their motives for play on men's courses and his attitude was that if women wanted to play it should be on terms dictated by men and they should be kept well out of sight. He need not have agitated so as the North Berwick ladies had already been provided with their own course in 1888 so that 'the flutter of petticoats' did not add to the distraction of the male players. [16] However women had an ally in the Reverend John Kerr who was more supportive and encouraging than Wellwood. As minister of Dirleton Parish Church in East Lothian, he had observed that North Berwick ladies who appeared to be serious and even rather competent at golf, playing '(. . .) in a style which some gentlemen themselves might well have tried to emulate'. [17] His supportive view was confirmed by Eustace White, the sport journalist, who rejected those men who 'eyed them with disproval' as 'their aptitude for the game was too evident and their quality of play too fine to permit the continuance of such a reproach'. [18] Indeed Mabel Stringer, a golfer and journalist, was of the opinion that men would eventually 'come to eat their words as the majority of the men who became converted to women's golf were as vehement in their support as they had been violent in their prejudice'. [19]

So it was in these circumstances that women began to take to the links, some with trepidation but others with more determination. They were no doubt influenced to some extent in their pursuit by popular literature and fashionable magazines of the day such as *The Gentlewoman* and *Ladies' Field* specifically aimed at the upper middle classes. With the journalistic aim to expound 'traditional virtues' and entertain the readership with gossip from court, tittle-tattle from society and promote the latest fashions in couture and in the arts, one would think there would be little heed paid to the interests of sportswomen. But in more serious mode in an attempt to encourage a healthy lifestyle, the editors devoted some space to features on sport, health and fitness. Illustrated notes began to appear on hunting, tennis, archery and golf with golf being seen as 'an excellent means of combining fresh air, exercise and society'. [20] The Rt. Honourable Arthur Balfour, a keen exponent of the game, reiterated the importance of outdoor exercise and the aim of achieving '. . . a degree of excellence which will give great satisfaction to themselves and considerable embarrassment to their opponents!' [21]

Pioneering leadership

Despite the fact that women were playing informal games, joining clubs, as well as getting involved in competition at club and inter-club level, there was no infrastructure in place to promote the game, oversee the vagaries of club handicapping or to bring together the best players to challenge each other in a national competition. The motivation to develop women's golf along separate lines and create a formal national body which would help to raise standards of play and proficiency came from Miss Issette Pearson (later Mrs T.H. Miller). Miss Pearson born in 1861, the daughter of a businessman, was one of the 'movers and shakers' of the ladies' golfing world in the 1890s. Her credentials as a golfer were well respected and she had always been a competitive player. Having already led a group of ladies at Wimbledon Golf Club in reforming the ailing ladies' section in the late 1880s, her primary interest was to establish a national structure to further women's golf and engage interest in national competition. This she felt necessary if women's golf was to progress and develop.

Having circulated all the known ladies' golf clubs in Britain Miss Pearson called those who might be interested to a preliminary meeting in London at the Grand Hotel, Northumberland Avenue on 19 April 1893. [22] As a safeguard she enlisted the support of Mr Laidlaw Purves, a Scot and one of the leading players from the Wimbledon Club, to assist with the initial organisation of the meeting. Purves was sympathetic with the objectives of the ladies as he had tried to establish a similar golfing association for men, albeit unsuccessfully. Paying tribute to the ladies present at the meeting he indicated that their presence signified 'the welfare of present and future golfers, which had not been evinced to the majority of the other sex'. His attention was now to support the ladies and give his backing to the scheme. [23] The meeting also received support from *The Gentlewoman*, which reported the instigation of the Ladies Golf Union (LGU) as 'a much needed movement for lady golfers'. [24] Thus the LGU was formed on 19 April 1893 and within two months had made all the necessary arrangements for the first Ladies' British Open Amateur Championship to take place from 13 to 18 June 1893, indicating just how efficient women were as organisers. As Joyce Wethered, the champion golfer of the 1920s claimed, 'women have an innate love for doing things thoroughly in matters of organisation and no less so in ladies' golf'. [25]

The formidable Miss Pearson was often criticised for the autocratic way she wielded power and would not tolerate interference from 'outsiders' when it came to matters concerning women's golf, and was reputedly 'as despotic as the Czar of Russia'. [26] While she could not have envisaged the change she would bring to golf in Britain, Miss Pearson's strong will and domineering manner gave women's golf the leader it needed.

Competition and society

The majority of women who participated in golf in the late nineteenth and early twentieth century viewed the game as a social activity while those with a competitive nature welcomed the chance to increase their skill in friendly competition. At this level golf was strictly amateur. Winning at all costs was not in the spirit of the game but taking part and exchanging news over tea in the clubhouse afterwards was far more important. If ladies entered competitions or tournaments in their locale or further afield, a small entry fee was paid and if successful the reward might be a trophy or more personalised prizes of silverware in the form of jewellery, trinket boxes or compacts. They were not expecting monetary prizes of any kind and vouchers to redeem in the professionals' shop were a long way off.

But the idea of determining the best golfer had been first muted by the ladies of St Anne's Golf Club in Lancashire in April 1893. They had visualised an 'open' competition and had already received contributions towards the purchase of a challenge cup. That several ladies' clubs were wealthy enough and willing to subscribe generously towards a cup indicates that there was some interest in the idea of a Ladies Championship which would be an 'open' championship to decide the best golfer. Combining forces, the newly formed LGU agreed to organise the national championship with St Anne's providing hospitality and the use of their course. This club had a reputation of 'treating its female members with fairness', which indicates that they could rely on assistance from the male members of the club. [27] The Ladies' Championship week from 13 to 18 June 1893 provided the opportunity for 38 ladies to compete on a short but tricky course as well as socialise before and after which of course was an important aspect of golf in the 1890s.

The inaugural championship attracted a few spectators 'largely motivated by curiosity about how women could play'. [28] This was the first opportunity for the general public to witness an official golfing event involving women. Mabel Stringer, an LGU official and instigator of county golf, recollected being present at the inaugural championship as a child and recalled with hindsight that it was 'a great occasion complete with marquees, flags, brass bands, etc.' [29] Subsequent championships established themselves as serious and viable events and were played over men's courses quickly disproving Horace Hutchison's sceptical mutterings that, 'they will never last through two rounds of a long course in a day'. [30]

When the championship ventured north of the border to Gullane in east Lothian in May 1897, the ladies had a chance to combine competition with local hospitality. As in previous years, an important element in the build up to the actual Championship was the garden parties and other social activities organised in the grounds of large local houses. On this occasion James Law, proprietor of *The Scotsman* invited participants to his home at Archerfield, a large estate with a private golf links, and organised a pre-championship competition with prizes donated by eminent local dignitaries. Seventy-two ladies played in a stroke play competition and were entertained to tea afterwards where, according to a report, everything was organised with 'great attention to detail'. [31] The competitors were also given access to practice on the course at Gullane prior to the championship and play in a stroke play competition. The competition, held on a local holiday, in recognition of the queen's birthday (24th May) gave the 100 competitors who entered a chance to familiarise themselves with the course, as well as to compete for prizes. This practise of playing for material as opposed to monetary prizes was well established by 1897 and the value of these material objects indicates the wealth of those who were part of the golfing establishment. While the members of Gullane Golf Club donated a necklace (valued at 10 guineas) and a pair of silver-mounted scent bottles, the captain of the club contributed a gold bangle. Not to be outdone, the LGU presented a silver hand mirror and a silver toilet box to the winners of the driving and pitching competitions. [32]

The 'ideal' lady golfer

If lady golfers wanted to emulate anyone in the 1890s they had a role model in Lady Margaret Scott. Lady Margaret born in 1874 was the second daughter in a family of seven and grew up playing golf with her father, Lord Eldon and brothers on a private nine-hole course on the family estate at Stowell Park in Gloucestershire. At the age of eighteen Lord Eldon's daughter set a standard for women by demonstrating that she could combine golfing stylishness with elegance; a stylist with a graceful swing, despite being hampered by tight fitting undergarments, she presented an image of grace and beauty at the first Ladies' Championship in 1893. Conventionally and acceptably attired in a blouse with leg of mutton sleeves, tight fitting to the wrists and wasp-waisted, a heavy full length skirt, a pair of leather gloves to protect her hands and a straw boater (no doubt held securely in place with hat pins), she played her way through the preliminary rounds in a confident manner. Her victory over LGU honorary secretary, Issette Pearson in the final round by seven and five, delighted the spectators showing to 'what pitch of perfection a lady golfer might rise' as well as reassuring the critics that golf could be competitive as well as fashionable. [33] Lady Margaret stood out in a class of her own among those competitors in the early championships by winning three consecutive titles relatively effortlessly, although at Royal Portrush in 1895, she had more of a contest in the semi-final when Mrs Ryder Richardson (at one point being four holes up) looked like defeating her. But her concentration, coolness and self-possession pulled her through and in the final she gained a 'runaway' victory over Miss E. Lythgoe. [34] Horace Hutchison, an amateur champion himself, previously dismissive of women golfers generally, admired Lady Margaret's accuracy and her ability to 'pick the ball off an indifferent, unsympathetic lie ... and send it flying straight to the mark'. [35] Arguably the quality of her game set the standard for other women to aim for and with her unbeaten record intact, she retired gracefully from championship golf in Britain leaving the way clear for others.

Dress sense and playing style

Women who took up golf in the 1890s appeared to accept that wearing clothes which restricted freedom and ease of movement merely signified the restrictions of their gender. Appearing on the links at St Andrews and elsewhere 'conventionally' attired, dressed for daytime visiting, it was clear that they were handicapped and unable to play with real freedom of movement or any degree of abandon. The question might be asked, why then, if they wanted to pursue a game which required a certain degree of physicality, would they want to constrain themselves in the conventional fashions of the day? As McCrone argues, 'prevailing fashions seemed purposely designed to prevent women from performing aesthetically'. [36] Tight corsets, blouses or jackets with leg of mutton sleeves, high tight-necked collars and full length skirts inhibited the manner of play and although women might have questioned the point of wearing 'fashionable' clothing for golf, it was the general belief that conventional dress must be worn. Were they demonstrating to society that they were women first and golfers second? It would appear that it was important for these players to observe convention rather than look out of place or deliberately shock.

The question of achieving liberty and freedom in the golf swing with respect to a woman's restraining undergarments also took time to resolve. If women were to be taken seriously in sport and progress from merely 'playing at golf' in polite society to playing golf with more purpose and zeal, then their underwear as well as their outer clothing must alter in order to accommodate more freedom. But how to maintain femininity in their shape along with the desire for more freedom in clothing gave designers some headaches. Dress reformers had tried to persuade women of the damage constricting undergarments might do to their bodies, but as Roberts concedes, 'an uncorseted woman was in danger of being accused of loose morals' and that would have been de rigueur in the 1890s. [37] Loose clothing was associated with loose living and at a time when behaviour of a moral as well as a physical nature was rigidly controlled, women had to contend with a variety of opinions in relation to preconceived conventions concerning their position in society. A solution was found in devising an athletic corset constructed in a strong linen with an elastic belt and an elastic gore at the front and side which allowed for the movements required in golfing. Altering the existing form of restrictive undergarment to incorporate the freedom to swing a golf club ensured therefore the comfort of golfers.

Playing with smooth and elegant strokes without exerting any obvious force and pressure was viewed as a primary consideration in maintaining femininity. From the tee, a full swing would deliver a longer drive if cleanly hit but a half swing could also cover the same distance with as much accuracy and did not call for more exertion than 'the push of a punt pole'. [38] When reference was made to women golfers in newspapers and golfing journals, remarks were frequently directed towards their appearance and demeanour. As Hargreaves observed of sportswomen, 'on the one hand they are newsworthy for their athletic efforts and successes, but because sport still poses a threat to popular ideas about femininity, readers are assured in various ways that they remain 'real' women'. [39] This is reflected by one newspaper reporter commenting on the 'femininity', grace and beauty of the winner of the Scottish Ladies' Championship played over the Old Course, St Andrews in 1903. Miss Alexa Glover is credited with qualities similarly attributed to Lady Margaret Scott and depicted as '(. . .) a typical athletic girl of the newest school . . . with her rose-leaf complexion, golden hair and pretty air of aloofness. Not the sunburnt hoyden who used to come to the front in active exercises'. Additionally it also pointed out that her 'gait' had 'a certain masculinity' – perhaps a taste of things to come. [40]

On the question of fashionable outer wear there was the male attitude to consider as well. From the early 1900s rather than wearing tight fitting blouses, golfers who wanted to be taken seriously began to appear at tournaments and championships attired in stiff-starched collar shirts with ties or cravats and jackets which sported their club insignia. This gave them a distinctly mannish appearance. McCrone identifies this gesture of incorporating a masculine image as 'a kind of contradictory tribute and challenge to the male world that was being invaded'. [41] These symbols of masculinity did not, however, have the same significance for women as for men. While women might adopt this type of 'club uniform', the symbolism of the 'old school tie' only had connotations in a man's world. Jackets and ties gave a more distinguished appearance to the upper half of the body but women were only prepared to sacrifice their feminine appearance above the waist. The retention of a skirt safeguarded their femininity and was the dominating image of the female golfer for several more decades. While a few daring female cyclists had taken to wearing bloomers, women golfers tended to be rather wary of causing provocation and felt it was their duty to counteract the women who 'showed six inches of her stocking beneath her skirts and loosened her corsets'. [42] They were guided by the authoritative voice of the LGU and other commentators who offered advice on what was considered correct and appropriate. First and foremost, a smart appearance was considered to be essential in protecting golfers from being ridiculed. It was the duty of the leaders in women's golf to make the position clear on this.

Playing together

It is evident from written sources as well as interviews conducted with women golfers that the prime motivation for girls to play golf came from the family. [43] Young girls whose parents were golfers had more likelihood of developing an interest in the game than those who had no golfing connections. Parents, especially fathers, were often considered as role models by their daughters while other male family members such as brothers and uncles played a prominent part in encouraging girls into golf. [44] Girls had a tendency to admire the sporting prowess of their fathers and brothers and wanted to emulate them as shown by Lady Margaret Scott. Similarly, Alexa Glover from Fife was another young woman who benefitted from watching and learning from her father and brother. She also learned to play at a young age in the 1890s round the links at Elie and was also fortunate enough to play regularly in Europe in the company of her father. [45]

While early depictions of mixed golf in cartoon form often trivialised and emphasised the flirtatious nature 'spawned by a desire to attract a husband', playing alongside men actually helped increase their skill and improve the standard of women's golf. [46] The policy at Bishop Auckland Golf Club was for all competitions to be mixed until the first mention of a 'ladies only' competition in 1908. [47] The Edinburgh club, Craigmillar Park, known for its equality from the outset, reported that the Mixed Championship on Finals Day in 1896 was by far and away the most popular of the competitions with 53 couples entering. [48] This club also recorded that the first match played in May of that year was a 'mixed doubles' against Edinburgh Ladies' Golf Club. [49] However gentlemen could also be ambivalent towards female golfers as is evident at Blackburn Golf Club where the ladies were refused permission to join the LGU in 1894 as the club felt it could not justify the entrance fee and subscription, but were eventually allowed to join 19 years later with the club providing the fee. [50] Sometimes incentives backfired as at Braemar Golf Club when in 1903 local ladies were allowed to play free of charge only to have the privilege withdrawn the following year as the club's debts increased. [51] To help bail out the club, the ladies were called on to help to raise the sum of £600 at a Grand Bazaar held on 17 and 18 August 1905. Sadly there is no record to indicate if the target was achieved but the club must have benefitted from the ladies' organisational skills as stallholders as the club incurred no debts the following year. [52]

It was the policy at some clubs to positively encourage families to participate together especially in the holiday season. Blairgowrie was proving to be one such popular destination for families where the golf club welcomed seasonal visitors. During the summer of 1894 this enterprising golf club offered the incentive of a reduced daily ticket of 1 shilling rather than 5 shillings and a special competition for visitors in August with the reward of substantial prizes; for ladies, a first prize of a patent driver and a second prize of six golf balls and for the gentlemen, a first prize of a dozen golf balls with a second prize of a golf bag. [53] In 1905, the *Golf Annual* reported that the Royal Hotel in Blairgowrie was offering a special tariff for golfers of 10 shillings a day or 2 pounds, 10 shillings a week. [54]

Ultimately women's golf would develop independently and separately from the men's game both at club and national level.

'Ladies' or 'Amazons'?

While the young and elegant Lady Margaret set the standard for the 'ideal' woman golfer, another female was in danger of usurping this image in the form of a precociously talented upstart by the name of Cecilia Leitch – Cecil for short. Something of a 'trailblazer' for women's golf, Cecil been introduced to golf at the age of nine by her father, a doctor from Fife, and along with her five sisters was encouraged to play on the exposed links of Silloth in Cumbria. She was a natural player and self taught with a style which had developed along independent lines. Wind was almost the normal condition at Silloth, and her game adapted accordingly to suit the conditions. Adopting a wide stance and taking a loose flat swing which emphasised her power, she drove aggressively through the ball finishing with a full follow-through. Her father and Eustace White, sports editor of the *Ladies' Field* thought her good enough at the age of 17 to enter the Ladies' Championship at St Andrews in 1908, where she reached the semi-final. [55] This was her first ever competitive event. Cecil certainly stood out as being 'ahead of her time' and different from the rest of the competitors appearing hatless with a large bow holding back her hair, a mid-calf length skirt and a shirt and tie. Her appearance attracted just as much attention as her style of play. Both sartorially and stylistically she seemed uninhibited having abandoned the restrictions of tight clothing and the graceful elegance of other golfers. Leitch as 'the first of the Amazons' was more powerful and in marked stylistic contrast to Lady Margaret Scott. [56] Reflecting on the impact made by Cecil, Eleanor Helme, a golf journalist, opined in 1955 that '(. . .) it was [Cecil] a mere semi-finalist, who made history once and for all at St Andrews in 1908, and made it because she went out to hit the ball with might and main, not merely trying to persuade it away by beauty of swing and timing'. [57] This was a new and startling doctrine that a woman should hit the ball so ferociously and so far. Bodily strength and muscularity symbolically associated with masculine power was uncharacteristic of the majority of women golfers at this time.

A potential role model for introducing younger women into golf, the precocious Cecil, at the age of 19 took on a male opponent, Harold Hilton in October 1910. Hilton was something of a sporting superhero having twice gained victory in the Open Championship as an amateur, and also in winning the Amateur Championship. But this was not the first time Cecil had played against men. She had already encountered James Braid at Walton Heath in 1909 and in February of the following year, had beaten Tom Ball, the professional, by one hole at Blundellsands. [58] The purpose of the Hilton match was to promote women's golf and with sponsorship from the *Ladies' Field*, the event was played over two rounds of 36 holes. Driving from the same tees on two fairly long courses (Walton Heath 6,322 yards and Sunningdale, 6,306 yards), interest was directed on the strength of each golfer. But what was equally important was the question of whether a young woman would have the mental capacity to withstand a competitive match of 72 holes against an experienced man. Miss Leitch was allowed nine strokes per 18 holes, according to Hilton's estimate of handicapping, receiving a stroke on the even-numbered holes. The first round of 36 holes was played at Walton Heath on 11 October. This event at the height of the women's suffrage campaign appeared to have caught the public imagination and attracted an estimated 3,000–4,000 spectators, no doubt enjoying the fine weather as well as the golf. [59] The result of the first day's play was a lead of one hole for Hilton with the players given a day's rest before resuming the second half of the match. The weather conditions on 13 October could not have been worse with a strong wind and drenching rain and a depleted crowd of around 1,500. Miss Leitch who looked like being defeated came back from being five holes down to win two up with one to play and this was celebrated by some as a victory for women's liberation. As Cecil later commented, the match 'certainly increased the interest taken in ladies' golf by the amateurs [meaning the male players], and vice versa, and before long a Ladies v. Men Match became an annual event at Stoke Poges'. [60]

Miss Leitch regularly offered instructional advice to the novice in the columns of the *Ladies' Field*. In 1911 she published *Golf for Girls* where she imparted to the young her advice on the type of clubs to suit the individual, as well as her experience of the competitive game, conceding that she had received many valuable tips from men, including Harold Hilton, Tom Ball and Arnaud Massy. This advice she considered greatly encouraging and valuable. Cecil was the number one lady golfer in the first decades of the twentieth century winning her first Ladies' Championship at Hunstanton in 1914. Had the First World War not intervened she might have achieved more but her run of victories continued in 1920 and 1921 with the final one coming in 1926. By the 1920s, her great rival Joyce Wethered was mounting a serious challenge.

Advice to would-be 'professionals'

To reflect the interest in ladies' golf in the 1890s, a collection of essays and reports along with profiles of prominent players were included in the first book on ladies' golf in Britain published in 1899. [61] Edited by Louie Mackern and M. Boys with contributions from other well-known golfers including Issette Pearson and Amy Bennet Pascoe, advice was given on the management of clubs, the etiquette of the game, and the merits of being taught golf by women. Also included in the book was a directory of ladies's clubs and courses which provided useful information for those who wished to join or visit a specific club.

On the subject of raising playing standards, it was the belief of Miss Boys and others that women were quite capable of instructing other women. Having consulted a golf professional (male) on this matter, she concurred with his opinion that a lady would understand more fully than a man 'the limitation of her own sex in strength' and conceivably be better qualified in this respect to teach than a man. [62] Miss Boys did not deem it necessary for an aspiring instructor to be a 'scratch' golfer in order to become a first-class expert of golf. There should of course be some standard of competence and she suggested that the LGU might vet women who aspired to be teaching professionals by organising 'authorized inspectors' from their ranks to 'put the applicant through her paces in every branch of the game'. As she explained '(. . .) the technicalities of golf tax a brain of no mean calibre, and for those who aspire to become professionals, the science of the game must be minutely studied and completely mastered'. [63] By becoming a female 'professional' those who did undertake this would have to realise that their social relationship with other ladies would change as a result and '. . . [they] must realise at the outset that once a "pro", they are no longer on the same par as their amateur friends'. [64] There could be no question of a professional entering an amateur competition. The concept of professionalism did not lie easily with Miss Boys who differentiated here between ladies who played golf purely for pleasure and those who considered it as their profession. There was obviously a question of social status involved as well with the lady golfer assuming superiority over the professional. She considered that if women took up golf as a trade they would 'have to begin as caddies and rise by degrees to notoriety and championships'. [65] Miss Boys thought that there might be few if any 'lady' golfers who would consider earning their living this way as this would have lost them their social status and in the eyes of a middle-class woman, would have lowered golf to the level of a trade. While men had a tradition of caddying and playing for prizes this would have been problematical for women as there was no tradition of females caddying in the men's championships and no championship where women would have been welcomed as 'professional' competitors. Rather optimistically she concluded that:

> No doubt the pioneer lady professional will meet with many difficulties and considerable opposition at the start, but, as in all cases of similar innovations, time will smooth over the strangeness, until it is a recognised thing for each lady's golf club to have its own woman club-maker and professional duly certificated by the Ladies' Golf Union. [66]

This was entirely speculative as there is no record of the LGU having certificated anyone as a club maker. Whether many ladies would have considered undertaking the duties of an instructor along with the duties of greenkeeper or caretaker in the clubhouse is another matter. There was something rather distasteful about doing something which involved a degree of manual or menial work. Club making in addition to club repairing would ensure that earnings might amount to about £90 a year, but this was an income which a 'lady' would have great difficulty living on. [67] Vamplew records that club professionals (as opposed to playing professionals) were employed by golf clubs and were required not only to teach but to make and repair clubs, sell clubs and other equipment, train assistants and apprentices and often be responsible for the duties of greenkeeping as well as club caretaking. [68] The hardship and drudgery of these duties would not have appealed to women, therefore earning a living from golf was never a consideration for women. The LGU records indicate there were no female 'professionals' as such at this time. They were not on a par with men as far as becoming a club 'professional' was concerned and they would never have been invited to give exhibition matches or play in professional tournaments. However giving instruction was another matter. Mrs Maud Gordon Robertson, daughter of the Rev. Fortescue Anderson of North Berwick was a 'professional teacher' at the Prince's Ladies' Club in Surrey from 1905. With a membership of over 300 ladies, Mrs Robertson would not have been short of work. [69] A few other women with golfing family connections were also known to have become female instructors. Miss Lily Freemantle, for example, the daughter of a professional, was employed by Sunningdale Ladies in 1911. At the same time Miss D.M. Smyth who had for some years been a member of the Barnehurst Golf Club, Bexley Heath, was appointed as a professional to Le Touquet Ladies' Club in the south of France. [70] However these 'professionals' were purely instructors for ladies and were not employed to take on other duties associated with club professionals such as club repair or club making.

Interestingly Mrs Robertson hailed from a family of keen golfers and it is known that her elder brother was secretary of Royal Portrush. [71] As well as teaching at Prince's where one of her pupils was Mrs Herbert Fowler, wife of the golf course architect who designed Walton Heath and West Surrey, Mrs Robertson also arranged tuition at schools and private homes and advertised her services in a sporting journal. [72] To assist newcomers to golf, her booklet of instruction, *Hints to Lady Golfers*, offered practical advice to those who had taken up golf 'for the sake of pleasure and health'. [73] This must have been a godsend for the golfing novice. Like male professionals she was not averse to a spot of commercial promotion and endorsement recommending that ladies should play with Dunlop balls. This particular brand of golf ball she considered 'most excellent' and advised that lady golfers would find that they could get maximum length with minimum exertion by using them. [74]

With an expansion in the number of women joining golf clubs, there was obviously a need for instructors to teach female members. A golf school (the first of its kind) opened in London in 1908 and this gave employment to Scottish male professionals from north of the border. However there is no evidence of female instructors being employed here, although of the 100 pupils who attended lessons, a large percentage were ladies. The head instructor at the New Golf School in Regent's Park, David Anderson of St Andrews, charged 5 shillings and 6 pence (about 52 pence) for a single lesson of one hour, or 3 guineas for a course of 12 lessons. [75] Private clubs however did not always take into account the domestic circumstances of women as at Ilford Golf Club where tuition was on offer to ladies only on Saturday evenings after 5 pm and Sundays after 1 pm. But as Vamplew indicates, this might have simply reflected the subordinate position of women in most clubs. [76]

Conclusion

Whether purely for recreation or to achieve equality with men, participating in golf was only part of the revolution in sport for women in the late nineteenth and the early twentieth centuries. As argued by Parratt, the involvement of women in sport was not inevitably restricted by ideological constraints, although the 'angel in the house' syndrome certainly influenced the nature and extent of their participation. [77] Park has also pointed out that, '... sport provided women with a wider social space' but '... owed nothing to the conscientious efforts on the part of feminists'. [78] Clearly women had to maintain a sense of balance in the organisation of their lives combining the responsibilities of home life with their desire for sport and leisure. By learning the rudiments of golf and accepting instruction, women could participate at a competitive level as well as enjoying the social aspects of the game amongst family and like-minded friends. As has been seen, Lady Margaret Scott and Cecil Leitch each offered a different presentation and style as role models for aspiring golfers to emulate.

While there were those who agitated on the political front for representation in winning the franchise, female golfers were more concerned in getting recognition for their sex on the fairways. Furthermore, that women were prepared to involve themselves in the organisation of golf in the late nineteenth century indicates their determination to promote the game for their own sex. At a time when women had little experience of administrative duties (apart from those associated with the running of a household), it could be argued that recognition for women's golf might have been more difficult to achieve without determined and self-confident individuals like Issette Pearson leading the way. But even these pioneering women felt restricted by convention at times and lacked complete control in their endeavours to establish themselves in their own right on the links and in the clubs. In an address to the Scottish Ladies' Golfing Association in 1928, Cecil Leitch recognised how much golf owed a debt to pioneering women. She claimed that 'the players of today should remember that the standard of the game has only been acquired by the efforts of the players of yesterday'. [79] While it has been shown that golf was 'an excellent means of combining fresh air, exercise and society', the acceptance of women at both recreational and elite level in golf was not without a certain amount of conflict and controversy.

Notes

[1] P.H. Chavasse's *Advice to a wife*, revised by Farncourt Barnes (London, 1906), p. 14.

[2] Important exceptions are Allen Guttmann, *Women's sports: A history* (New York, 1991), who devotes his account to women only, while two general studies of sport Richard Holt's *Sport and the British* (Oxford, 1989), pp. 117–34 and John Lowerson's *Sport and the English middle classes, 1870–1914* (Manchester, 1993), pp. 203–20 are important in highlighting the extent of women's contribution to sport.

[3] Neil Tranter, 'Women and sport in the 19th century Scotland' in Grant Jarvie and Graham Walker, eds., *Scottish sport in the making of the nation* (Leicester, 1994), p. 35.

[4] Jennifer Hargreaves, *Sporting females* (London, 1994), p. 51.

[5] Richard Holt, *Sport and the British* (Oxford, 1989), pp. 117–8.

[6] Ada Ballin, 'Introduction' in H. Spicer, ed., *Sport for girls* (London, 1900), p. 15.

[7] Ada Ballin, 'Physical health and culture', *Womanhood*, vol. I (Dec. 1898), p. iii.

[8] Louie Mackern and M. Boys, eds., *Our lady of the green. A book of ladies' golf* (London, 1899), p. 108.

[9] Marilyn Constanzo, '"One can't shake off the women": Images of sport and gender in *Punch*, 1901–10', *International Journal for the History of Sport*, 19 (1) (2002), p. 39.

[10] See Jane George, Joyce Kay and Wray Vamplew 'Women to the fore: gender accommodation and resistance at the British golf club before 1914', *Sporting Traditions*, 23 (2) (2007), pp. 79–98, for the role of gender power relationships.

[11] Quoted in David Hamilton, *Golf: Scotland's game* (Kilmalcolm, 1998), p. 156.

[12] There are numerous examples of ladies having to 'give way' to men even although they were within their rights as paid-up members of the same club. The author is in the process of preparing a forthcoming article on the treatment of women in golf clubs in the twentieth century.

[13] Harry and Alfie Ward, *A history of Biggar Golf Club through 100 eventful years, 1895–1995* (Biggar, 1995), p. 23.

[14] Peter MacPhee, *Ballater Golf Club 1892–1992* (Ballater, 1992), p. 45.

[15] George Fullerton Carnegie, 'The Golfiad' in *Golfiani: or niceties connected with the game of gold* (Edinburgh, 1842), pp. 5–10. 'The Golfiad' was originally published by Blackwood in 1842.

[16] John Kerr, *The golf book of east Lothian* (Edinburgh, 1896), pp. 133–4.

[17] Ibid., p. 133.

[18] Eustace White, 'Lady golfers', *Golfing*, IX (56) (1908), p. 439.

[19] Mabel Stringer, *Golfing reminiscences* (London, 1924), p. 33.
[20] *The Ladies' Field*, 25 Feb. 1899, p. 493.
[21] Quoted in *C.B. Fry's Magazine of Sports and Outdoor Life*, 3 (16) (July 1905), p. 314.
[22] There were approximately 65 ladies' clubs prior to 1893 as noted by Rosalind Cossey, *Golfing ladies: Five centuries of golf in Great Britain and northern Ireland* (London, 1984), p. 244.
[23] Mackern and Boys, eds., *Our lady of the green*, p. 14.
[24] *The Gentlewoman*, 29 Apr. 1893.
[25] Joyce Wethered, *Golfing memories and methods* (London, 1933), p. 182.
[26] Cossey, *Golfing ladies*, p. 26.
[27] Malcolm Crane, *The story of ladies' golf* (London, 1991), p. 18.
[28] Kathleen McCrone, *Sport and the physical emancipation of English women, 1870–1914* (London, 1988), p. 171.
[29] Quoted from *Fairway and Hazard*, Apr. 1943, pp. 40–1.
[30] Letter to Blanche Martin, LGU treasurer, from Horace Hutchison, 9 Apr. 1893, cited in Lewine Mair, *One hundred years of women's golf* (Edinburgh, 1992), p. 13.
[31] *The Scotsman*, 24 May 1897, p. 4.
[32] *The Gentlewoman*, 5 June 1897, p. 796.
[33] A. Starkie-Bence, 'Golf', in F. Slaughter, ed., *The sportswoman's library*, vol. I (2 vols., London, 1898), p. 313.
[34] Mackern and Boys, eds., *Our lady of the green*, p. 27.
[35] Horace Hutchison, *The book of golf and golfers* (2 vols., London, 1899), p. 202.
[36] McCrone, *Sport and the physical emancipation of English women*, p. 235.
[37] H. Roberts, 'The exquisite slave: The role of clothes in the making of Victorian woman', *Signs*, 2(3) (1977), p. 565.
[38] *The Gentlewoman*, 4 Mar. 1893, p. 266.
[39] Hargreaves, *Sporting females*, p. 164.
[40] *St Andrews Citizen*, 20 June 1903, p. 5.
[41] McCrone, *Sport and the physical emancipation of English women*, p. 240.
[42] Jihang Park, 'Sport, dress reform and the emancipation of women in Victorian England: A reappraisal', *International Journal of the History of Sport*, 6 (1), p. 10.
[43] Jane George, 'Women and golf in Scotland' (unpublished PhD thesis, University of Edinburgh, 2003), pp. 77–107.
[44] Ibid., pp. i–ii. Evidence to suggest this came from approximately 50 British women born between 1906 and 1985.
[45] A collection of Miss Glover's press cuttings in the Scottish Ladies' Golfing Association archive indicates the extent of her frequent trips to play at golf clubs in the south of France in the early 1900s.
[46] Constanzo, 'One can't shake off the women', pp. 40–2.
[47] J.R. Longstaff, *The first hundred years of Bishop Auckland Golf Club, 1894–1994.* (Bishop Auckland, 1994), p. 55.
[48] William Russell, *A history of Craigmillar Park Golf Club 1895–1995* (Craigmillar, 1995), p. 5.
[49] Ibid.
[50] R.B. Smith, *Blackburn Golf Club 100 years, 1894–1994* (Blackburn, 1993), p. 19.

[51] Eve M. Soulsby, *Braemar Golf Club. The story of the first 100 years* (Braemar, 1902), p. 9.
[52] Ibid., p. 15.
[53] Alex McIntosh, *Blairgowrie Golf Club 1889–1989* (Blairgowrie, 1989), p. 17.
[54] Ibid., p. 19.
[55] Douglas Caird, 'Miss Leitch looks back . . .', *Fairway and Hazard*, Apr. 1969, p. 42.
[56] Enid Wilson, *A gallery of women golfers* (London, 1961), p. 53.
[57] Eleanor Helme quoted in *Fairway and Hazard*, Dec. 1955, p. 210.
[58] Douglas Caird, 'Miss Leitch looks back . . .', *Fairway and Hazard*, Apr. 1969, p. 43.
[59] Alan Jackson, 'The oldest contest of all', *Through the Green*, Mar. 2000, p. 29.
[60] Cecil Leitch, *Golf* (London, 1922), p. 59.
[61] Mackern and Boys, eds., *Our lady of the green* (London, 1899) includes some articles which had already appeared in the *Badminton Magazine* and *Golf* publications.
[62] Ibid., p. 95.
[63] Ibid., p. 94.
[64] Ibid., p. 96.
[65] Ibid., p. 101.
[66] Ibid., p. 100.
[67] Ibid., p. 97.
[68] Wray Vamplew, 'Successful workers or exploited labour? Golf professionals and professional golfers in Great Britain, 1888–1914', *Economic History Review* 61 (1) (2008), p. 57.
[69] Prince's Ladies' Golf Club on Mitcham Common was instituted in 1894. Nisbet's *Golf year book* (London, 1906), p. 364, notes that Mrs Gordon Robertson and Mr Philpot were instructors at that time.
[70] Robert Browning, *History of golf* (London, 1955), p. 196.
[71] Alan Jackson, 'Mitcham's mystery unmasked', *Through the Green*, June 1998, p. 20.
[72] *The Hockey Field*, 8 Oct. 1908, p. 428.
[73] Jackson, 'Mitcham's mystery unmasked', p. 20.
[74] *The Hockey Field*, 8 Oct. 1908, p. 428.
[75] *Ladies' Field*, 10 Oct. 1908.
[76] Vamplew, 'Successful workers or exploited labour? pp. 62–63.
[77] Catriona Parratt, 'Athletic "womanhood": exploring sources for female sport in Victorian and Edwardian England', *Journal of Sport History*, 16 (2) (1989), p. 155.
[78] Park, 'Sport, dress reform and the emancipation of women in Victorian England', p. 10.
[79] Noel Dunlop-Hill, *History of the Scottish Ladies' Golfing Association* (London, 1930), pp. 44–5.

Still Going After All These Years: Text, Truth and the *Racing Calendar*

Joyce Kay

The Racing Calendar, *the 'bible' of the British turf, is one of the longest continuous series of sporting records in the world. Yet it is unlikely to receive the widespread recognition it deserves as a sporting text because it reflects a relatively minor sport in twenty-first century terms. This article will briefly outline its history, analyse its contents and attempt to evaluate its worth to historians of sport. Its reliability as a source will be scrutinised in the light of current debate, and the information it can supply with regard to gender and racing abroad will be assessed.*

When *The Turf* was published in 1976, Wray Vamplew could not have imagined that his contribution to the economic and social history of horseracing had only just begun and was to span the next 30 years. [1] None of his subsequent books, articles or conference papers on racing topics as diverse as the impact of the Victorian railways, the demise of the Edwardian gentleman rider, the bizarre and often dangerous life of the twentieth-century professional jockey or the rise and fall of the Jockey Club could have been written – let alone quantified – without recourse to 'the official organ of the racing authorities', the *Racing Calendar*. [2] This paper will briefly outline its history, analyse its contents and attempt to evaluate its worth as a comprehensive and reliable source. It will then seek to illustrate some ways in which historians of racing can still use this extraordinary sporting series.

Joyce Kay, University of Stirling.

Time after time

'Horseracing is one of the oldest sports in the world' and the *Racing Calendar* is a time-honoured chronicle of its evolution in Britain. [3] Although it has been claimed that 'no other branch of sport can boast of records dating back in this unbroken manner for two centuries', [4] this refers only to Weatherbys' volumes. It is now nearly 300 years since John Cheny published his original *Account of all the Horse-matches Run and of all the Plates and Prizes Run for in England (of the Value of Ten Pounds or Upwards)* in 1727. The scope of this *Racing Calendar* – advertised as including the owners, the names and colours of the horses, the winners and places, and the 'conditions of running as to weight, age, size etc.', together with a list of the principal cock fights – had entailed considerable travelling around the country as Cheny built up a network of acquaintance who thereafter supplied him with reports of local meetings and matches. In this way he obtained 'a fairly complete return' but the limitations of the work are obvious, with races restricted not only by his personal information gathering but also, as the title-page suggests, by value and geography. ('England' was later to become Great Britain and Ireland.) From 1732 he employed two or three servants to ride out collecting intelligence during the flat racing season and was therefore able to supplement the annual with a fortnightly 'sheet calendar' from mid-April to the end of October containing details of racing for the previous two weeks. For these services he charged subscribers half a guinea. [5]

Cheny continued to publish his *Racing Calendar* yearly until his death in 1751. By then the contents had been expanded to include the pedigrees of principal runners, a list and description of the 'places of sport' and a rudimentary index of horses. The following two decades saw various entrepreneurs carry on a similar format but with several significant additions. John Pond's *Kalendar* (1751–1758) included the first set of general rules of racing and the first mention of the Jockey Club, later to become the regulatory authority of horseracing in Britain. *Heber's Calendar* (1751–1768) contained the original list of racing colours registered by owners and the earliest reference to racing overseas (Philadelphia). [6] A period of intense rivalry, amounting even to skulduggery and threatened law-suits, followed Heber's death in 1768, during which partnerships involving Messrs Thomas Fawconer, William Tuting and James Weatherby were formed and dissolved. The eventual winner of this publishing contest was Weatherby, now 'keeper of the match book' at Newmarket. His initial format retained some features of earlier *Racing Calendars* including a list of meetings and of racing colours, an index of horses and the fortnightly production of the sheet calendar. It dispensed with others, notably Pond's general rules of racing, and added a register of subscribers and an expanded set of Jockey Club rules. By the time of Fawconer's death in 1778 Weatherby's *Racing Calendar* had established itself as the sole heir to Cheny's original work.

It is still going 230 years later, although aesthetically it is a mere shadow of its former self. Until the late 1960s it was bound in hard brown covers with red and black leather title strips on the spine, the lettering and decorative bars in shiny gold – a fat, seductive volume, fit to grace the library of any Georgian aristocrat or line the study walls of any Victorian squire. It had continued to expand in size throughout the twentieth century, reflecting the growth of British horseracing – some editions were over three inches thick. In its final years, however, its appearance metamorphosed to a rather nasty shade of sickly yellow and its contents were radically reduced, focusing almost exclusively on race results and racehorses. It eventually ceased to appear in book form in 1989 but continues to be published weekly for the benefit of the modern multi-million pound racing industry. Over the years it has evolved from a privately printed commercial venture by the Weatherby family, through a lengthy period of semi-autonomy in which it clearly acted as the unofficial mouthpiece of the Jockey Club, to a point in 1902 when it was purchased by racing's governing body. For much of the twentieth century it continued to be 'published for the Jockey Club by Weatherby and Sons', while the expanding firm cemented its position in racing administration – registering owners, horses and racing colours, receiving entries and declarations, allocating weights, issuing official lists of runners and riders, and collecting and distributing prize money. Weatherbys is still responsible for the day-to-day running of British horseracing under contract to the present regulators, the British Horseracing Authority, but the traditional form of the *Racing Calendar* is no more.

Times they are a-changin'?

One of the remarkable aspects of the *Racing Calendar* is how little it changed for much of its history. A Georgian racehorse owner would still have recognised many of the basic contents of the annual volume two hundred years later, even if the terminology had altered. The index of meetings held, the results of past races, the details of stallions' fees, the lengths of the racecourses and the register of winning horses were still there in 1968 as they had been in 1778. Gone were the references to cocking: banned in 1840; future races: printed separately from 1846; King's or Queen's Plates: a type of race abandoned in 1887; subscribers: subscription lists ceased to be published in 1888; and racing colours: ended in 1963 when the details of registered owners' silks had reached 106 pages.

What would probably have surprised him was the sheer amount of official information included. General rules and regulations of horse-racing, a wealth of data relating to the Jockey Club and lists of licensed racing personnel such as trainers, officials and jockeys had turned the annual *Racing Calendar* into a substantial and authoritative-looking publication by the twentieth century. Seven pages of rules in 1807 had become 21 in 1852, 56 in 1904 and 88 by 1968 – the index of rules alone ran to 21 pages. A list of Jockey Club members, first introduced in 1835, was later augmented by committee membership, reports of proceedings and over 50 pages of stewards' enquiries. Jockeys, too lowly to even be named in the race results until 1823, had to apply for annual licences from 1879 and those authorised to ride had their names printed each year. Their numbers peaked at just over 300 in the 1920s, falling back to around 220 in the post-1945 decades, a period at which apprentices reached double that figure and licensed trainers numbered over 250.

The potential for charting the growth and development of horseracing through the pages of this continuous series would therefore seem to be considerable and economic and social historians of the sport such as Wray Vamplew, Mike Huggins and John Tolson have used it extensively. It is possible to analyse the changing geography, extent and gradual concentration of racing in certain parts of the country as some traditional courses and meetings faded into obscurity or oblivion while others took their place. Numbers of race meetings, when they were held and for how many days, lengths of jockey or racehorse careers and their success rates, changing patterns of racing such as the demise of heats and yearling races or the proportion of two-year-old racers, can all be discovered. An economic historian can calculate the amount and growth of prize money within the sport over a period of time; a social historian can find out who won it and who donated the many racing trophies to successful owners. It is a racing anorak's paradise.

There's just one problem

Historians of horseracing have not needed a deconstructionist to alert them to possible flaws in the *Racing Calendar* as a source. Over 30 years ago, Wray Vamplew recognised that the race meetings contained in its nineteenth-century volumes did not amount to a comprehensive register of racing in Britain and that there was, additionally, a 'fluctuating set of lesser events, extremely local in character and seldom having a permanent date in the *Racing Calendar*'. [7] Mike Huggins cast an even more critical eye over its contents and possible defects as a barometer of horseracing, pointing out, for example, that the annual list of racing colours contained so many lifetime registrations that it was an imperfect gauge of upper-class, titled participation: it did not guarantee that owners were active in any particular year. [8] The most problematic issue with Weatherbys' tomes, however, is that they might easily be characterised as 'sites of power', in the terminology of Doug Booth. Before they can be approved as historical sources, we have to consider who they were written for, why they were written, who might benefit from their publication and what material was included or omitted. [9]

When Cheny first published his *Calendar*, he suggested that 'in the midst of Winter, [it] will be an agreeable Amusement, in that dull, inactive season, rendering Gentlemen capable, even in their Chambers, of diverting themselves with a Prospect, as it were, of the Sport of each past year . . .' [10] His was a commercial, money-making enterprise that aimed to supply information to racegoers, owners and bettors throughout the country. When James Weatherby began to compile his own work in 1773 he undertook the same task but with an important difference: he had been an official at Newmarket, already the headquarters of horseracing, for some years. Undoubtedly known as 'keeper of the match book' – a title printed on the frontispiece of his *Racing Calendars* – he may also have been secretary to the Jockey Club by this time, a designation previously used by his erstwhile publishing partner, Thomas Fawconer. Several sources are of the opinion that a member of the Weatherby family held this post continuously for 200 years from the early 1770s; Wray Vamplew himself considered James Weatherby to be 'keeper of the match book' and club secretary from 1771. [11]

In his second volume, Mr Weatherby thought fit to trade on his official position, advising prospective clients that this gave him singular advantages over any rival publisher. Furthermore, he continued the item introduced by Messrs Tuting and Fawconer in their 1770 *Racing Calendar* under the heading 'Orders Settled by the Jockey Club'. This became 'Rules and Orders of the Jockey Club' from 1773 and although some were merely regulations applying to the members of that organisation, such as annual dinners or appointments of stewards, others suggest an embryonic code to cover races at Newmarket. [12] Even at this stage the *Racing Calendar* was a means of disseminating information about the body that was to become the sole arbiter of the sport in Britain; subscribers throughout the country were made aware not only of club affairs but of the opinions and strictures of elite racing men. Cognisance, however, is a long way from control. Although the Jockey Club was occasionally asked to adjudicate on race disputes outwith Newmarket, it was a further 100 years before it sought to extend its authority over the conduct of racing beyond its home base. [13] Weatherby's early *Racing Calendars* are therefore unlikely to be any more biased than those of Cheny and other predecessors: their limitations are largely those of geography and awareness. From 1797 till 1858 they even included Pond's general rules of racing, something which suggests that the Jockey Club was in no hurry to exert a regulatory influence over the sport.

Mike Huggins, however, has been critical of the *Racing Calendar* as a historical source from the second half of the nineteenth century onwards as it increasingly became the 'de facto mouthpiece of the Club', publishing 'details of such matters as the Club wished to make known more generally, and not those it wished to keep dark.' [14]. As such it appears to represent the type of 'official' document of which Booth cautions us to beware. [15] From the 1870s it could be said to have provided a partial view of British horseracing, concentrating on the financially and socially superior end of the sport to the exclusion of the small, local – and possibly corrupt – meetings that flourished in areas of the country remote from Newmarket. The Jockey Club ruling of 1870 – that only those events that were advertised as subject to its revised, and now extensive, 'Rules Concerning Horse-racing in General', published in the *Racing Calendar*, would have their programmes and results included therein – led to a 30% drop in reported meetings within five years. It would seem, nevertheless, that many of the small country fixtures continued 'pretty much on the old lines . . . a law unto themselves,' at which 'the local officials constituted themselves into a self-contained Jockey Club and a Messrs Weatherby's of their own.' [16]

The way in which the *Racing Calendar* was used to validate approved aspects of British horseracing – the 1870 ruling was followed by an even more draconian edict from Newmarket in 1877, banning the advertisement within its covers of any meeting that failed to award prize money of more than £300 – certainly suggests that it increasingly operated as an official digest as well as a commercial undertaking. A two-tier picture of British racing thus emerged: the regulated, relatively wealthy, often multi-day event of licensed horses, jockeys and trainers that attracted members of polite society, and the little, one-day local meet of doubtful nags, dubious organisation and possible dishonesty that continued to provide entertainment for rural or distant communities. From this time on, the *Racing Calendar* might be viewed as a less than comprehensive record of race meetings and results, although it could be argued that it had probably omitted some of the least noteworthy race days throughout its history.

However, there is no reason to suppose that its official lists – of owners, trainers, jockeys, apprentices, registered colours, rules – or its record of 'approved' race meetings are in any way flawed. It may increasingly have spread the gospel according to the Jockey Club from the middle of the nineteenth century and its omissions may present a rather distorted picture of racing for the ordinary punter but its statistical evidence probably offers the most comprehensive view of British horseracing over a period of 200 years.

Against all odds?

One aspect of racing that has not been considered so far is betting, the *raison d'être* of the sport according to Huggins, its lifeblood as described by Vamplew. [17] In Cheny's original *Racing Calendar* the detailed information about horses and their 'form' was proclaimed as a means of assisting subscribers in 'reducing their Calculations nearer to perfection, and consequently of matching or betting with greater advantage.' [18] His was essentially the first form guide for punters; one historian of the Jockey Club likens it to the *Timeform* or *Raceform* publications of today. [19] The 1732 edition noted that the methods of deciding bets are 'frequently attended with Disputes and Contentions, too many of which proceed to expensive Law Suits'; it was therefore Cheny's intention to publish the rules of betting founded 'on the Dictates or Judgment of Newmarket.' Nothing came of this proposal. [20]

Although John Pond's *Kalendar* contained the first published rules of racing and betting, Weatherby, as already noted, initially dispensed with these. When they were re-introduced in 1797, over one-third related to betting, and a further minimum of 12 were to be found amongst the 'Rules and Orders of the Jockey Club' – that is, only applicable to racing at Newmarket – from 1809 to1857. Yet the club itself was allegedly 'not interested in betting as such, acting only to ensure that . . . debts of honour were settled.' [21] As if to emphasise this statement, the revised general and club rules of 1858 removed references to betting to an appendix; nearly half of the 19 regulations listed there had originated with Pond a century earlier. While the majority of these had been published under the 'Rules of Horse-racing in General' – for example rule four, 'Confirmed bets cannot be "off" except by mutual consent' or rule eight,

'The person who lays the odds has a right to choose a horse or the field: when a person has chosen a horse, the field is what starts against him' – some had previously been included under the Jockey Club code. Rule five, relating to matches or private sweepstakes between any two horses being rendered null and void if both subsequently became the property of one person, is a Jockey Club ruling; so is the edict that all bets made on the Derby, Oaks, St Leger and several other major races – these change over time – 'shall be considered "play or pay" '. Why these were previously part of separate codes is unknown and the significance of that separation is lost on the author! [22]

A further revision of the rules of racing in 1889 saw the disappearance of the appendix on betting and the re-instatement of two items (out of 184) on 'Bets, defaulters for'. Rule 18 stated that 'the Stewards of the Jockey Club take no cognisance of any disputes or claims with respect to bets', a re-iteration of the original 'hands-off' stance adopted in 1842 which had freed them from any responsibility for gambling matters, even at Newmarket. [23] Rule 177 noted that defaulters would be 'warned off'. These two remained part of the general rules printed in the *Racing Calendar* until they ceased to be published in 1970. The removal of the archaic and unnecessary 'Colours Worn by the Riders' in 1963 made space for the publication of a 'Raceform Index' – 'the horses, their breeding, dams' sires and racing records', an idea proposed but not completed by Cheny 230 years earlier.

In spite of the reservations expressed above, there are many ways in which the *Racing Calendar* can be mined for information about the social and economic history of horseracing. What follows is based solely on the flat racing calendars (Weatherby also became responsible for publishing details of national hunt rules and fixtures) from which two areas have been selected for closer examination. The first concerns the origins of female participation in the sport, the second looks at international aspects of racing.

Always a woman?

It has always been asserted that women were not allowed to take part in racing. [24] Yet there is no rule published in the *Racing Calendar* to that effect; if women were 'banned' from racing horses this was an unwritten law or social convention not a Jockey Club requirement. It was not uncommon in the second half of the nineteenth century for owners to race under a pseudonym and the usual story in circulation is that those women who were interested in the sport bought, owned and ran horses under male names. The examples most frequently cited are the formidable Duchess of Montrose, an acknowledged expert on thoroughbred racehorses who raced under the name 'Mr Manton' in the 1880s, and the actress Lillie Langtry, who was known as 'Mr Jersey' in the 1890s. These two 'gentlemen' can certainly be found in the lists of registered owners' colours printed annually in the *Racing Calendar*, Mr Manton's jockeys wearing scarlet and Mr Jersey's decked out in turquoise and fawn hoops. Their real identities were an open secret and it seems strange that they felt it necessary to 'disguise' themselves in this manner, particularly when other women were boldly registering silks under their own names and had been doing so for decades.

A careful scrutiny of both Weatherby's *Racing Calendar* and *Ruffs Guide to the Turf*, another annual racing publication, shows that one or two female names crop up in the lists of colours from the late 1850s. In 1855 a Mr Osbaldeston raced in green with a red cap; by 1858 this combination has been assigned to Mrs Osbaldeston, her husband having presumably died, and she features for a number of years thereafter. In 1868 Mr C. Snewing, owner of 1862 Derby winner, Caractacus, registered his colours as light blue with a white cap but Mrs W. Snewing preferred a gold jacket and green velvet cap with a gold tassel. From the late 1880s onwards, lady owners appear more often and more regularly: there are eight in 1889, 14 in 1902 and 33 in 1910. Even Lillie Langtry had finally relinquished her pseudonym by 1907.

It might be suggested that marital status or social rank were factors inhibiting open disclosure of horse ownership. Yet single women such as Miss Isabella Graham (1887) and Miss J. Nicholl (1888), and others with titles – Lady Anne Blunt (1884), Lady Meux (1892) – rejected secrecy. Some husbands may have preferred their wives to race incognito but there are several examples of both spouses registering colours: Mr and Mrs T. Chaloner for over 30 years from the 1890s (she had two sets of racing silks), Mr and Mrs J. Shepherd and Mr and Mrs J. Collins (both from 1902). It may be that some names using the style 'Mrs' were, in fact, not their own – something that cannot now be ascertained. It is scarcely conceivable that any man would have taken a female pseudonym if he wished to remain anonymous: there were so few female titles in this period that they stood out sharply amongst the lords, sirs and misters. The most likely explanation is that some women felt bound to observe a supposed convention for family or societal reasons but that a small group of female owners in the late Victorian and Edwardian years were willing to flout this practice. The growth in numbers coincides with the gathering momentum of the women's suffrage movement, many supporters of which joined ladies' clubs, formed in imitation of male establishments, were actively engaged in sporting activities, and took an increasing interest in what had previously been seen as masculine preserves. [25] After World War I – and the partial granting of the vote for women – the number of female owners grew more rapidly; 160 were registered in 1921, (8% of the total), 467 in 1936 (18%). By 1958 nearly 30% of owners registering colours were women.

The *Racing Calendar* also provides information about women in other branches of horseracing, as subscribers to the volume (names were listed until 1888) and as thoroughbred breeders, firstly under the annual 'List of Foals', later in the reports of bloodstock sales. Initially most of the women named in subscription lists were associated with inns and hotels – Mrs Howard of the Coach and Horses, Dover Street, London is mentioned in 1846, along with Mrs W. Smith of the Albion Hotel, Liverpool and five others. By the 1880s a few notables such as the Duchess of Montrose, Lady C. Ker, the Honourable Mrs Ramsay and the Honourable Mrs H. Pigott-Carleton are listed but they remain a tiny group. Breeders had also been represented from the 1840s, seldom more than six each year until the 1880s, but thereafter their numbers increased in a similar fashion to lady owners: 22 (including five members of the aristocracy) in 1888, 39 in 1910, 83 in 1921. Women may not have played a significant part in the nineteenth- and early twentieth-century business of horseracing but they were not completely excluded, as generally believed.

Far, far away

The *Racing Calendar* is not a purely British affair; the list of subscribers demonstrates an overseas interest in the English turf from the late eighteenth century. Nine subscriptions in 1804, mostly from North America, had become 56 by 1839, 82 by 1865 and 125 – over 10% of the total – by 1888. Most copies found their way to France, Germany and America but a few were destined for Australia, New Zealand, South Africa and the East Indies. Some were purchased by overseas racing organisations and turf authorities – the Bombay Turf Club, the Moscow Racing Society and the Jockey Clubs of Argentina and the United States. Others became the property of Russian princes, Hungarian counts and Prussian barons. From the 1860s onwards, however, between one-third and one-half went to France, reflecting not only French interest – and considerable success – in English racing but the fact that there was a sizeable community of Englishmen training horses across the channel, particularly at the Newmarket of French racing, Chantilly. Here generations of Pratts and Carters trained for local owners and introduced their English customs – *le* five o'clock tea, *le* Harvest Festival and *le* Cricket Club – to the local community. [26] Six individual Pratts subscribed to the *Racing Calendar* in 1880.

Overseas racing featured briefly in earlier *Racing Calendars*, but it was 1864 before European meetings, mostly in France, were regularly reported. The number of French meetings covered in the later nineteenth century seems surprising, not just the important fixtures at Chantilly and Paris but racing at provincial courses the length and breadth of the country, from Pau and Avignon in the south to Brest in the northwest and Nancy in the northeast. In 1868, 54 places in France were mentioned in the *Racing Calendar* together with six in Belgium. This is perhaps less strange when the jockeys are considered – the majority appear to be English. Browns, Hunters, Pratts, Whittakers, Giffords, Flatmans, Smiths, Greens, Thomsons and Barlows are only a few of the Anglo-Saxon names to appear and it seems probably that, like the trainers mentioned above, they were based in France. For the most prestigious races such as the Grand Prix de Paris they were sometimes joined by top English jockeys. George Fordham, winner of 16 English Classics, won the Prix du Jockey-Club – the French Derby – in 1868; he was able to do so without jeopardising his English rides because the major French races took place on Sundays, a rest day at home. Nevertheless, in an era of steam train, boat and horse-drawn carriage, a trip to Chantilly or Paris for the day was not to be undertaken lightly.

By the beginning of the twentieth century, reports of 'Continental racing' in the *Racing Calendar* had become increasingly selective. Only 25 'places of sport' were listed in 1902. The small French country courses had gone the way of their English counterparts, leaving eighteen of the more significant venues – Saint Cloud, Maisons Laffitte, Deauville, Chantilly – and several of the larger tracks around Europe (Baden Baden, Cologne, Vienna and Turin). British jockeys were still in evidence but they had now been joined by a number of Americans including Johnny Reiff and Danny Maher. Both were licensed to ride in Britain – Maher was third in the jockeys' championship in 1902 – but Reiff seems to have spent a large part of the year in France where he won the Prix du Jockey-Club and the French Two Thousand Guineas, and was third in the French Oaks. [27]

'Continental racing' ceased in 1914. French races re-appeared in 1938 for two seasons, and recommenced in 1945 but the reports were scanty, normally featuring only the French classics and a few other major races at Longchamp, such as the Prix de l'Arc de Triomphe. English jockeys earning a living in France had virtually disappeared, although a couple of Australians – 'Scobie' Breasley and 'Rae' Johnstone – were successful in major French races in the post-war period. In a complete reversal of fortune, French jockeys regularly obtained temporary licences to ride in Britain; the 1950s saw up to a dozen plying their trade at the major racecourses in the south of England and meeting with considerable success. Roger Poincelet won the Two Thousand Guineas in 1952, the One Thousand Guineas and Oaks in 1960, the Derby in 1961 and the King George VI and Queen Elizabeth Diamond Stakes twice, in 1955 and 1961. French owner/trainer partnerships also won the Derby in 1950, 1955, 1956, 1963 and 1965, and the Oaks in 1947, 1950, 1956, 1958 and 1962 while British raids to France appear to have ceased. By the mid-1960s reports of European races were no longer included in the *Racing Calendar.*

A simple twist of fate?

The *Racing Calendar* will never receive widespread recognition as a sporting text because it is fated to reflect a relatively minority sport in twenty-first century terms. The British Horseracing Authority may paint a rosy picture – 5.86 million people went racing in 2006; the industry had an overall economic impact of £2.86 billion in 2004–2005; racing is second only to football measured by revenue and spectator numbers (including television viewers) – but most racegoers are simply interested in a day out with food, drink and an opportunity to gamble. [28] Very few have any knowledge of the sport's lengthy history; few sports historians have any interest at all in either horseracing or equestrian events in general.

One reason for this may be that horses are no longer part of everyday life as they were in Victorian and Edwardian times. Another is that racing does not have a genuine 'fan base' – spectators are not there to follow a team or a star athlete, or share in the communal experience of winning or losing. There are no amateur racing historians or statisticians out there, no fanzines. Nor, unlike most sports, can horseracing encourage participation – there is no 'grass roots' and most fans of racing will never even have ridden a horse, let alone raced one. There are also those who think that racing is a form of cruelty to animals and should be next in line for a ban, following the suppression of foxhunting. Who, outwith the narrow confines of the industry and the day-trippers, actually cares about horseracing?

The *Racing Calendar* is a remarkable record of one of our oldest national sports. There is scope within its pages for revealing much more, especially about twentieth-century racing which has so far been under-researched. The texts are there, the evidence is waiting to be unearthed but unless another Wray Vamplew comes to the fore hundreds of volumes of the *Racing Calendar* will simply gather dust in library vaults.

Notes

[1] Wray Vamplew, *The turf: a social and economic history of horse racing* (London, 1976).
[2] Wray Vamplew, 'Still crazy after all those years: Continuity in a changing labour market for professional jockeys', *Contemporary British History*, 14 (2) (2000), p. 140.
[3] Mike Huggins, *Flat racing and British society, 1750–1914* (London, 2000), p. xi.
[4] Tim Fitzgeorge-Parker, *The spoilsports* (London, 1968), p. 18.
[5] C.M. Prior, *The history of the Racing Calendar and Stud Book* (London, 1926), pp. 94, 108–9.
[6] Ibid., p. 147.
[7] Vamplew, *The turf*, p. 33.
[8] Huggins, *Flat racing*, p. 65. A change in the rules from 1936 removed the entitlement to colours for life. Thereafter owners had to register their colours annually.
[9] Douglas Booth, *The field; truth and fiction in sport history* (London, 2005), p. 85. Briefly, Booth reminds historians that official documents should not be viewed as neutral sites of information but as 'managed' sources, open to manipulation and concealment, dependent on purpose, personnel and policy for their retention.
[10] Prior, *The history of the Racing Calendar*, p. 95.
[11] Norman Barrett, *The Daily Telegraph chronicle of horse racing* (Enfield, 1995), p. 9; Barry Campbell, *Horse racing in Britain* (London, 1977), p. 202; Roger Mortimer, *The encyclopaedia of flat racing* (London, 1971), p. 389; Wray Vamplew, 'Reduced horse power: The Jockey Club and the regulation of British horseracing', *Entertainment Law*, 2 (3) (2003), p. 109.
[12] Prior, *The history of the Racing Calendar*, pp. 151–8.
[13] Huggins, *Flat racing*, p. 174; Vamplew, 'Reduced horse power', p. 100.
[14] Huggins, *Flat racing*, p. 175.
[15] Booth, *The field*, pp. 84–6. The *Racing Calendar* is an interesting historical record: is it an 'official' publication or a 'document of mass communication' in Booth's terms? (It is classified as a 'journal' in the catalogue of the copyright National Library of Scotland).
[16] John Fairfax-Blakeborough, *The analysis of the turf* (London, 1927), p. 162.
[17] Huggins, *Flat racing*, p. 20; Wray Vamplew and Joyce Kay, *Encyclopedia of British horseracing* (Abingdon, 2005), p. 44.
[18] Quoted in Prior, *The history of the Racing Calendar*, p. 95.
[19] John Tyrrel, *Running racing: The Jockey Club years since 1750* (London, 1997), p. 9.
[20] Prior, *The history of the Racing Calendar*, p. 107.
[21] Tyrrel, *Running racing*, p. 29.

[22] For an explanation of nineteenth-century betting practices and the Jockey Club attitude to bets and bettors, see Huggins, *Flat racing*, pp. 185–91.

[23] Tyrrel, *Running racing*, p. 60.

[24] For example, Caroline Ramsden, *Ladies in racing* (London, 1973), pp. 21–2; Gillian Newsum, *Women and horses* (London, 1988), pp. 111–12; Huggins, *Flat racing*, p. 45.

[25] For ladies's clubs, see Joyce Kay, 'No time for recreations till the vote is won? Suffrage activists and leisure in Edwardian Britain', *Women's History Review*, 16 (4) (2007), pp. 15–23; for sporting activities, see Joyce Kay, 'It wasn't just Emily Davison! Sport, suffrage and society in Edwardian Britain', *International Journal of the History of Sport*, 25 (10) (2008), pp. 9–13.

[26] Jean-Pierre Blay, 'Industrie hippique, immigration anglaise et structures sociales à Chantilly au XIX siècle', *Revue Européenne des Migrations Internationales*, 8 (2) (1992), pp. 123–4, 127.

[27] For a detailed examination of the 'American invasion', see Wray Vamplew, 'The American invasion of the English turf: A study in sporting technological transfer' in J. Toleneer and R. Renson, eds., *Old borders, new borders, no borders* (Leuven, 2000).

[28] British Horseracing Authority website, http://www.britishhorseracing.com/inside_horseracing/media/2.5.7.1.asp?item=001579, accessed 21 Apr. 2009.

The Proto-globalisation of Horseracing 1730–1900: Anglo–American Interconnections

Mike Huggins

This study explores racing's global interconnectedness through an analysis of the ways in which English racing was represented, exploited and engaged by the American horseracing and thoroughbred breeding groups from c.1730 to 1900. It examines the American importation of British bloodstock; the formation of jockey clubs and rules and regulations of racing on the English model; the emigration to America of English jockeys and grooms; visits of English racing men; and media coverage of English racing. Finally it briefly examines the ways whereby American racing began in its turn to impinge upon England as American-bred horses began to compete on the English turf from the 1850s onward.

Introduction

The academic study of horseracing is relatively young. As Wray Vamplew recently pointed out, it still features infrequently in leading historical journals. [1] Journalistic works, largely written by racing insiders, still dominate the field, often showing little sense of the wider historical context, employing a limited range of historical sources and heavily over-focused on leading horses, owners, jockeys and trainers. In England, there have been important academic studies by Huggins, Vamplew and others in recent years, but there are still chronological and thematic gaps. [2]

Mike Huggins, University of Cumbria.

Australia, another traditional racing centre, only began serious exploration of the history of the sport in the last couple of decades. [3] The United States, the third of the leading longstanding thoroughbred racing countries, still lacks a major academic study focusing solely on racing. [4]

Although modern racing experts have regularly stressed the significant globalisation of thoroughbred racing and breeding, academic historians have been slower to stress that racing and breeding have had global interconnections since at least the eighteenth century, though their nature, direction, pace and velocity have varied from place to place and from time to time, depending on economic, political and cultural circumstances. Globalisation has become a dominant concept in the social sciences, and students of sports studies, whilst accepting that globalisation is not new, tend to stress 'its increasing momentum during the twentieth century'. [5] Most discussion is present-centred and has little or no historical dimension. [6] Racing on the English model was spreading throughout much of the world by the later nineteenth century, one of several such 'proto-globalised' sports, although the links were often mediated, challenged or opposed. In America, for example, hunting with horses and hounds became highly stylised and ritualised in the Eastern states from the late 1860s on as it increasingly emulated British models.

As recently as 2007, Rebecca Cassidy wrote that 'the stories of racing in the UK and US are told separately' and rarely brought together. [7] So this study sets out to explore one dimension of racing's global interconnectedness. It provides an analysis of the ways in which English racing was represented, exploited and engaged with in America from *c.*1730 to 1900. It begins by exploring the many ways in which English racing impacted upon America: importation of bloodstock; the formation of jockey clubs and rules and regulations of racing on the English model; emigration to America of English jockeys and grooms; visits of English racing men; and coverage of English racing in the media. Finally it briefly examines the ways whereby American racing began in its turn to impinge upon England: when American-bred horses began to compete on the English turf from the 1850s onward; the increased success of American horses, symbolised by the victory of Iroquois in the 1881 Derby and St Leger; and the growing numbers of American owners, jockeys and trainers on the English turf, especially at Newmarket, at the end of the nineteenth century.

Importation of English horses into the American states

Stallions had been imported into England for many centuries to improve racing quality, and by the beginning of the eighteenth century what was later to be known as the 'thoroughbred' or 'blood' horse, bred for racing, had emerged. 'Barb' (north African) and Arabian stallions such as the three major 'taproot' stallions, the Byerley Turk (imported into England in 1689), the Godolphin Arabian (imported in 1706) and the Darley Arabian (imported in 1730) covered 'foundation' Yorkshire-bred mares, and over time produced a much-improved racing breed. [8] Despite fluctuations in popularity, increasing numbers of English towns had annual races during the 1700s. Owners of racehorses often maintained their own studs, whilst by the end of the century specific training and breeding areas had emerged, not only at Newmarket but also in many other areas. Amongst upper-class families, interest in breeding was widespread. But such interest was not confined to England. It was also found in America.

For early sporting colonists England was a role model, and they were keenly interested in importing British racehorses. One authority has estimated that 386 stallions and 168 mares had been imported from England by the end of the eighteenth century. [9] The first thoroughbred to arrive in Virginia, in 1730, Bulle Rocke, was sired by the Darley Arabian, and from then on thoroughbreds were regularly imported, initially largely into Virginia and North Carolina, though a few horses entered New York state in the 1760s. By then, as a British traveller noted, the Virginians 'spared no expense or trouble to improve the breed ... by importing great numbers from England'. [10] Despite the distance between the two countries, there were close cultural connections between America and England. Some governors, staff and military men brought their racing interests with them from England. Governor Ogle (1694–1752) was governor of Maryland three times between 1731 and 1752. He organised English-style races at Annapolis, involving several horses, rather than matches between two horses, and in 1747 he brought over the stallion Spark, and a brood mare, Queen Mab, setting the fashion for English thoroughbreds. The area round his house at Bel Air became a horse breeding area, and included many early turf patrons. [11] Breeding and racing thoroughbreds became a key indicator of gentility, and added depth to a planter's status.

As more thoroughbreds were imported, they largely took part in the longer-distance two-mile or four-mile races for older horses, on one- or two-mile dirt courses, often in heats, on the English model. There were also more socially-mixed forms of racing with horses of no particular breeding, but these were less fashionable. Thoroughbred racing was popular across the southern states of Virginia, the Carolinas and Maryland. For those from established families, wealthy southern plantation owners and merchants, it provided a way of preserving continuity with England. Planters preferred bloodlines traced back to England's first Arabian stallions. Wealthy breeders got pleasure out of watching the practical test of their theories, the joy of achievement, a view shared on both sides of the Atlantic. [12]

As Gems *et al.* stressed races 'held cultural, social and legal significance'. [13] Racing was a symbol of gentility. Betting and support for a horse by owner, neighbours and tenants asserted status as well as enjoyment. [14] More important race meetings increasingly lasted three days, attracting wives and daughters to the tracks in Virginia, Maryland and South Carolina. Nancy Struna has argued that this was less the case in the northern states, though it should be pointed out that Philadelphia and New York had similar meetings. [15] Well-bred running horses required substantial capital outlay, and these early races often involved legal contracts. Arranging matches involved personal honour and glory, entailed 'heavy' high-status betting, attracted deference and generated widespread local community interest and involvement. Success conferred distinction. Indeed Breen has argued that even in the seventeenth century, the 'horse was an extension of his owner; indeed a man was only as good as his horse'. [16] Appearances were important: both in the homes planters built and the horses they imported, so for those with means no expense was spared. Racing divided as well as united owners, offering the excitements of risk, competition and negotiation both within and between social groups. The market economy of wagering, exchange and selling of horses that racing generated created confrontation, complexity and confusion. [17] Prize money and the glory of winning were valued, though ownership of a 'great' horse, especially of one's own breeding, conferred higher status. [18]

Surviving horse and studbooks, correspondence, account books and probate inventories indicate the importance that the higher status American colonists placed on well-bred running horses bred from English stock. But the exact details of how many stallions and mares were imported, when, where from, and of what British (or occasionally Spanish) background, are often lacking, and the data are highly problematic, not least since it could be in a breeder's interest to create a fictitious pedigree. It may be for this reason that early twentieth-century studies concentrate on leading 'tap-root' sires to the exclusion of others. [19] Few owners's studbooks or early newspapers survive.

American collections of detailed genealogies and stud records took time to model themselves on British exemplars, and the earlier nineteenth-century American attempts to create more general stud books are unreliable. *The American Race-Turf Register... and General Stud Book.*

Vol I (New York, 1833), for example, has been described as unreliable, uncritical, and incomplete. It failed to cover much Southside stock, and many pedigree claims prior to the second decade of the nineteenth century could not be substantiated. [20] There were still major problems of definition, authentication and reliability once better data began to be collected after the Civil War, when Sanders Bruce, editor of *Turf, Field and Farm,* began to put together his unofficial series, *The American Stud Book.* In his introduction to volume three in 1878 he wrote that he had 'not attempted to fix any standard of what constitutes a thoroughbred. It is the custom to call those "thoroughbred" which have five uncontaminated crosses to a thoroughbred [but] many in this volume as well as in the first two cannot be traced for the requisite five crosses'. [21] Many races lacked records. All brood mares were not recorded.

In general we know more about foaling dates of imported stock than date of importation, but neither set of data allows us to produce accurate tables. The foaling dates from the admittedly unreliable material surveyed, tentatively suggests that peak years for stallions were for those born in the 1750s, 1780s, 1790s, 1820s, 1830s and from the 1860s onwards. The cessation of racing in 1774 due to the American Revolution meant breeding was neglected, and imports only revived after 1783. There were, for example, probably nearly 60 imported stallions that had been foaled in the 1790s, and about the same foaled in the 1830s, both peak decades, but after Civil War decline numbers then rose, with at least 67 imported stallions born in the 1870s.

Mare numbers followed a different pattern. By and large mare importations were few per decade before the Revolution, with around twenty imported mares having been foaled in the 1890s. But thereafter breeders consistently began importing far more English mares than stallions. Over 60 imported mares were foaled in the 1820s and about 170 in the 1830s, both peak decades. After the Civil War imports rose. Nearly 140 imported mares were foaled in the 1860s and about 170 in the 1870s, for example.

Data based on date of importation is also problematic. So when Hervey, in his study of eighteenth-century racing, told his readers that '20 mares or more were imported into Virginia in the 1780s' while between 1784 and 1800 94 stallions and 40 mares were imported from England' such figures must be treated with great care, as indicative rather than exact. [22]

The mechanisms through which importations were organised are clearer. Family connections with England were exploited. Where wealth was coupled with expertise men might purchase horses on visits. Edward

Fenwick (1720–1775) of South Carolina, related to a landowning Northumberland racing family, imported no less than eight stallions and six mares. Though born in Virginia, he spent much time in England, and spent much time there carefully selecting horses for his John's Island stud. [23] William Constable of New York visited England in 1795 and imported two horses, one, the stallion Baronet, bought from James Weatherby, while a three-year-old filly was bought via Tattersalls, the leading London horse dealers. John Randulph of Roanoke, a subscriber to the English *General Stud Book* by 1808, first visited England in 1822, and subsequently made biennial visits and cultivated acquaintance in the fraternity of English horsemen, visiting Newmarket and Epsom, and country houses in the south and east. Sons of wealthy colonists were often sent to England for education, gaining knowledge and contacts there. Two pioneer importers, John Carter (1696–1742) of Virginia and James DeLancey (1732–1800) of New York, who had racing stables, paddocks and training track in the Bowery, had both attended Cambridge, and learned horse life at Newmarket.

Many commercial breeders employed agents in England to purchase horses, specifying price and pedigree: their agents were usually leading thoroughbred-horse dealers and racing men, such as members of the Weatherby and Tattersall families, central to the administration of English breeding, betting and elite racing. Where possible, Americans would ask a referee to run a final check on the horses such recommended. British grooms were commonly hired to bring horses across. The Virginian John Baylor (1705–1772), a commercial breeder, imported English horses, including Fearnought, an influential sire, and wrote to his English agent John Backhouse specifying wanting a big, strong bay, to be brought by his groom, paid by trip or a year's wages.

American buyers were keenly competitive. They wanted the best blood at the best price, provided detailed instructions to agents and wrote regularly to them. They could not afford to be over-prescriptive, since though horses were often bought directly from owners through private treaty, such negotiations were often long and detailed. It was easy too to be outbid. In general the best purchase was a horse with 'good' bloodline, a proved foal getter, who could be bought at a reasonable price because currently unfashionable in England. Often Americans were forced to buy cheaper, older horses, since the costs of getting a horse to the USA could double the price.

Importation was problematic. Overheads were high, and commercial breeders had to be able to sell at a price that incorporated the initial purchase costs of the horse in England, plus very significant transportation and shipping costs. It could take anything up to six months for an imported horse to recover from the weight loss and other effects of the sea voyage, cope with American climate, water and feed and get into condition. The risks of shipping were high, and horses regularly died. Voyages under sail generally took around six weeks right up to the 1850s, though a horse could be at sea up to three months if gales seriously delayed the vessel. Following the advent of steamships travel was quicker and more comfortable, though there were still deaths. The death of Cobham, imported by W.H. Wilson, during a gale 10 days out of Liverpool, was the third for his owner in two years, and was not insured. [24]

Better-bred horses may have increased the chances of winning and breeding future good quality stock, but even wealthy owners, apparently less interested in making money, still recognized the financial benefits of hiring their stallion out. For the rich, breeding may have been in part a hobby, but even in the later 1700s some colonists imported stallions for more purely commercial reasons, either to breed from them and sell their stock, or sell them on at a substantial profit. After the American Revolution, power in Virginia, for example, was moving from planters and the older ruling classes to merchants, traders and commercial groups. Breeding continued, but became more commercial, though the contrast can be overstated, and there were still many wealthy gentlemen breeders, and elite members of jockey clubs. As in England there was often a mixture of motives, philosophies and approaches. [25]

The market for importations widened and blossomed up to the 1790s, though most stallions imported were bought relatively cheaply. But it declined substantially across the first two decades of the nineteenth century, whether because of antipathy and bitterness towards England, as in anti-British South Carolina, or because of the economic effects of the American Revolution, especially in Virginia. With few importations, the Diomed bloodline dominated, emphasising inbreeding. By the later 1820s, fresh demand meant breeders needed new outcrosses, and there was a renewed sentiment in favour of English bloodstock. This soon became a fashionable craze. Earlier imported horses sometimes raced before turning to breeding. The early nineteenth-century importations were exclusively for breeding, to provide new arrivals of fresh in-bred, out-bred and hybrid strains of 'blood'. When progeny were successful racing on the American turf, this allowed breeders to charge more for their stallion's coverings.

Stallion importations increased substantially in the 1820s and 1830s, years when mare importations also increased. These further crosses of newly imported English bloodstock with existing American horses (themselves with substantial English pedigree) further raised American standards.

The years from 1830 to 1839 were ones of growth and prosperity in racing, especially in the south. Over 80 stallions were imported, and over 210 mares, more than in the previous 100 years. Many importations were commercial in their scope, sometimes buying expensive and successful stallions from the best stables to then sell on. Several short-lived companies such as the Kentucky Import Company cashed in on demand. In the 1830s many imported stallions could generate an income of up to $2,000 in stud fees per annum, so importation could be more profitable and less risky, while Atlantic crossings were becoming less problematic. The Americans were ahead of the British in being able to get insurance against loss of a horse, though prices were high enough to deter many from taking it.

British stock was highly prized amongst breeders. A survey of stallion advertisements in the 1839 *Spirit of the Times*, though an unknown proportion of successful stallions standing at stud in America indicated that 29 out of 80 stallions were imported and often highly bred. A wider sample of 160 public stallions the same year, largely in Tennessee, Kentucky, Virginia and Alabama, showed 45 were imported.[26] By the 1840s, the evidence of stallion advertisements suggests that around half the stallions with offspring running on the American turf came from England (Table 1).

Some importers were highly successful, and able to afford the risk of purchasing Classic winners from England. James Jackson (1782–1840), a leading Tennessee businessman, landowner, Alabama senator and later state president, imported the stallion Leviathan in 1830, employing the Weatherbys as agents. The horse soon became the leading American sire. In 1835 Jackson sent a commission to the Tattersalls, by then the leading purchasing agents, to buy the best horse available from a list of several leading horses. In 1836 he obtained Glencoe, a 2000 Guineas and Ascot Gold Cup winner. Glencoe became an outstanding foal getter, especially of mares, and immensely influential in American bloodstock breeding,

Table 1 Numbers of imported and American-bred stallions with offspring running on the American turf 1829–1855

Date: 18-	29	31	33	35	37	39	41	43	45	47	49	51	53	55
Imported stallions	2	1	3	6	9	17	23	28	31	16	16	12	10	8
American-born	42	36	71	90	104	113	94	56	50	47	30	29	46	48

Source: Frank Forester, *Horse and Horsemanship of the United States*, vol. 1 (1857).

though not all Jackson's investments went so well. A later importation, St Giles, the 1839 Derby winner, was a failure. [27] Failure was not uncommon. The Alabama mill-owner, E.H. Boardman, produced few winners from the two stallions and 19 mares he was first sent by Richard Tattersall or from later imports.

In the southern states the quality of horses had become significantly higher by the 1840s, but inflated fees for stallions meant foals were now overpriced, and sires that turned out poorly meant some major losses. In the north the decades following the depression of 1837 had a major impact on thoroughbred racing and on sales, while anti-gambling groups became better organised. Racing collapsed throughout the northern states in the 1840s, and in the 1850s there was little or no racing in Pennsylvania, New Jersey or New York.

American breeders were slow to emulate annual yearling auction sales. In 1857 wealthy, English-educated breeder Robertson Aitcheson Alexander (1819– 1867), who had estates and relations in Scotland as well as the USA, acknowledged his intention of following 'the plan adopted by some of the English breeders, of having an Annual Sale of young horses, the produce of my horses and mares' on his Woodburn Farm estate in Kentucky. His leading stud farm auctions were soon widely imitated and became the accepted system. [28] By this time Kentucky had taken over from Virginia as the leading breeding centre, thanks to a potent combination of climate, environment, bluegrass, investment and expertise. Alexander, Keene Richards and others were rich gentlemen breeders, but there were also many with strongly commercial approaches.

In the late 1850s stallions were imported that further developed the American breeding scheme by establishing three key bloodlines. The first, Bonnie Scotland, foaled in 1853, did not perform well in England due to injuries, though he came second in the St Leger. Consequently he was not in demand at stud and was exported to America in 1857. His offspring soon got a reputation for speed and after the Civil War he was consistently amongst America's leading sires. The second, Australian, arrived in America in 1858 for wealthy magnate A. Keene Richards (1827–1881), of Kentucky, along with a number of English brood mares. The horse was second in the list of winning sires six times, between 1871 and 1877. Richards also imported St Leger winner The Knight of St George, in 1859, but he was not a success. The third stallion, Eclipse, arrived in 1859, after having been bought in England by Richard Ten Broeck in 1858. In 1867 and 1869 the horse stood second in the list of winning stallions.

The Civil War hit racing hard, and had a major impact on breeding, not least since many horses in the east were taken from studs for cavalry

Table 2 Racing in America 1874–1886: numbers of races

No. of races in	1874	1878	1886
Half mile and under	246	191	352
Five furlongs to a mile	459	476	1968
Above a mile to two miles	216	284	812
From two miles to four miles	37	35	14
Races	958	986	3146

Source: H.G. Crickmore, *Krik's Guide to the Turf* (New York).

purposes. There was much uncertainty and confusion through the 1860s. When racing revived, American racing changed to follow that in England, where long-distance heats had been falling out of favour by the 1840s, in favour of sprints of under a mile by younger horses, which were more attractive to the betting public, while numbers of races grew rapidly in the 1880s. [29]

This meant that horses bred for pure speed rather than stamina became fashionable, and this necessitated fresh waves of English imports, as Americans assimilated to English models. By the 1880s demand for such horses meant, according to *Spirit of the Times*, that buyers 'were willing to pay any price for the get of English sires'. And this resulted in 'a general importation of English sires', many of which were cheap but also of poor quality. [30] But by the 1880s, as racing expanded and more elite meetings and jockey clubs emerged, rich men were paying top prices for top English bloodstock.

Richer owners spent substantial sums to support their breeding theories. J.R. Keene, for instance, who believed that the best way of improving his Castleton Stud outside Lexington, Kentucky was to mate American sires with English mares, sent his commissioner to spend £20,000 buying mares from Tattersalls in 1894. He wanted the best that could be had in England regardless of cost as the nucleus of a stud for his stallion Spendthrift. Over the next two decades he probably imported more than 50 mares from England.

A select few had sufficient interest to purchase Weatherby's *Racing Calendar* to check details of English performances. Before the Civil War there were never more than six American subscribers listed annually, but by 1882 there were 20. And some breeders were even going further afield to strengthen their studs. During the 1880s there were regular importations from France as well as England, but also two stallions from New Zealand, from Australia, and two from Prussia and this trend continued thereafter. [31] In America, racing was sufficiently popular that even in 1901 it was still being described as 'the National sport of the country'. [32]

But if America was still importing British horses in the 1890s, American standards were such that some English owners and breeders began to import American horses, and American owners, trainers and jockeys began to appear in England in large numbers. Termed by the British, 'the American invasion', this is an area that Vamplew has explored in some detail in a recent paper. [33] By 1900, though British horses continued to be imported to America, the thoroughbred trade and trans-Atlantic racing influences had become very much two-way.

Racing clubs and regulations

Americans were often ambiguous in their feelings about England. For much of the nineteenth century some newspaper material talked of English racing in terms of 'the motherland' or 'our cousins' using the analogy of being part of the same family. Others, however, talked of England as a competitor or an imperial power whose sway over America had been illegitimate.

But for many racing men, England provided an idealised model. So, for example, when there were complaints in 1885 about the starts and the poor jockey behaviour at Saratoga, the *Chicago Horseman* reported that one 'often hears the question "why don't we do it here as they do in England. You never hear all this fuss over there about bad starts" '. [34] The same paper pointed out that names of races were often directly copied from famous English examples, such as the Derby, even if the actual conditions were completely different. [35] Race meetings were sometimes named after English exemplars. At least twenty American racecourses were called Newmarket between 1740 and 1840. And press descriptions of race meetings often used English analogies: Saratoga was described as 'the Ascot of the American turf', while Monmouth Park was the 'Newmarket of America'.

It might be thought that since America had many jockey clubs they had only too clearly emulated the British model. In fact however, Charleston in South Carolina had a Jockey Club in 1734, well before the English Jockey Club was founded. [36] Such clubs were already common before the American Revolution, when Stafford County in Virginia, for example, had jockey clubs at Fredericksburg and six other towns. [37] Kentucky's first club was formed in 1797. Since, as both Huggins and Vamplew have shown, the English Jockey Club took a long time to gain high status in

England, there is no reason to believe that it was very influential in America. [38]

There is a far stronger argument for the early impact of English rules. Rules and regulations of racing in America varied from place to place to a certain extent. But it is clear that by the early nineteenth century their various rules of racing drew heavily on English practice, though only the elite courses in England followed Newmarket rules, and England had local and regional variations. So rules from a variety of English race meetings would have been taken to America. In turn, as new American racing clubs were formed they appropriated rules from nearby. In Virginia the Richmond Jockey Club rules and the New-Market rules had much in common. [39]

One might have expected Americans to follow the English example provided by the Jockey Club, which by 1870 dominated and controlled mainstream British racing. By contrast in America, states and towns exercised more independence. New jockey clubs were formed in individual towns, and old ones revived, throughout the nineteenth century. As racing became a pursuit for the wealthy once again, after the Civil War, these organisations could have very high status. In 1883, for example, 500 leading Chicago citizens, about one third of which were millionaires, founded the highly prestigious Washington Park Jockey Club.

But a centralised rule-making body in America on British lines took a long time to emerge. The economic, social and cultural divisions between northern and southern, eastern and western USA after the Civil War, meant that calls for a national Jockey Club, run by gentlemen on the English model went unheeded. The regular press editorials that supported such a move had little effect. *Turf, Field and Farm* argued in 1868 that 'if we wish to make the turf a permanent institution in America we must adhere to the English plan of racing, make it a gentleman's amusement by confining its management exclusively to the keeping of gentlemen'. [40] A movement in New York in the 1880s to bring jockey clubs together 'with the purpose of forming a board of Stewards similar to that existing in England for the purpose of having control of the affairs of racing in the Eastern states' proved abortive due to friction between clubs, though an unsuccessful Board of Control was formed in 1891. [41]

In 1894 James R. Keene proposed a new organisation deliberately patterned on the English Jockey Club. By this time a wealthy group of largely New York-based owners were involved in racing and breeding. They had made millions in mining, transportation and finance. Newly rich families such as the Belmonts, Whitneys and Vanderbilts were preoccupied with legitimacy and emulated the lifestyle and trappings of the wealthy British aristocrats, buying the finest horses and forming a new Jockey Club. The club wrote and enforced rules of racing, licensed jockeys and trainers, appointed officials and allocated racing dates, kept forfeit list and published a racing calendar on the English model. In 1896 they took over publication of the *American Stud Book*, in the name of improving the breed and rendering racing respectable. This was very much a bid for power on English lines. [42]

But its power only extended as far as some of the eastern racecourses. Unlike England there was no central organisation to dominate rule making. So as late as the early 1900s in the north some tracks followed the rules of the Western Jockey Club, others the American Turf Association, and still others more regional variations.

British racing incomers

American courses regularly hosted visitors from England, and British racing men from Tyrone Power to Abingdon Baird could be found at Saratoga, Jerome Park and other prestigious courses near New York. [43] Southern courses were less accessible, and when Richard Tattersall of Hyde Park, London, visited the South Carolina Jockey Club races, in 1837 he was elected an honorary member of the club, a very rare honour as there were only five honorary members. However this was probably as a result of his presentation of a whip 'to be run for annually upon the principle which governs the Whip in England'. [44]

The English horse-dealing firm Tattersalls tried to set up an American version under Richard Brooke Tattersall in the late 1870s with a capital of about £10,000.[45] When a branch was set up in New York in 1880 William Easton became its auctioneer. He was New York born but educated in Clifton, Bristol. He later studied law and enrolled in the Middle Temple in London. He was a skilful auctioneer and ran auctions on the English manner in New York and Kentucky. Easton's exact relationship with the English firm in later years remains to be researched, but certainly the Tattersall name continued to have symbolic power in helping to sell stock. In 1893 there was also a Tattersalls (of Chicago) Ltd in Dearborn, and a Tattersalls–Brasfield organisation based in Lexington, Kentucky.

There were also significant numbers of British horsemen and stud grooms finding work in the American racing and breeding industry. Quite often grooms came over with the horses and then found employment in the USA. When Col. John Tayloe III received a shipment of two stallions, a brood mare, and two fillies, via the Tyne, in 1799, an English groom named Larkin came over and stayed on at a plantation stud. [46] Head grooms of top American owners were often English and Irish men hired away from British owners.

English jockeys also found employment, though courses were different and races run differently so it could take time to regain form. In the early nineteenth century, Arthur Taylor, of English birth, was originally a lightweight jockey for William R. Johnson (1782–1849) a major turf magnate, who had a very large stable at Oaklands, and allowed other owners to share it, at a price. Taylor later became his head trainer. [47]

After the Civil War, as transport links improved, more jockeys came across, a number at the invitation of American owners. By the 1870s, according to Edward Hotaling, America was 'now attracting top Newmarket riders', as well as some from Yorkshire, and certainly Barratt, Hughes, Sayers, Holloway and Meany were all riding in the later 1870s. [48] English jockeys such as Hayward, Barbee, or Evans assimilated to the American system, were successful and stayed in America, much favoured by northern and Maryland stables. Englishman Billy Haywood, who came from Mat Dawson's Newmarket stable in *c.*1867, became the leading American jockey of his generation and later a good trainer. He was described in 1888 in the *Spirit of the Times* as 'the best race rider we have ever known'.[49] As in England, jockeys moved round to seek employment. The English lightweight Charles Morton originally was engaged to John Hyland in the east in 1887, but in early 1888 went to California and got work.[50] Sam Loates reportedly spent some time in the USA in the early 1890s, where 'his forte was in winning the short races'. [51] Owners were prepared to offer good money for good jockeys, no matter whether English or American. In 1888 James Woodburn the well-known northern English lightweight jockey, 25 years old, declined a 'handsome offer' from a leading American stable, which reportedly involved a 'handsome' salary and 5% prize money of the races he won. [52]

Interest in British racing in media

Interest in British racing was very strong even in the eighteenth century. Early plantation owners with English family connections often had paintings of English horses displayed on their walls. Right through the nineteenth century most American painters of thoroughbreds copied the British tradition of painting champions amidst a bucolic, tranquil landscape. Edward Troyes (1808–1874) was a leading painter of throughbreds, especially in Kentucky, and produced engravings of many of the leading foundation sires and mares for the *American Turf Register and Sporting Magazine.* He was very influenced by British and French sporting art, and had worked in England. Likewise, the humorous prints which lampooned racing, its dishonesty and the greed of gamblers, tended to follow British models. The walls of major racecourse clubhouses and jockey club rooms were often decorated with paintings and etchings of English horses. Some wealthy owners bought the work of English painters too. Lorillard, at his home at Rancocas, had 'a magnificent oil painting' of his horse Parole, ridden by Archer, 'painted in England'. [53]

But from the 1820s it was the American sporting press that most stimulated a wider interest in British performances and pedigree of imported horses. Illustrations now provided information on conformation. The various weekly and monthly turf magazines and newspapers all drew heavily on British material for information about breeding, pedigrees and blood lines, fashionable stallions and prices; and England's leading races and owners. There was less interest in their trainers and jockeys.

The pre-Civil War coverage consistently assumed its readers (or indicated that the editors) had a major interest in British racing. Material relied largely on reports from English papers shipped across and perhaps six weeks out of date. J.S. Skinner's rurally-oriented monthly *American Turf Register* provided the key early example. It was first published in 1829, and was modelled on the English *Sporting Magazine*, which had been founded in 1792, but had more emphasis on horseracing, breeding and breeding history, and did much to standardise thoroughbred racing nationwide.

The first significant American horseracing weekly was published in 1831. This was William T. Porter and his brothers's more urban-oriented weekly *Spirit of the Times*, aimed, according to historian Steven A. Reiss, at 'gentlemen of property and standing'. Its style was based in large part on the English sporting paper *Bell's Life in London*, and it promoted all forms of horseracing, including harness racing, which was America's leading spectator sport until at least the 1870s, and thus more popular than thoroughbred racing. The paper soon had a circulation of 40,000 copies. [54] It regularly drew on the London sporting press for reports. By 1839 it was powerful enough to buy up its rival the *American Turf Register.* [55] It had a brief spell of anti-British sentiment in the 1840s, but in the 1850s still had regular reports on 'Foreign Sporting Intelligence' from all the leading London sporting papers, and employed a special correspondent in London. The paper was a propagandist for thoroughbred racing, noting signs of revival or expansion, and regularly using English examples as benchmarks, to be aspired to. An editorial in 1856, for example, noted the 'reviving inclination throughout our country for the enjoyments of the turf' and then stated:

> We turn the reader's attention for a moment to the summary of the York (English) Races in another column, in order that he may test, by his pulse, if he have any game blood in him, and see if he do not stir with emulation for a sport which is the chosen enjoyment of all others of the most distinguished and cultivated gentlemen in the British realm. [56]

Despite changes of editor and a brief split *Spirit of the Times* continued until suspending publication in June 1861, due to the Civil War. After the Civil War there was still interest in British racing. Results of major English races were soon rapidly available via 'ocean telegraph'. The editor George Wilkes and his successor William Curtis continued an elitist English-style amateur approach and the paper still provided significant English racing material in the 1880s. In 1888, for example, it contained advertisements for English stallions inserted by William Allinson, of the International Bloodstock Agency, in London, and aimed at 'American Breeders and Owners of Thoroughbred Horses who wish to Import the Best Blood from England on the Most Reasonable Terms'. [57] There were also reprints from inter alia *St Stephens Review*; *London Sporting and Dramatic News* and *Sporting Life*; engravings of English classic winners and reports on their races, 'Gossip from England' by Uncle Ben and similar material.

Turf, Field and Farm: the Sportsman's Oracle and Country Gentleman's Newspaper became a major rival to *Spirit of the Times* from 1865, but was more essentially a thoroughbred journal. Its New York proprietors, S.D. and B.G. Bruce, laboured hard to clear up pedigrees of thoroughbreds, and admired English racing, incorporating regular columns on 'The Turf in England', and details of English horses, jockeys and owners, largely plagiarised from their racing contemporaries in London. S.D. Bruce also published an American studbook based on the English models.

Later sporting papers also provided English racing news and information. *Livestock Record*, later the *Thoroughbred Record*, a weekly turf publication, published in the breeding centre of Lexington, Kentucky from 1876, gave such material from its beginnings. In the 1890s it regularly had two columns of 'Foreign Turf News', largely British, as well as reprinting English articles from *Sporting Life* and the *Sportsman*, and a regular feature, 'Our English Letter'. The illustrated weekly *Chicago Horseman* was 'devoted to the interests of the Horse, His owner and his Friends', printed in Chicago and New York, and begun in 1881. It had a special correspondent, Break o'Day, based in Manchester, travelling the racing circuit in England to provide news. By the 1890s there were even occasional English bookmakers advertising postal bets in the American press. However, as racing's expansion slowed and American horses, owners and jockeys became more successful in England, there was less interest in English racing in general, and more in the results of Anglo–American racing competition.

Emerging rivalry with England

Up to the 1850s and often beyond American racing men saw England as a source of better-quality thoroughbreds. It was a model to emulate and look up to. Most people assumed that English racing was superior. But increasingly, as standards of racing rose and the commercial rivalries between the two countries increased, some rich Americans began to consider testing their horses against English opposition, as a measure of progress. English owners would not consider bringing their supposedly superior horses to America for the relatively low prize money offered. They had too much to lose in both money and status if beaten. So Americans would have to take on the English on their own ground. From the 1840s Americans accepted that England horses were superior in terms of sprint races. [58] But they regularly questioned whether that superiority was more general.

This first significant test of this proposition, and an 'assault on the British turf', as Vamplew and Kay describe it, was by Richard Ten Broeck (1811–1892), from a rich Dutch New York family. [59] He was a sporting adventurer and professional gambler who mixed well socially with leading figures in both sides of the Atlantic, such as the English Jockey Club steward and handicapper Admiral Rous. [60] Ten Broeck spent much time in England, and in August 1856 took across his string of American horses, his trainer Palmer; his jockey Gilpatrick and other staff. The first races of his best horses, Lecompte, Prioress and Pryon, were followed closely in the American sporting press, who identified the horses as representing American breeding against the English, and so described them as 'distinguished', and as 'cracks' contending for 'superiority'. The horses had no success in 1856 and early 1857, and as expectations went unfulfilled, despite generous English weight allowances, blame was attached to the trainer and jockeys as well as the horses, though the horses may also have needed more time to acclimatise to English climate, weather, feeding, exercise and tracks. A Porter's *Spirit of the Times*'s correspondent suggested that all defeat proved was that 'a second class

American horse (and out of condition at that) must receive more than 14 lbs in a race of two and a half miles from first and second class English horses'. [61] In September 1857, when Lecompte came last in the Warwick Cup, there were calls for the horses to be send home, and for America to compete with 'superior stock', since 'national pride has been deeply wounded by the defeats of our horses'. [62] By October 1857, only the four-year-old Prioress was still racing. Sent off in the leading handicap event of the season, the Cesarewitch, at 100–1, she dead heated for first place, and then won the run-off by half a length. George Fordham, the English star, had replaced her American jockey to help ensure victory, and she had been favourably handicapped. As the first American thoroughbred to win in England, this win was rapturously received back home.

Summing up the season, the *New York Herald* described the stable as 'peculiarly unfortunate' but pointed out that whilst the horses were the best in the stable 'they were not selections from the best stables in the country', and so the races were not really a 'national affair', suggesting that the question of superiority between English and American horses had yet to be decided. [63] By early 1858 the American press had generally swung against the attempt and disparaged the horses. Failure had hurt national vanity. The *Spirit of the Times* bemoaned the way American writers were now 'so ready to admit and claim superiority for the English racers' and was 'somewhat surprised at the avidity with which a certain set of writers seized every occasion on which the American horses were defeated, to disparage their pretensions as racers, and the readiness and eagerness with which they claimed superiority for the English racer'. [64] Ten Broeck continued his attempts for several further years, but with only limited success.

The improvements in American thoroughbreds's speed and stamina after the Civil War led to further consideration and debate about standards. The Hon. James Beck claimed English horses arriving in Kentucky 'seemed to improve upon themselves' when put into the breeding stud. He felt English grazing centres were less good. Milton Sanford, a leading owner who had made his fortune manufacturing blankets and carpets at his Massachusetts mills during the Civil War, was not fixed in his view, but thought Kentucky was 'the first grazing state in America', though it was an open question 'whether the best bred of American horses were equal to the best breed of English horses'. General Robinson believed that 'a select stable of horses could be taken to England that would beat the English on their own tracks'. Mr Frank Hunt felt that would be 'hazardous'. Eventually Mr Sanford announced that he had engaged some of his colts in England. He was not confident as 'the English have money, brains and experience', and felt that they had 'three times as many horses to experiment with and ten times more money'. [65]

Sanford's string set off by steamer in late October 1875 with trainer and jockeys, and settled at Newmarket. The following year they were engaged in a number of prestigious races. In America the press settled to watch with interest, keen for the horses to be a credit to the country. Sanford tried to play this down, arguing that his enterprise was personal, not a national one, and that his visit should not be considered an invasion, or 'on the slightest degree in the light of rivalry. . .he bred, reared and ran simply for amusement'. [66] His horses had limited success in 1876, but in 1877 Brown Prince came second in the 2000 Guineas. This intensified interest back in the USA, though the horse ran unplaced in the Derby. [67] Sanford shipped further horses across in June 1877 and entered horses for the Oaks, Derby and St Leger in 1878, but had very limited success. He returned home believing that American horses were not yet on equal terms.

Whilst there were still claims that 'America was not inferior to any other country in the world in the purity of blood and high quality of [her] thoroughbreds', Sanford's lack of success caused despondency in American ranks. [68] Even so, there was increased belief that even if the English horses were bred for speed, the stamina and soundness of American horses was superior. [69]

The assault gathered further momentum in 1879, when Pierre Lorillard (1833–1901), a millionaire tobacco merchant, sent a small string to England to compete. Lorillard's name became 'more widely known to the general public than any other turfman' when his horse Parole won five races, including the Newmarket Handicap. [70] So in 1880 he sent a further string, trained by American Jacob Pincus. Between 1879 and 1883 Lorillard's horses won thirty races, worth £29,295, in England. In 1881 his colt Iroquois won the Epsom Derby and the Doncaster St Leger, wins which shocked both nations but delighted America. Winning the Derby had long been the ultimate measure of American breeding progress. It proved American horses could cross the Atlantic and win Classic races. As one correspondent had foretold,

> When we have a winner of the Derby, as we shall have sometime, the heart of the country will throb with joy and exultation from the centre to the uttermost limits. There is not one thing we can think of that would please all classes of the American people so much. [71]

The race had generated substantial American interest. According to a *New York Sportsman* editorial there was 'more interest felt in this country respecting the great three year old race to be run on Epsom Downs next Wednesday than there has been since Umpire started 25 years ago and ran unplaced'. [72] The telegraphed result got major coverage. New York went wild. The New York Stock Exchange closed. The *Sportman* printed two full columns, despite lacking details of the race, explaining how everyone was 'delighted and enthused', especially since the English press had claimed that 'no American horse could ever reach Derby form'. [73] Lorrillard got as much publicity as his horse. Both were heroes. He was regarded as 'the man who had put the USA on the map'. [74] Thereafter Lorillard continued to contest races in England until his death in 1901. The same year, 1881, another owner, English-born multimillionaire James Robert Keene (1838–1913), who had made several fortunes in America, had major success with one of his American-bred horses. He had taken horses to race in England from the late 1870s. His horse Foxhall won the two leading Newmarket handicaps in 1881 against strong fields, leading many English sporting writers to speak of 1881 as 'the American year'.

Success changed American attitudes. Once Americans recognised that they could compete effectively in England they came across in larger numbers, racing their stronger strings and sometimes breeding from their mares. The horses of August Belmont, the Whitneys and other rich American owners were soon racing in England. Weatherby's *General Stud Book Volume XVIII*, published in 1897, demonstrated clearly the many American horses were now being exploited. By 1900 the two leading American prize-winning owners, J.R. Keene and W.C. Whitney, were taking the cream of their horses to Europe, and writers were looking forward to their performances, which 'would result in more reliable deductions as to the relative merits of the English and American thoroughbred'. [75] In 1901 Whitney won the Derby and thirty-nine other English races with American-bred horses, proving their effectiveness.

Many American owners, trainers and jockeys saw an opportunity to make money. Owners could sell good American-bred horses to the English. Trainers, such as John Huggins, who trained the winners of 162 English races between 1898 and 1900, introduced effective American training methods and racing practices, including more fresh air, lighter racing plates and healthier environments. In 1900 American trainers Duke and Wishart trained 31 and 54 winners respectively. Wishart trained more winners than any English trainer, although some successes were due to doping techniques. [76] American jockeys were also successful. Willie

Sims, the African-American who was champion jockey in the USA in 1893 and 1894, introduced the short-stirrup riding style to England when riding there in 1895, and the American seat and tactics proved more effective, especially in short sprints. By 1900 five of the top 10 jockeys in England were American, including the champion jockey, Lester Reiff. Americans were now competing with the English and holding their own.

Conclusion

Clearly this study has not explored how Americans in general saw British racing. The sources interrogated here represented the views of a section of American society whose interests already lay in horseracing, breeding and betting, often through the twin lens of heredity and class. The American scholar of harness racing, Melvin Edelman, has argued that while harness racing was seen by nineteenth-century contemporaries as the 'democratic, utilitarian and by logical extension, the American horse', the thoroughbred was 'aristocratic and foreign' (i.e. English). [77] Such a view is overdrawn. Certainly there was substantial support for England and its horses amongst this group, most of whom were wealthy men and/or people from established families.

Globalisation entails a growth in the sharing of ideas and cultures, and it is clear that this process was well underway in racing in the later eighteen and nineteenth centuries, and that the direction of flow was by no means one-way, no least since interpenetration was linked to changing structures of power. My views are shaped by my background, my substantial earlier published work on British racing and through spending longer in Virginian archives than elsewhere. But even given such caveats, it is clear that throughout the period from 1730 to *c.*1900 many American racing men and breeders placed great store by certain branches of English bloodstock and imported significant numbers of stallions and mares. American rules and regulations borrowed from English models; jockeys, stablemen and stud grooms came from England and contributed expertise; and the American sporting media reprinted substantial amounts of English material. In the later nineteenth century power began to shift, and as more American horses, owners, trainers and jockeys competed on the British turf their fortunes were followed avidly back home, and this in turn acted back to make racing widely popular in America, though racing remained under attack from opposition groups. By the late nineteenth century some Americans believed that their turf had become just as much 'a national institution' as it was 'in England' and that their best horses could compete with the English. [78]

Acknowledgements

I would like to acknowledge the help of the National Sporting Library, Middleburg, Virginia, whose Fellowship scheme and outstanding collections of equestrian and field sport material were an immense help in facilitating the wider research on which this essay is based. I'd also like to thank Tony Collins, Ken Cohen and Elizabeth Tobey for helpful advice. Finally I'd like to thank Wray Vamplew whom I first met teaching social science statistics when I was studying for a part-time first degree. Wray was kind enough to offer a reference for a higher degree if ever I needed one. Many years later, whilst working for OFSTED, I was considering a part-time PhD and remembered Wray's 1976 book on horseracing. So I chose racing. Thanks Wray!

Notes

[1] Wray Vamplew, 'Horses, history and heritage: The state of the going', in Chris McConville, ed., *A global racecourse: Work, culture and horse sports* (Melbourne, 2008), p. vii.

[2] For an example of the traditional approach see John Hervey, *Racing in America, 1665–1865* (2 vols., New York, 1944). Steven A. Riess has incorporated material on racing into his studies of Chicago and more general studies, e.g. *City games: The evolution of American urban society and the rise of sports* (Urbana, IL, 1989). He is currently completing a study of gambling and horseracing in Chicago and New York from 1865 to 1897. Melvin Adelman's *A sporting time: New York City and the rise of modern athletics* (Urbana, IL, 1986) contains much material on horseracing. See also Melvin L. Adelman, 'The first modern sport in America: Harness racing in New York City 1825–1870', *Journal of Sport History* 8 (1) (1981), pp. 5–32.

[3] Roger Munting, *Hedges and hurdles: A social and economic history of national hunt racing* (London, 1987); Fergus D'Arcy, *Heroes, lords and racing men: The Turf Club, 1790–1990* (Curragh, 1991); Mike Huggins, *Flat racing and British society, 1790–1914* (London, 2000); Rebecca Cassidy, *The sport of kings* (Cambridge, 2002); Mike Huggins, *Horse racing and the British 1919–1939* (Manchester, 2004); Wray Vamplew and Joyce Kay, eds., *The encyclopaedia of British horse racing* (Abingdon, 2005).

[4] Andrew Lemon with Harold Freedman, *The history of Australian thoroughbred racing*, vol. 1 (Melbourne, 1987); Andrew Lemon with Harold Freedman, *The history of Australian thoroughbred racing*, vol. 2 (Melbourne, 1990). Wray Vamplew and Brian Stoddard, eds., *Sport in Australia: A social history* (London, 1994); and Wray Vamplew *et al.*, *Oxford companion to Australian sport*, 2nd ed. (Oxford, 1997) both contain useful material. See also Wayne Peake, 'The significance of unregistered proprietary pony racing in the social history of Sydney horse racing', *Sporting Traditions* 20 (2) (2004), pp. 1–18.

[5] Dominic Malcolm, *The Sage dictionary of sports studies* (London, 2008), p. 119.

[6] Barry Houlihan, *Sport and society: A student introduction* (London, 2008), pp. 553–73.

[7] See Rebecca Cassidy, *Horse people: Thoroughbred breeding culture in Lexington and Newmarket* (Baltimore MA, 2007), p. 194.

[8] See C.M. Prior, *The history of the Racing Calendar and Stud Book* (London, 1936).

[9] Frank Forester, *The horse of America*, vol. 1 (New York, 1857), p. 435.

[10] Andrew Burnaby, *Travels through the middle settlements of North America in 1759 and 1760* (London, 1775), p. 78.

[11] Francis Barnum Culver, *Blooded horses of colonial days* (Baltimore, MA, 1922), p. 37.

[12] See V.C. Johnson and Barbara Cruickshanks, *Virginia horse racing: Triumphs of the turf* (Charleston SC, 2008).

[13] Gerald Gems, Linda Borish and Gertrud Pfister, *Sports in American history* (Champaign IL, 2008) p. 20.

[14] Timothy Breen, 'Horses and gentlemen: The cultural significance of gambling amongst the gentry of Virginia', in *William and Mary Quarterly*, 3rd series (33) (1979), pp. 239–57.

[15] Nancy L. Struna, 'Gender and sporting practice in early America, 1750–1810', *Journal of Sport History* 18 (1) (1991), pp. 25–6.

[16] Breen, 'Horses and gentlemen'.

[17] Kenneth Cohen, 'Well calculated for the farmer: Thoroughbreds in the Early National Chesapeake, 1790–1850', *Virginia Magazine of History and Biography*, 115 (4) (2007) pp. 370–411.

[18] Heidi Weber, 'Pride of ownership: 19th century South Carolina planters and their horses', *Our Story: Journal of the New Jersey Council for History Education* (Fall 2006), web extra.

[19] Lyman H. Weeks, *The American turf: A historical account of racing in the United States* (New York, 1898); T.B. Merry, *The American thoroughbred* (New York, 1905); James Douglas Anderson, *Making the American thoroughbred* (Norwood, 1916); Francis Barnum Culver, *Blooded horses of colonial days* (Baltimore, MA, 1922); Robert L. Gery, *The matriarchy of the American turf* (New York, 1931).

[20] Fairfax Harrison, *The background of the American Stud Book* (Richmond, VA, 1933), p. 28; Frank Forrester (psuedonym of Henry William Herbert, 1807–1858), *Horse and horsemanship of the United States* (2 vols., New York, 1857).

[21] Sanders D. Bruce, *The American stud book*, vol. 3 (New York, 1878), p. 5.

[22] Hervey, *Racing in America*, vol. 1, p. 243.

[23] *South Carolina General Gazette*, 21 July 1775; Fairfax Harrison, *The Johns Island Stud South Carolina, 1750–1788* (Richmond, VA, 1931), esp. pp. 6, 34, 54.

[24] *Turf, Field and Farm*, 26 May 1876.

[25] See Rebecca Cassidy, *Horse people: Thoroughbred breeding culture in Lexington and Newmarket* (Baltimore, MA, 2007), pp. 15–16.

[26] Anderson, *Making the American thoroughbred*, p. 10.

[27] Hervey, *Racing in America*, vol. 1, p. 139.

[28] Hervey, *Racing in America*, vol. 1, pp. 321 ff.

[29] Huggins, *Flat racing and British society*, p. 33.

[30] *Spirit of the Times*, 15 Jan. 1887.

[31] Sanders D. Bruce, *The American stud book*, vol. 4 (New York, 1884).

[32] Vosburgh, 'Preface', in W.C. Whitney, *H.G. Crickmore's Racing Calendars, 1861–1869* (New York, 1901).

[33] Wray Vamplew, 'Sporting innovation: The American invasion of the British turf and links 1895–1905', *Sport History Review* 35 (2) (2004), pp. 122–37.

[34] *Chicago Horseman*, 6 Aug. 1885.
[35] *Chicago Horseman*, 25 May 1893.
[36] John B. Irving, *The South Carolina Jockey Club* (Charleston, SC, 1857).
[37] Jerrilynn Eby, *They called Stafford home: The development of Stafford County, Virginia, from 1600 until 1865* (Garrisonville, VA, 1997), pp. 253–4.
[38] Huggins, *Flat racing and British society*, pp. 174–203; Wray Vamplew, 'Reduced horse power: The Jockey Club and the regulation of British horseracing' *Entertainment Law* 2 (3) (2003), pp. 94–111.
[39] Richard Mason, *The gentleman's new pocket companion* (Petersburg, VA, 1811) gives both English and local rules. See also *Fairfield Jockey Club: Rules and regulations of the Fairfield Jockey Club* (Richmond, VA, 1853).
[40] *Turf, Field and Farm*, 18 Sept. 1868.
[41] *Spirit of the Times*, 18 Feb. 1888.
[42] Bernard Livingston, *Their turf: America's horsey set and its princely dynasties* (New York, 1973); Carol Case, *The right blood: America's aristocrats in thoroughbred racing* (New Brunswick, NJ, 2001).
[43] George Waller, *Saratoga: Saga of an impious era* (Englewood Cliffs, NJ, 1966).
[44] Irving, *The South Carolina Jockey Club*, pp. 147, 151.
[45] Vincent Orchard, *Tattersalls* (London, 1953), p. 274.
[46] Hervey, *Racing in America*, vol. 1, p 195.
[47] Hervey, *Racing in America*, vol. 2, p. 82.
[48] Edward Hotaling, *They're off: Racing in Saratoga* (Syracuse, NY, 1995), p. 106; Edward Hotaling, *The great black jockeys* (Rockling, CA, 1999), p. 224.
[49] *Spirit of the Times*, 19 May 1888.
[50] *Spirit of the Times*, 18 Feb. 1888.
[51] *Livestock Record*, 16 Feb. 1895.
[52] *Spirit of the Times*, 17 April 1888.
[53] *New York Sportsman*, 24 Dec. 1881.
[54] Steven A. Riess, *Sport in industrial America* (Wheeling, IL, 1995), p. 31.
[55] Arthur A. Raney and Jennings Bryant, *Handbook of sports and media* (Abingdon, 2006) p. 23.
[56] *Spirit of the Times*, 20 Sept. 1856.
[57] *Spirit of the Times*, 11 Feb. 1888.
[58] J.S. Skinner, 'Introduction', in William Yuoatt, *The horse* (Philadelphia, PA, 1843), p. 17.
[59] Vamplew and Kay, *Encyclopaedia of British horseracing*, p. 215.
[60] T.H. Bird, *Admiral Rous and the British turf* (London, 1939), pp. 199–202.
[61] *Porter's Spirit of the Times*, 19 Sept. 1857.
[62] *Porter's Spirit of the Times*, 26 Sept. 1857; 10 Oct. 1857.
[63] *New York Herald*, 26 Nov. 1857.
[64] *Porter's Spirit of the Times*, 27 Feb. 1858.
[65] *Turf, Field and Farm*, 1 Oct. 1875.
[66] *Turf, Field and Farm*, 3 Dec. 1875.
[67] *New York Times*, 30 May 1877.
[68] *Spirit of the Times*, 8 Jan. 1876.
[69] *New York Sportsman*, 22 Jan. 1881.
[70] *New York Times*, 22 March 1880.
[71] *New York Sportsman*, 11 Sept. 1880.

[72] *New York Sportsman*, 28 May 1881.
[73] *New York Sportsman*, 4 June 1881.
[74] Samuel Hildreth and James R Crowell, *The spell of the turf* (Philadelphia, PA, 1926), p. 128.
[75] W.R. Rowe, 'The Thoroughbred', *Outing* XXXVII (5 Feb., 1900).
[76] Wray Vamplew, *The turf* (London, 1976), pp. 50–51.
[77] Adelman, 'The first modern sport in America', p. 10.
[78] *New York Sportsman*, 12 Feb. 1881.

What Went Wrong with Counting? Thinking about Sport and Class in Britain and Ireland

Mike Cronin

This paper argues that the methodologies employed in much of Wray Vamplew's work, that of a 'traditional' economic historian, have great relevance in current studies of sports history. The issue of class, and in particular, the middle classes, have been a central theme in much recent sports history work, yet the work presented to date has not been underpinned by the kind of empirical work which Vamplew excelled at. The paper concludes that without a double approach – both empirical and cultural – our understanding of class and other key questions in sports history will be weakened.

I began working with Wray Vamplew at the International Centre for Sports History and Culture, De Montfort University, in 1998. I viewed him at one level as a leader in the writing and development of sports history, but at another, as a strange, perhaps outdated creature: the economic historian. Having been trained in the late 1980s and early 1990s in the field of Irish history, where we waded through the bloodshed of the battles over revisionism, and were aware of the developing trends in cultural history, the study of economic history seemed a side discipline that had seen its day. To my mind studying the world of the industrial revolution, economic downturns and upswings and the arena of business seemed both irrelevant and dull. Certainly when I had to teach such subjects I found that students were largely disengaged, and the texts that

Mike Cronin, Boston College, Dublin.

we used unappealing due to the countless tables, graphs and statistics. While I knew that Wray had wider interests than economic history alone, I was always amused by his opening question to any student: 'what are you going to count?'

By counting I knew what Wray meant. He considered it vital to any appreciation of history that the figures supported any argument or thesis. However, such work, involving as it did hours in the archives, population statistics, census reports, accounting books and so on, always seemed to me to be old fashioned and laborious. Did those hours in the archive counting things really advance our knowledge? It appeared as if the need for definite statistics was a search for some kind of absolute truth in history. By the mid-1990s it seemed that we, as a profession, had agreed that this was not possible. We had turned to the archive, to literature, popular culture and so on, not in search of hard facts, but looking instead for 'texts' that could be 'read'. There was no truth, only a variety of discourses, power dynamics and a welter of culture that had to be decoded.

I still stand by the impulses that lay behind what we can term the cultural turn, but have come to understand Wray's perspective. We do indeed need to count things. What I want to argue in this article is that while the new historiography of the late twentieth and early twenty first century has been vitally important to the study of sport, we too often followed wider historical trends without one eye on what was actually necessary. We applied contemporary models and practices to sports history even though, as a young discipline, we often failed to accept that there were certain things we didn't *know*. As a discipline that emerged from the demand for history from below, but one that simply did not have a critical mass of practitioners nor high numbers of Masters and PhD students, the amount of material that was sourced in relation to sport through social and economic history methodologies was relatively low. A key issue here is class. A subject that dominated the historiography of early British sports history – in line with wider patterns in 'mainstream' history – class quickly became unfashionable. The need to study history from below had dovetailed with the high levels of trade union activity in the 1970s, and had seemed important during the class struggles of the Thatcher years. However, by the late 1980s the unions were dead, and the home owning, service industry and free market dreams of Thatcherism had won out. Enter New Labour and their much vaunted appeal to an ideal of a classless Britain (or at least one where the majority could be middle class), and the study of class (and the concomitant interest in Marxism) as a central defining issue in history seemed an irrelevance.

We were left with a body of sports history that had begun by looking at the working classes in the development of the main professional sports of the late nineteenth century, and then rushed off to consider all kinds of other weighty issues empowered by ideas of culture, postmodernism, deconstruction, political theory and even a smattering of sociology. Sports history could be whatever you wanted it to be, and the whole issue of class was locked away to be revisited at some future date.

Perhaps it was the Blairite appeal to 'middle England' that led to some sports historians – notably Huggins, Mangan, Lowerson and others – to return to class. [1] However, this would not be a study of class in terms of struggle and conflict (the workers), but would instead focus on those that Blair was seeking to capture: the middle classes. Led by Huggins, and a wide range of books and articles that he has published, the sports history of the twenty-first century (especially in the pages of the *International Journal of the History of Sport (IJHS)*) seems obsessed with the middle classes. Even the other main theme in recent years in the *IJHS*, that of colonial sports, particularly India and neighbouring countries, has worked through issues of colonial discourse and power in the context of a wider understanding of the middle class. [2] Both coloniser (the civil servant, army officer and so on) and the colonised (elite royalty, indigenous administrators and leaders of commerce) are all fashioned as middle class. And what does middle class mean? In much of the literature that has been published of late, no matter how it has been problematised, middle class stands as short hand for respectable, upwardly mobile, conservative and decent – the very people that the sports revolution depended on for its long-term success.

My issue with much of the middle class literature is that they have forgotten Wray's argument: there needs to be some counting. While I understand and applaud many of the arguments that have been made in terms of the middle classes and sport, I am always left feeling uneasy. There are too many claims made in the various books and articles that are left un-investigated. It is as if the authors have discovered a lost tribe or city and that the act of discovery alone is the value of the mission. I would argue that it is not enough to have 'rediscovered' the middle classes and proceed to argue for their importance. Time has to be spent so that we know *who* these middle classes were in terms of their occupations, their property status, social and associational lives, their habits and customs, religious affiliation, political affiliation, and level of education. What do we mean by the term, who was included and excluded, how did people move in and out of the middle classes and how did that group come to connect with sport? Put simply: we have to count.

This article isn't simply critiquing recent work on the middle classes. Indeed it accepts two salient points made by Huggins. First, that the middle class involvement in sport 'constantly receive ritual reference yet frequently are not carefully considered or enterprisingly explored'; and second, that 'models of middle class involvement with leisure and sport thus far have been insufficiently comprehensive and precise, largely due to insufficient empirical research'. [3] My argument is that while there is a need to push forward new boundaries in terms of class-based research, it is impossible to imagine such being done without the 'empirical research', i.e. the counting, as argued for by Huggins. And this is not simply an issue for the middle classes. It applies to the involvement of the upper classes in sport, institutional elites and many variants of working-class sport that have not to date been covered (i.e. those sports which were not centred around teams of professionals). In the arena of working-class sports, that were based around professionalism, we do know a lot. Work by Tony Mason, Matthew Taylor and Neil Carter on football, Tony Collins on rugby league and union, Wray Vamplew on cricket and golf (amongst others) and Martin Johnes on pigeon racing has all, at different levels, revealed much about the socio-economic background of those workers who took part in sport. [4] This work has emerged from long hours uncovering who played, managed and directed sport, and matching names against census returns and trade directories. As a result, it is possible to *know* who was involved in working-class sport and, as Wray Vamplew did in *Pay Up and Play the Game: Professional Sport in Britain, 1875-1914* [5] and Hugh Cunningham in the *Cambridge Social History of Britain* [6] begin suggesting a taxonomy for distinguishing between different sub-groups within broad class categories.

It is not, as most scholars accept, desirable to talk about a three-class system (in Britain or anywhere else), and most attempt to problematise the internal workings of different classes as well as seeking to understand issues of transference at the borderlands between classes. However, until the research is undertaken that will allow us to know who formed the various groups, then any other conclusions as to the definitions or taxonomies of class in a sporting context can only ever be speculative. While any employment of cultural approaches to sports history in the realm of class can make useful contributions to our knowledge, the power of any conclusions will remain effectively sterile until the empirical information exists to support it.

The problem with empirical research is that it takes hard work. While I always applaud the fact that researchers head off to the archives to find out who really took part in sporting activity, it is never something that

I would undertake myself: I consider it a private matter for consenting adults. This is neither ignorance nor arrogance, just an acceptance of what interests me and the kinds of research I wish to pursue. However, I am always delighted that someone has conducted empirical research and encourage it – without it, other scholars, including myself, cannot make the forward strides in our research that we might envisage. Over recent years I have been blessed with a string of excellent graduate students, many of whom have gone to the libraries, archives and private holdings of many a sporting organisation and dug deep to reconstruct who played sport. Ian Clarke, while working on Cornish cricket cross-referenced team lists with the various census returns of the second half of the nineteenth century, and was able to reconstruct, in class terms *who* played cricket in that county. [7] Such research cast light not only on Cornish cricket, but on the workings of the whole of society in professional and social terms. Those individuals who play sport do not exist in isolation, and by understanding who they were it is possible to reconstruct their working and social week, understand their associational lives and, in doing so, develop a taxonomy for social interaction, mobility and social choice. In a similar vein, Liam O'Callaghan is producing a social history of Munster rugby, and has matched disciplinary and county minutes with census material and trade directories. [8] In doing so he has tackled core foundation myths relating to Munster rugby, and in particular the binary division between Limerick (working class) and Cork (middle/upper class) rugby. Again, such close empirical research not only answers key questions about the place of sport in the past, but also sheds light on key questions of agency, civil society and social networking.

Perhaps the best exponent of class-based empirical research in recent years has been Tom Hunt. [9] Working on an Irish topic always, in a British context, throws one to the margins. I have always reminded colleagues, in whatever history department I have worked in, and at conferences and seminars, that Ireland, until 1922, was part of Britain (not matter how contested that status was) and should be included in their work. However, for most British historians, including those working on sport, the Act of Union never happened, and for 'Britain' read England plus small pockets of Wales and Scotland. Ireland, north or south, may as well never have existed. It is because of long-standing attitudes towards Irish material that many sports historians have failed to read or understand the value of Hunt's work. He built directly on the work of Vamplew and undertook, in his work on Westmeath, the most extensive reconstruction of socio-economic groups involved in sport that has ever been completed. In a recent work, Hunt tackled one of the central facts that had underpinned our understanding of sport in Ireland: that the Gaelic Athletic Association (GAA), when founded in 1884, appealed to the landless labourer in line with the organisation's stated political and cultural objectives. Hunt, in a survey of 500 players from the first two decades of the organisation, which matched player names with census returns, land valuations, trade directories and Ordnance Surveys, was able to demonstrate that the number of landless labourers in the GAA was negligible (and thereby killed a foundation myth that has sustained itself for 125 years), and that the real strength of the organisation was in its ability to attract a group of young men who had left the farms of their family and changed their work attire to a collar and jacket. [10] The roots of the GAA, in terms of personnel, was not the men of the land, but rather the men who stood and sat behind the counters of shops and the desks of service agencies.

An ongoing project in Ireland, of which Wray would approve, is underpinned by a counting process, and examines associational life from the middle of the eighteenth century to the 1940s. Funded by the Irish Research Council for the Humanities and Social Sciences, and led by Vincent Comerford at NUI Maynooth, Associational Culture in Ireland is a vast project. As the project outline states: 'the Associational Culture in Ireland Project explores the culture of Irish associational life from 1750 to 1940, not merely from the point of view of who, what, where and when, but also the "hidden culture" of social networking which operated behind many different clubs and societies throughout the period'. [11] The project, which will continue beyond the life of its funding, is delivered in the form of a searchable database. Local papers from across Ireland have been examined, and details of any associational activity have been entered into the database. This allows us to view the sheer amount of associational activity across the period, who the people were that were involved in such organisations, and where they held their meetings. As the introduction to the database suggests: 'How central was Kiely's public house on the Quays in Waterford to eighteenth-century club life in that city? Or, what were the associations between the Mecklenburgh Musical Society and the debtors of the *marshalseas* in 1760s Dublin? Another important feature of the ACI database is its ability to search for individual members of clubs and societies as well as the associations themselves. In this way, it is possible for the historian to trace the networks that bound Amyas Griffith, master of the Fethard lodge of Freemasons in the early 1770s, to the Belfast Amicable Society in the 1780s'. [12] This is a highly significant development in our understanding of associational life in Ireland, and in this, the project reveals much (and a similar project of this scale is badly needed for Britain). As it is not simply restricted to sport, but does include it, the project builds on the work of Peter Clark in a British context and offers a series of interconnections as to what people did with their leisure, or non-work time. [13]

The problem with much sports history, especially in its discussion of class, is that it deals with sporting activity and clubs in isolation. The value of the Associational Culture Project is that is sees sport as one activity partaken by individuals in their week, and also explores what else they do. This has profound implications for the study of sport and class. A late nineteenth-century man may well have played cricket at the weekend, and may have even attended a committee meeting during the week. But this was not his only social outlet. As Clarke showed with respect of Cornwall (a work which, while local, had a similar breadth to that of the Associational Culture Project), the man of standing who played cricket, would have also visited during the week the local meetings of the National Geographic Society and the Royal Society, taken part in amateur dramatics (especially the craze for Gilbert and Sullivan) and also attended a range of meetings that while associated with their jobs, would have been primarily social and associational activities such as guild meetings. [14] What such a hectic social week tells us is that the middle classes (and the range here is wide, as will be discussed below) are constantly active, are not focused on a single activity such as sport and, given the nature of the social networks of all but the largest cities, are in daily social contact with the same group of people albeit in a variety of settings. As such sporting activity or membership does not define or shape class. It is simply one more activity which contributes to the definition of class. Also, we have to question how far a sporting choice, by any class group, is driven by a love and desire for any given sport. Acknowledging the wide range of activities that emerge in the Associational Culture Project, it is clear that class solidarity and exclusiveness, as well as a desire to be connected with the right group, also informed people's leisure choices. As such, does a man join the local cricket or tennis club because he has a strong need to play that sport, or is his membership a product of fitting in, extending or sustaining social networks and of improving business and social connections? In a similar vein to the Associational Culture Project, I am currently involved in a major oral history project examining the GAA in Ireland and across the diaspora. [15] The aim of the four-year project is to question people about their lives in the GAA through the use of questionnaires and interviews, as well as through different projects at schools and college level. In its entirety the project aims to gather the recollections of *c*.20,000 people. What underpins each questionnaire or interview is a series of questions relating to education, occupation, religion, location and so on. This will allow a database to be constructed that will produce the largest historical record of socio-economic backgrounds for people involved in a sporting organisation, as well as contextualising them in a broader social frame. In its entirety the project will allow us to say *who* was involved in the GAA and *what* they were in terms of socio-economic background. Once a useful taxonomy has been designed, which will not centre on a three-tier version of class (as such categories are not suited to the Irish context), a socio-economic reading of the groups and networks involved in the GAA since the 1930s will emerge.

What I am arguing here is that the very act of counting, of doing the empirical research, which something as large scale as the Associational Culture Project or the GAA Oral History Project allows, helps us understand who did what and with whom. As a result we can begin mapping that person through their individual occupation and circumstances, as well as locating them within their social milieu. This longitudinal approach has to inform any discussion of class and sport and also places it in context. It also sheds light on how macro-social forces are played out and inform matters at the local level.

The problem for much British sports history is that it has been primarily (irrespective of class focus) been informed by work on the urban conurbations that emerged from the industrial revolution. There are notable exceptions such as the work of Alan Metcalf and Neil Tranter who explored smaller communities, and obvious oversights such as any major consideration of sport in London (a point also made by Huggins) still exist. [16] Given that the industrial revolution, in those towns and cities that arose from it, was driven by capital, the simplistic three-tier class model works at the basic level. In large towns the mix of workers, suited professionals and factory/land owners is fairly straightforward and their sporting choices and associations can be followed accordingly. However, what do we do with peripheral spaces and places? In broad terms the sports history of Britain is focused on the towns and cities of the north and midlands of England, and the industrial and raw material towns of south Wales. There is little work that explores whole swathes of the country such as the southwest, East Anglia, the southern coastal counties, most of Scotland outside the Clyde region or central and northern Wales. As for the islands around Britain, and sport in Northern Ireland, there are wholesale gaps in our knowledge. These regions are however the most interesting, or so I would argue. They offer up smaller pockets of population, yet did 'benefit' from the macro forces that stemmed from the industrial revolution. All the regions mentioned above witnessed the arrival of the railway (even in limited form), the spread of an education system that heightened literacy levels, an increased level of industry and commerce (albeit on a small scale) and the growth and spread of the printed media. But in these regions, given the slightness and wide spread of population, issues of class in the sporting context are far more complex.

In a town where they may have been a single bank, doctor or solicitors office there is, strictly speaking, no grouping of the professional classes: there are simply individuals of standing. As such the idea that the 'middle classes' in such areas would underpin and sustain a sporting revolution is problematic as there is no critical mass. Equally, the presence of higher numbers of rural workers and dwellers also creates problems. Considerations of rurally-based sports movements are unusual in the written history of sport, and in such regions the coexistence of modern and pre-modern forms of sport survives for much longer than in urban areas. This is not to say that there is no sport, but research needs to be conducted (back to the counting) that explores and uncovers how sport (and society) in these peripheral areas functioned. How do the small number of middle-class professionals chart their way through their associational life when they are limited in numbers? Is there a blurring of lines between the upper and middle classes, so as to give them numerical sustainability and thereby exclude the workers; or do the middle classes find sporting allegiance with those same workers through games, such as cricket, which allow for an inbuilt stratification of the classes? I cannot answer those questions, but suggest them as future avenues for research. The point is that to understand the middle, or any other classes, we have to problematise how we approach different towns, cities and rural areas, to contextualise any findings in terms of the area under consideration (and this is where numbers are important) and accept that in terms of making national conclusions we have to have nationally diverse empirical research at hand. It is not enough to make conclusions about the working, middle or upper class (no matter how complex we are in our understanding of those terms) based on research from the pages of one town or city's newspapers and posit national conclusions on that basis.

To work briefly through an example of some of the problems of understanding who played sport, and what this meant in terms of class, I turn to one quick example. At present I am working on a re-reading of the bodyline test series between England and Australia. What I am primarily interested in is how the English team, and in particular its captain, Douglas Jardine, were presented to and understood by the English public. This is a view completely at odds with the Australian version (that the English were cheats led by the devilish, win at all costs mentality of Jardine), and instead posits the team as much-needed national heroes during a time of depression and crisis. Further, I argue that Jardine can be understood as possessing heroic values which were commonly inscribed in both the popular fictional heroes of the time and those real-life English heroes who were travelling the world exploring or else breaking all kinds of records in planes and cars. Essentially my argument is that Jardine is a modernist hero who represents, rather than subverts, the prevailing English characteristics of the period. That is not the issue here however, and instead I want to turn to the English team.

If we take the eleven men who appeared for England at the infamous Adelaide test in January 1933 we see that they included various post-test professions such as sports outfitting proprietor (Sutcliffe), bank clerk (Jardine), sports administrator (Hammond), professional cricketer (Ames, Leyland, Wyatt, Verity, Voce and Larwood), manual worker (Paynter) and cricket administrator (Allen). In this we have, at first glance, a mix of middle-class professions, as well as members of the working classes – a fairly standard mix for inter-war test teams. However, a deeper series of questions suggests itself. Admittedly the careers of all these men were shaped and interrupted by both world wars, and their elevation to the test team meant that all of them, directly or indirectly benefitted from cricket. Despite the classes that separated them, what is the real difference (in an age where professional sportsmen could make a living) between Hammond securing a role within the Marylebone Cricket Club (MCC) and international cricket, and Larwood and others making a living from playing the game and later securing coaching positions? All of them benefit from the game, and it is here that class labels begin to get problematic. Jardine, born in India, from an affluent family and well schooled, appears upper class. And yet he chooses a moderate life in banking over one in the law. He marries well, and makes some money from writing about cricket. Does he remain the upper class man of his Edwardian birth, or does he become something else? The very reason that Jardine cites for quitting cricket is that he cannot devote the time to the game when he has a living to earn; he is a gentleman cricketer, but not a gentleman with independent means. Likewise Voce and Larwood – born as they were in coal mining towns, and beginning their working lives in the pits – remain working class men by the end of their careers? Both benefit from their professionalism, and live a very different life from their pit village counterparts. These are however broad-brush portraits without context.

The context for all these eleven men is where they fit within the counting game. Because of *Wisden* and the *Dictionary of National Biography* we know much about their lives, and their monetary vale at their death. But what does Jardine's apparent downward spiral from son of imperial privilege to comfortable middle-class man, or Sutcliffe's acquired wealth as a shop proprietor tell us? In themselves, they tell us the story of changing socio-economic times, of a drift from inherited position and schooling for some, a rise from manual labour to the relative luxury of professional sport, and all that it afforded, for others. I would argue however that to truly understand the context of the team, in socio-economic terms, we would have to revisit their origins. What happened to Voce's fellow pupils at Annesley Woodhouse School or his many teammates at Nottinghamshire? The same question could be applied to Jardine's classmates at Winchester or Allen's at Eton, and their respective professional colleagues in banking and stockbroking. The point of this exercise would be to understand the socio-economic background of those surrounding elite sportsmen at that point in history. Are Voce's classmates all destined for the pit? Do some of Jardine's schoolmates, many of them sons of empire like himself, suffer an inter-war readjustment so that they become part of the new suburban middle classes?

My argument then simply is this: without the counting – the empirical research – answering complex questions about class will be an empty exercise. Yes, I can write about the cultural context of the reception of Jardine's bodyline team, but I cannot make conclusions as to their respective class positions and the response to them, without understanding their lives and the socio-economic structures (schools, workplace, teams and so on) from which they sprung. Without comparisons to their fellow travellers in life, it would be impossible to contextualise them, or understand questions that relate to their social mobility, their supposedly privileged place as sports heroes and, in some cases, professionals. Equally, it is difficult to envisage any understanding of their social networks and ties to place and space without some comparative understanding of their peers. So, alongside our cultural readings and our problematisation of the very idea and taxonomy of class, we need the hard work with the records to create a true understanding of how the individual sportsman (or woman) can be located within the ever changing social circumstances of their life and their times.

To conclude, I have to be honest, and still say that there is something about all the figures and tables, such as in Wray's recent article in the *Economic History Review* that leaves me a little cold. Perhaps it is my failing, and I don't really understand them. However, I do appreciate them. In that article, the lives of golf professionals are presented so that we *know* those men and the lives they lead. We do not rely, as perhaps we may have done before, on socio-economic shorthand and presumption, i.e.

golf equals middle- and upper-class socialisation in the confines of private clubs. Instead, what Wray offers us in this, and much of his other work, is a window on those men who staffed sporting places. In doing so he shows how even elite private spaces, such as golf courses, actually offer a series of complex mediations between different classes who are present within the golfing space. They are not all privileged, and they are not all there for the same reason. Sports clubs and organisations are complex bodies and contain, in different locales and at various times, a whole range of different social classes who are present to enable the game to be played and consumed. If we are to truly move sports history forward once more, to appreciate and problematise class, and to add to our cultural readings of sport, we have to know who played, who was employed and who served. In doing so, we can understand a whole series of inter-relationships and can move on to make international, national and regional comparisons. Perhaps then, Wray was right all along. We have to ask ourselves: 'what am I going to count?'

Notes

[1] The weight of this work is impressive, especially in the *IJHS*, but see for example in book form, Mike Huggins, *Victorians and sport* (Hambledon, 2007); J.A. Mangan, ed., *Reformers, sports modernisers: Middle class revolutionaries* (London, 2002); John Lowerson, *Sport and the English middle classes* (1995); John Lowerson, *Sport and the English middle classes* (Manchester, 1995).

[2] See the many articles by Boria Majumdar, for example, 'Tom Brown goes global: The Brown ethic in colonial and postcolonial India', *International Journal for the History of Sport*, 23 (5) (2006), pp. 805–20.

[3] Mike Huggins, 'Second-class citizens? English middle-class culture and sport, 1850–1910: A reconsideration', *International Journal of the History of Sport*, 17 (1) (2000), pp. 1, 5.

[4] Tony Mason, *Association Football and English society, 1863–1915* (Brighton, 1980); Matthew Taylor, *The leaguers: The making of professional football in England, 1900–39* (Liverpool, 2005); Neil Carter, *The football manager: A history* (London, 2006); Tony Collins, *Rugby league in twentieth century Britain* (Abingdon, 2006); Tony Collins, *Rugby's great split* (London, 2006); Tony Collins, *A social history of English rugby union* (Abingdon, 2009); Wray Vamplew, 'Successful workers or exploited labour? Golf professionals and professional golfers in Britain, 1888–1914', *Economic History Review*, 61 (1) (2008), pp. 54–79; Keith A.P. Sandiford and Wray Vamplew, 'County cricketers' benefits and testimonials, 1946–85', *International Journal of the History of Sport*, 16 (1) (1999), pp. 87–116; and Martin Johnes, 'Pigeon racing and working-class culture in Britain, *c.*1850–1950', *Cultural and Social History*, 4 (3) (2007), pp. 361–83.

[5] Wray Vamplew, *Pay up and play the game: Professional sport in Britain, 1875–1914* (Cambridge, 2008).

[6] Hugh Cunningham, 'Leisure and culture', in F.M.L. Thompson, ed., *The Cambridge social history of Britain, 1870–1960*, vol. 2: *People and their environment* (Cambridge, 1990).

[7] Ian Clarke, 'Social history of Cornish cricket' (unpublished PhD thesis, De Montfort University, 2004), ch. 4.

[8] Liam O'Callaghan, 'A social history of Munster rugby' (unpublished PhD thesis, Leeds Metropolitan University, 2010).

[9] Tom Hunt, *Sport and society in Victorian Ireland: The case of Westmeath* (Cork, 2007); and for an assessment of its importance see IHR reviews in history, available online at http://www.history.ac.uk/reviews/paper/rouse.html, accessed 6 May 2009.

[10] Tom Hunt, 'The GAA: Social structure and associated clubs', in Mike Cronin, William Murphy and Paul Rouse, eds., *The Gaelic Athletic Association, 1884–2009* (Cork, 2009), pp. 183–202.

[11] See http://irishassociations.ie/wordpress/

[12] Ibid.

[13] Peter Clark, *British clubs and societies, 1580–1800: The origins of an associational world* (Oxford, 2000).

[14] Clark, 'Cornish cricket', ch. 3.

[15] See www.gaahistory.com for details

[16] Alan Metcalfe, *Leisure and recreation in a Victorian mining community: The social economy of leisure in rural north-east England, 1820–1914* (London, 2005); for example, Neil Tranter, 'The patronage of organised sport in central Scotland, 1820–1900', *Journal of Sport History*, 16 (3) (1989), pp. 227–47; and Neil Tranter, 'The social and occupational structure of sport in central Scotland in the nineteenth century', *International Journal of the History of Sport*, 4 (3) (1987), pp. 301–14.

Australian Sport History: From the Founding Years to Today

Daryl Adair

The academic study of sport history in Australia is a relatively recent initiative, dating back to the 1970s. It was inspired by a handful of enterprising scholars, each of whom is now retired. The following paper has two aims. First, it reflects on the efforts of early sport historians to carve out a research niche within the Australian academy. In keeping with the festschrift theme, it also dwells upon the profound influence of Wray Vamplew – a Yorkshireman who had the temerity to help pioneer sport history in an Antipodean setting. Second, the main body of the paper goes on to identify three key areas of research developed over the past thirty years by scholars of Australian sport history, then concludes with recommendations for further research.

Fascinated by sport; underwhelmed by its history

Despite the high profile of sport in Australian culture, the historical analysis of sport in this country has a low profile, whether in terms of academic research, media interest, or the reading public. Australian sport fans are eager to recount glorious performances by the nation's teams and athletes, and certainly indulge themselves in eulogistic books and magazines about sport. But these enthusiasts have comparatively little knowledge about, nor interest in, Australian history and the role of sport in shaping its evolution. This is, in large part, a reflection of inadequate education: in many schools history has been supplanted as a key area of study, with the Australian story conveyed as part of broad brush subjects like 'social studies' or 'civics and citizenship'. [1] Moreover, at university

Daryl Adair, University of Technology Sydney.

level Australian history is typically taught with scant regard for the explanatory potential of sport and physical culture. Too often, sport has been relegated by Australian academics to the 'toy department' rather than the history department where, incidentally, there are few scholars for whom sport is a serious focus of research. [2] This is illogical, because sport can provide important insights into themes and issues that have been pivotal to the evolution of Australian history. Indeed, as this article indicates, sport historians have carved out areas of research that contribute ably to the study of Australia's past.

It should be acknowledged that two of the best known chroniclers of Australian history, Manning Clark and Geoffrey Blainey, both recognised the role of sport in community and nation building. Clark's epic six-volume collection *A History of Australia* (1962–1999) includes numerous scattered references to major sports, such as cricket and Australian Rules football, as well as moments of high drama, such as the famous Anglo-Australian 'Bodyline' series. [3] But it would be an exaggeration to claim that sport was a key theme in Clark's narrative, despite his personal fondness for it and his passion for Carlton football club. Sport was simply not on the social history 'radar' when Clark was in his prime, and the fact that he actually gave it some profile was noteworthy in itself. Blainey, a long-time supporter of the Geelong football club, took a different route; his monographs of the Australian story barely mentioned sport, but he eventually produced *A Game of Own: The Origins of Australian Football* (1990). [4]

From within the academy, a lesser known but far more influential contributor to sports history laid the intellectual groundwork from which the sub-discipline would slowly emerge. W.F. 'Bill' Mandle read history at Oxford University and later accepted academic appointments in New Zealand and Australia. He has been described, in retrospect, as a 'giant' figure upon whose shoulders fledgling early sport historians stood. [5] In particular, Mandle's emerging interests in nationalism and identity allowed him to bring the subject of sport firmly into new discussions of Australian history. [6] Fittingly, Mandle was a key contributor to the first academic conference on sport history in Australia – 'Sporting Traditions', which was staged at Sydney in 1977. Several delegates recalled a feeling of 'coming out' from inside the history closet, admitting excitement, even 'exhilaration' at the opportunity to pursue seriously the role of sport in Australian history. [7] An edited book was a key outcome and, four such conferences later, the Australian Society for Sport History (ASSH) was formed in 1983. [8] The following year ASSH's refereed journal, *Sporting Traditions*, was launched with Wray Vamplew as the foundation editor. By the mid-1980s, therefore, a small but enterprising group of academics had begun a collaborative approach to the historical study of Australian sport. Names like Cashman, O'Hara, Murray, Stoddart, Tatz and Vamplew – to mention just a few – had the audacity to make sport a key part of their historical research. Significantly these trendsetters were typically situated in arts and humanities or social science faculties; thus they were part of intellectual environments within which the study of history was valued.

Wray Vamplew and Australian sport history

Among the 'team of 1977' Vamplew has been the last to retire, though his absence from Australian shores is not recent. Vamplew returned to the UK in 1993 after some 16 years at Flinders University in Adelaide. During his early career from the mid-1970s onward, Vamplew's expertise in economic history led him to quantitative methodology and empirical data collection, both of which allowed him to make statistical analyses of sport in Britain, as well as the rise of commercialism and professionalism in sport during the late Victorian era. That research was not only pathbreaking, it was prolific: the quality and quantity of Vamplew's economic studies of British sport history were without peer. [9] He also brought skills of quantitative analysis to Australian sport history, producing statistical interpretations of sport crowd figures and investigations into the commercial operation of local sport enterprises. [10] Vamplew's reputation soon led him to be appointed the editor of *Australian Historical Statistics*, a 470-page volume in the prestigious *Australians: A Historical Library* series produced to mark the 1988 bicentennial of white settlement. [11]

Ever the pragmatist, Vamplew embraced the social history of sport, and there he made outstanding contributions to that emerging sub-discipline in Australia. He led a team of researchers to produce the germinal *Oxford Companion to Australian Sports History* (1992); with Brian Stoddart he edited *Sport in Australia: A Social History* (1994), which covered 13 types of sport; and with Daryl Adair he co-authored the synthesis study *Sport in Australian History* (1997). The last of these books was part of Oxford University Press's Retrospective Series which required authors 'to examine formative issues' in Australian history 'in a style accessible to non-specialists'. [12] This particular text attracted very mixed reviews with readers seemingly polarised in their support or opposition to the Adair-Vamplew offering. [13] The excitement diminished quickly, though, after the authors produced a lengthy rebuttal to the most serious charges – which included male chauvinism, disrespect for ethnic minorities, and racism. [14]

Vamplew has taken a particular interest in player and spectator violence in Australian sport, which in the days of World Series Cricket and some jingoistic 'ethnic minority' soccer clubs in Sydney and Melbourne seemed endemic. His research coincided with studies of crowd behaviour in British soccer where problems were much more serious. [15] After returning to the UK in 1993 Vamplew developed four areas of inquiry – sport and alcohol consumption, [16] the establishment and purposes of sport museums, [17] the impact of weather and climate on sport, [18] and the impact of rules changes on sport over time. [19] These are topics that could be usefully explored in an Australian context. Finally, it is important to acknowledge that Wray Vamplew served as either president of ASSH or editor of *Sporting Traditions* for a number of years, and fittingly was guest editor of the special issue 'Commemorating 30 years of ASSH Conferences' (2007). As a keen observer of Vamplew's work for nearly 20 years, my single regret is that he returned too soon to the UK. An economic history of Australian sport still beckons. [20]

Academic sport history: A profession in limbo

By the early twenty-first century, as exponents of Australian sport history have either moved on or retired from academia, they were not being replaced by scholars with similar research or teaching interests. At the University of New South Wales, for example, Richard Cashman had successfully taught sport history for many years, and established the Australian Centre for Olympic Studies (ACOS). When he retired in 2004, UNSW not only put an end to the sport history program – which was popular with students – it also closed down ACOS, despite it having contributed significantly to research on the Sydney Olympic Games and their legacy. Cashman's swift transfer of ACOS to the Faculty of Business at University of Technology Sydney, and his appointment there as an adjunct professor, symbolised a wider trend for academic practitioners of sport history today. This current generation of academics resides almost solely in either business or human movement faculties, and none has the title 'historian'. They lecture in sport management or the socio-cultural dimensions of human movement, and do their best to infuse historical perspective into these teaching programs. They continue to pursue historical research into sport, but do so in working environments where colleagues typically focus on contemporary issues, such as sport marketing, sport pedagogy and the science of athletic performance.

In short, intellectual environments within which history is generally not valued.

It is, therefore, a credit to academics, past and present, whatever their disciplinary background or location, for ensuring that the subject of sport history has retained an identity as a discrete sub-discipline and, moreover, has contributed something tangible to the wider history of Australia. There have been noble efforts to produce synthesis studies of Australian sport history, with Cashman's *Paradise of Sport* (1995) the most comprehensive and Booth and Tatz's *One Eyed* the most argumentative. [21] Studies that include both sociology and an element of history include B. Stoddart, *Saturday Afternoon Fever: Sport in the Australian Culture* and P. Kell, *Good Sports: Australian Sport and the Myth of the Fair Go*. [22]

But no one can claim, after a little over two decades of ASSH-led exploratory study, to be an authority on Australian sport history. There is simply too much yet to be researched, and too few academics putting their shoulder to the sport history wheel. So, as the following survey indicates, there has been welcome progress but significant gaps remain. Three pivotal historical areas will be surveyed: geography and Australian self-image through sport; norms of participation in Australian sport; and Aboriginality, 'race' and ethnicity in a white-dominated sports culture. Analysis of these key areas of sport and society will enable educators to add value and depth to existing approaches to Australian history; and thus 'not', as Vamplew once put it, 'just its sports pages'. [23]

Geography and Australian self-image through sport

According to historian Geoffrey Blainey, Australia has been cursed by the 'tyranny of distance'. [24] As a British colonial outpost it was literally on the other side of the world, and, particularly before air travel and electronic communication, this meant separation from the so-called 'motherland'. Sport was one way in which Britain and its colonies, whether in Australia or elsewhere, could be connected. It was, as both Cashman and Daly have averred, part of the cultural baggage of migrants – particularly those who arrived as free settlers in the second half of the nineteenth century. [25] Efforts to establish race tracks, cricket fields and rugby pitches were part of the colonial drive to recreate – even if in the imagination – some of the cultural trappings of a distant 'homeland'. It was therefore of particular note when sports teams and competitors from Britain toured the colonies. The locals were initially in awe of visiting athletes, such as in cricket, where English sides toyed with their colonial counterparts. But, as historians have shown, from the 1860s onwards the tide slowly turned – most notably in cricket, rowing, and rugby union – with Antipodean teams and crews performing creditably in Anglo-Australian contests. [26] The importance of this sporting relationship was firmly established in 1882, when the legend of the 'Ashes' was born in the wake of a surprise Australian win over England at The Oval in London. That victory, together with other triumphs in sport, impacted positively on colonial self confidence: athletes and teams were eagerly representing 'Australia' abroad before the nation existed. [27] They were still fiercely pro-empire, but anxious to overcome negative attitudes about a convict past and rumblings about Antipodean inferiority. [28] Sport, with its immutable scoreboard, was thus an important way of establishing a sense of Anglo–Australian parity – and ultimately rivalry.

Mandle sees in sport, though most notably in cricket, seeds of a colonial nationalism that went beyond culture into politics. [29] Australians were for many years lukewarm about the idea of federation, and it took two referenda for that proposal to be passed – and eventually by only a small majority. [30] Mandle contends that inter-colonial and Anglo-Australian sport provided examples of effective administrative co-operation at the national level, which many had thought unlikely in an era when parochial colonies protected their local economies with tariffs and, by producing different sized railway gauges, effectively stymying regional trade and travel. [31] This rather 'reluctant' Commonwealth of 1901 provided a very hybrid sense of nationhood. [32] Australia remained a dominion of the British Empire and would continue to prove its loyalty to Britain by military service in the Boer War and two World Wars. Through 'Empire' sports like cricket, rugby union and rugby league, together with active support for British troops in Europe, Australians developed a formidable reputation on both playing fields and battle fields. This combination of sport and wartime service has received attention by scholars interested in questions of identity, loyalty and gender norms. [33] But the subject has not been treated exhaustively; surprisingly so given the depth of interest in military history in Australia and the elevation of the Australian and New Zealand Army Corps (ANZACs) to the status of legend. [34]

Use of space and response to climate are lynchpins of Australian history. With European annexation of land, many colonists looked to establish agricultural properties and mining operations in rural or remote areas. But they proved exceptional; most whites resided in urban centres along the outer rim of a vast, largely dry, island continent. There they had ready access to the ocean and regular supplies of water from coastal river systems – both of which also provided opportunities for aquatic sports. [35]

The city of Sydney, with its sunny weather, panoramic harbour and lengthy Parramatta river, provided regular opportunities for sailing and rowing regattas, which proved to be some of the most popular sporting spectacles of the nineteenth century. [36] Today, of course, some of the most iconic recreational spaces in Australia are beaches, with both surfers and surf lifesavers quintessential symbols of local aquatic culture. [37] Yet as historians have shown, during the colonial era there was conflict between picnickers and surf bathers, and efforts to proscribe swimming in public. For many moral conservatives, bathing at the beach in daylight hours was frowned upon as improper; exposing too much flesh at a time when modesty was acute. [38] Indeed, when public bathing eventually became more widely accepted, whether at the beach or in swimming pools, men and women were initially segregated. [39] Surf lifesaving – an Australian invention – dates from 1907, but until recent decades this was a male dominated institution. The timing and extent of gender reform is, however, still hotly debated by sport historians. [40]

As public space, the beach provides scholars with a fascinating resource for tracking changing perceptions about the human body and norms of public behaviour. Surfing, for example, became part of a 1960s beachside 'counterculture' in which self-expression and aesthetic movement in the surf were highly prized. New swimwear was intended to accentuate body display, and was soon commercialised as a fashion item. [41] Booth's research has revealed structural tensions at the modern beach. 'Surfies' preferred to stay aloof from formality and civic engagement, while surf lifesavers volunteered their time to clubs and the wider beach-going community. To the lifesavers the 'surfies' appeared self-indulgently radical; to 'surfies' the lifeguards seemed subservient to authority and conformist. These were convenient stereotypes; both of these male-dominated groups could, in their own way, be a law unto themselves. Lifesaving clubs were ideal places to drink heavily; many were sponsored by alcohol companies or pubs. Surfers, meanwhile, were more likely to experiment with illicit drugs. None of these substances was conducive to optimum motor skills or water safety. [42] Today many of the best Australian surfers are part of a global professional circuit, with style being rewarded in cash. [43] Concurrently, surf lifesaving clubs have sought to curb excess drinking, make membership more gender inclusive, and actively recruit volunteers from culturally and linguistically diverse backgrounds (CALDs). Indeed, a positive response to the infamous Cronulla Beach riots of 2005, which involved conflict between ultra-nationalist 'whites' and beachgoers of middle-eastern background, has been surf lifesaving's 'On the Same Wave' program, which has actively recruited volunteers from diverse ethnic and cultural backgrounds. [44]

While space, place and geography are pivotal to our understanding of Australian history, these subjects have yet to be developed extensively by sport historians. Indeed, although regional differences have been noted about sport around Australia, [45] there is no systematic geographically informed or comparative research – certainly nothing to rival the comprehensive work of John Bale in Britain. [46] Our notions about athleticism, identity and self-image are therefore lacking a demonstrated awareness of similarities *and* differences about sport and history across what is, after all, a vast continent with varying terrains, climates, populations and cultures. And, as is now discussed, there were key norms and power relationships in society that established social boundaries within sport.

Norms of participation in Australian sport

The Australian colonies did not reproduce a class system based on nobility. There were self-styled migrant aristocrats from Britain, but in the Antipodes elevated status was shaped overwhelmingly by holding public office or 'making good' economically. Australians were not equal in wealth or power, though there was a commitment to opportunity; an achievement culture. Those who 'made it' were, however, frowned upon if they adopted 'airs' and 'graces'. Hirst has described this as 'a democracy of manners'. He contends that 'it is the feel of Australian society that is markedly egalitarian, not its social structure'. [47] This hypothesis can also be usefully applied to Australian sport. Sociologists have done much to dispel widespread assumptions that sport is structurally egalitarian in contemporary society. Yet they also note the persistence of discourses that present sport as inherently 'open to all'. [48] Historians, meanwhile, have tried to put inequalities in context: class and status divides in sport were typically more pronounced in the nineteenth and twentieth centuries than today, and some sports were more elitist than others.

In late Victorian England there was a serious divide between professional and amateur versions of sport. This schism soon impacted on Australia, particularly as rules for the amateur code tended to be drawn up in Britain. [49] In the colonies there evolved amateur and professional versions of sports like rugby football, [50] athletics, [51] cycling, [52] and rowing. [53] A further sporting innovation from abroad was the Olympic Games, where amateur status was needed for eligibility to take part. Hence there was considerable surveillance of sports to which prize money and wagering were attached. [54] By and large, though, the amateur code was read and applied more stringently in Britain than in Australia. With rowing, for example, English clubs not only banned participants who had competed for a wager or prize money, they eventually imposed a test of status and privilege – anyone deemed working-class was proscribed from membership of an amateur club. [55] In Australia, however, non-pecuniary amateur status was more important than class background; hence the introduction of a manual labour amateur classification at many rowing clubs. [56] In Australian sport the amateur code was open to very different interpretations, and the penalties associated with transgressions varied; officials could be very harsh while some conveniently turned a blind eye. This was very much sport and politics. [57] It used to be thought that amateur and professional sport in Australia were entirely separate domains. Recent research, however, has thrown that easy assumption into disarray. In mid nineteenth century rowing, for example, it was quite common to offer prizes to amateur victors and this did not compromise their amateur status. What was more, they often competed on the same program (though generally in different events) as professional competitors. [58] Most startling of all, though, Stuart Ripley's PhD thesis has revealed that some of Australia's leading sport officials presided over both amateur and professional competitions during the late nineteenth and early twentieth centuries. [59]

In terms of the evolution of amateur and professional modes of elite sport in Australia, much has changed since the advent of live television broadcasts from the 1970s. Significantly, neither tennis nor cricket offered long-term professional careers within Australia until players sought, in effect, a slice of the TV revenue being earned by not-for-profit sporting bodies. However, while there has been much debate about the World Series Cricket 'revolution' that spawned the rise of full-time professional cricketers in Australia, [60] remarkably little has been written about the schism in Australian tennis, wherein some of the great players of the 1950s and 1960s turned professional at a time when the Majors were for amateurs only. [61] Golf provides another complex scenario: professionals in private clubs of the early twentieth century were modestly-paid coaches or lowly-paid caddies appointed to serve the interests of members, with many of the latter coming from wealthy backgrounds. This 'master and servant' relationship has now evolved to the point where a club professional holds a position of considerable status, and the burgeoning prize money offered on Australian and overseas circuits has raised the income of the elite golfer and caddy into the upper echelons of athletes worldwide. [62]

Tennis and golf are also interesting historically because they have long been sites of public access or private privilege. The fees associated with membership of a private club have always acted as an economic filter, but so too has social vetting of members by club boards. Curiously, though, too little is presently known about questions of inclusion and exclusion in two of Australia's largest participant sports. [63] Indeed, there is a general lack of systematic historical analysis into questions of class, status and privilege in a range of emergent elite sports like sailing, motor racing and horse racing, where wealth and social position impact on membership of private clubs and the capacity to own yachts, grand-prix cars, and thoroughbred horses. [64] The eminently popular Melbourne Cup is perhaps the quintessential example of Hirst's dictum about structural inequality and a 'democracy of manners' in Australia. This horse race literally stops much of the nation for two minutes on the first Tuesday in November; to that extent it is a shared celebration. However, Flemington racecourse separates spectators according to their status as club members, horse owners and 'ordinary' punters. They might be at the same event, but the idea that all classes 'rub shoulders together' on Melbourne Cup Day – whether at the race course or over a champagne lunch – is one of the nation's most alluring myths. [65]

Australian schools have long been nurseries for major sports like rugby union, rugby league, Australian Rules football, cricket and netball. Back in the nineteenth century there was a particular effort by denominational schools to instil in pupils the British-inspired athletic ideal of 'muscular Christianity', within which amateurism was a core value. This not only applied to Anglican and Protestant schools; amateurism was a hallmark of Irish sport too, hence its significance within Catholic education. [66] A major examination of sport, religion and ideology in Australian history none the less awaits. [67] Perhaps the biggest gap, though, is in our historical understanding of varying physical education and sport opportunities for children across the two educational systems: state-funded, secular schools and state-subsidised, private schools. [68] For example, in Sydney, a small elite clique known, from 1892, as the Athletic Association of the Great Public Schools of New South Wales (or Great Public Schools [GPS]) has provided sport facilities and resources, such as rowing sheds, swimming pools and tennis courts, that are typically absent from the grounds of non-selective state schools and second-tier independent schools. One of the major events on the GPS sporting calendar is the exclusive 'Head of the River' regatta, which dates back to 1893 and is modelled on boat races among the elite public schools of England. [69] Sydney's GPS schools have been a traditional nursery for recruitment into New South Wales rugby union clubs; and, since the majority of these schools catered for boys rather than girls, the social construction of masculinity through body contact sport. [70] This is not to suggest that girls have had no place in school sport, either in the state or private systems. But it has been very much a secondary place. For example, not until 1996 did female students in New South Wales have their own Head of the River regatta. [71]

Gender identities and associated norms of physicality are indeed keys to investigate sport in Australian history. It has been largely a male domain, as elsewhere. Scholars have shown that for many young boys sport has been a significant rite of passage into manhood. This reflects longstanding cultural assumptions that boys are 'inherently' combative and aggressive, and that sport provides a focus for such overtly 'masculine' behaviours. [72] For young females the reverse has been true; until the late twentieth century girls had fewer opportunities to participate in sport, and they were often encouraged to undertake 'female appropriate' activities, such as netball, that did not compromise traditional notions of femininity. [73] Even today, with important efforts to improve female access to a range of sports, the institution of sport itself remains a key to the gendering process. Not only are men and women typically separated in competitive physical activity, at the elite level females are celebrated as athletes of calibre on too few occasions, such as Olympic and Commonwealth Games, where they receive equal media coverage alongside men. [74] The history of women in Australian sport has been characterised, on the one hand, by radical feminist criticism of marginalisation and oppression by males; [75] to on the other hand, liberal feminist arguments that women have indeed been more active in sport than many (male) historians have bothered to notice. [76] There is, however, little debate about one point: as the work of Dennis Phillips has shown, Australian women have repeatedly outperformed their male counterparts in terms of procuring medals at the Olympic Games. His research offers an alternative way of recognising and valuing female sport achievement. [77] Similarly, Rob Hess has examined the historical importance of women as sports fans; their contribution as supporters of Australian Rules football, in particular, is unsurpassed by any other code. [78] Today, though, the analysis of women in Australian sport history seems to have reached a hiatus; the twenty-first century has yet to produce much in the way of new research. [79]

The historical analysis of group identity, inclusion and exclusion in Australian sport must also engage with societal issues for indigenous peoples, other non-whites, and ethnic minorities generally. As the following discussion indicates, this means taking seriously endemic problems of racism and stereotyping 'others' on the basis of their skin colour or ancestry.

Aborigines, non-whites, and ethnic minorities in Australian sport

Well before the arrival of Europeans and the subsequent British annexation of *Terra Australis*, a vast array of Aboriginal peoples were custodians of the land and sea. They were regionally disparate and spoke different languages, but had much in common. This included an ingenious capacity to observe, understand and respect the natural environment, a constructive mutualism that enabled co-existence for at least 40,000 years. Aborigines were spatially aware and physically dexterous; they needed these attributes when fishing and hunting for food. It was here that play, games and sports provided input. Within Aboriginal communities there were games of strategy and play activities requiring athleticism and dexterity. Footraces promoted speed, ball games fostered agility, while spear and boomerang throwing contests demanded eye-to-hand coordination important for hunting. [80] However, Aboriginal societies were fragmented by white annexation of land, with many Aborigines confined subsequently to colonial reserves and missions. This dislocation meant that traditional Aboriginal sports and games began to lose their functional relevance, with the meaning and significance of such activities not passed onto later generations. A decline in these customs was part of a wider diminution of Aboriginal culture and identity under European colonisation. [81]

Recently, there have been efforts to trace, record and revive traditional indigenous games. Using the medium of oral history, Queensland academic Ken Edwards has spent many years talking with Aboriginal and Torres Strait Islander elders. Through this dialogue, as well as by reading early anthropological accounts, he has established a formidable record of customary Aboriginal recreation. [82] That knowledge now has applied significance because Edwards, with the assistance of the Australian Sports Commission, has produced a user-friendly booklet for schools and community groups which explains the purpose of particular indigenous games and how they may be played today. [83] This is a significant development: through sport and recreation non-Aboriginal Australians can be introduced to aspects of a living culture. Too often indigenous history and customs are neglected as 'irrelevant' in discourses of modernity in Australia.

Histories of Aboriginal responses to colonialism, and the regime of controls exerted on indigenous peoples by representatives of the British Crown, have developed significantly over the past twenty years. [84] So too stories of the various missions that institutionalised Aborigines and separated them from white settlers. [85] This confinement introduced indigenous people to language, religion and customs from Britain. That process of colonial acculturation included sport – most notably the game of cricket – as a means of instilling in Aboriginal boys and men agreement on rules, respect for the decisions of those in authority, and a common goal of teamwork in a competitive setting. It seems remarkable, at first glance, that in 1868 the first 'Australian' cricket team which toured England consisted almost entirely of Aborigines. However, as historians have shown, this was an entrepreneurial initiative on the part of white sponsors and management, who saw an opportunity to draw big crowds and significant revenue for themselves from a series of exhibitions abroad – involving both cricket and displays of Aboriginal physical culture. [86] The Aboriginal cricketers performed ably, winning as many games as they lost. But this did not establish indigenous players in Australian cricket back home. Indeed, although there were some fine young Aboriginal cricketers in the late nineteenth and early twentieth centuries, they faced significant obstacles to play at the elite level. [87] There were logistical problems owing to laws that constrained the movement to cities of Aborigines impounded on rural missions and reserves. What was more, as sport historians have shown, the few indigenous players who did make it to first-class cricket had chequered experiences, such as outstanding bowlers Jack Marsh and Eddie Gilbert, both of whom had problems with cricket officials that negated their opportunity to play for Australia. [88]

Despite negative Aboriginal experiences in cricket, Newlin and Moran make the salient point that 'there have always been Aboriginal achievers in sport, but few people know this'. [89] Sport historians, led by Colin Tatz, have tried to rectify this lack of awareness, while also detailing ways in which Aborigines have been discriminated against in sport and society. [90] indigenous athletes were most likely to appear in activities that offered the prospect of financial reward; amateurism was a white, middle-class philosophy of privilege that was not relevant to their circumstances. No surprise then that Aborigines featured in prize-money events, particularly pedestrianism (sprinting), boxing, and as jockeys in horse racing. [91] But they were basically invisible in sports that required expensive equipment, such as sailing and rowing, or membership of a private club, such as golf and tennis.

When Australia was proclaimed a Commonwealth in 1901, the restrictive White Australia Policy (WAP) was enshrined in law. The focus of this federal legislation was non-English speaking immigrants and (de facto) people of 'colour' seeking to be residents of Australia. However, short-term visitors could, with the support of a local sponsor and the consent of immigration authorities, be provided with an 'exemption certificate' that temporarily overlooked their 'alien' or 'coloured' status. [92] Intriguingly, this loophole allowed occasional visits by non-white, 'foreign' athletes who performed publicly at Australian sport venues. Notwithstanding the racial separation implicit in the WAP, local sport fans typically appreciated the athletic skills and 'exotic' appearance of these 'coloured' competitors. However, there were also differences of opinion and reaction. African-American boxer Jack Johnson was admired for his boxing prowess, but hated by many for defeating a white title holder in Sydney in 1908. [93] Yet only two years earlier African-American cyclist Marshall 'Major' Taylor had beaten all comers in Sydney and was widely coveted by local sport fans. [94] In 1915, the man widely accredited with giving surfing a high profile, Hawaiian Duke Paoa Kahanamoku, was revered when he took to the waves in Australia. [95] Similarly, Alick Wickham, a Solomon Islander in Australia, became the most famous exponent of the 'crawl' stroke. [96] Athletes of Asian origin were less renowned in Australia but do not seem to have been excluded from local sporting culture. [97] Indeed, despite local fears of eventual invasion by the so-called 'yellow peril' from East Asia, swimmers from Japan and footballers from China were received very hospitably during the 1920s. [98] There is plenty of irony about athletes of non-white appearance being accorded such status; not only because of the WAP, but because in the first half of the twentieth century indigenous Australians then had such a low profile in the nation's sporting culture. [99]

There were signs of change in the 1960s and 1970s. When Aboriginal boxer Lionel Rose claimed the world bantamweight title in Japan in 1968, he was mobbed by well-wishers upon return to Australia. Not only was Rose the first Aborigine to win a world boxing title, he also became the first indigenous person to be awarded the prestigious title of 'Australian of the Year'. A year later he reached the top of the music charts with a country and western song 'I Thank You'. [100] Along with tennis player Evonne Goolagong, who twice won the Wimbledon singles crown, Rose presented the image of an Aborigine who had 'made it' in white society. Like Cathy Freeman, who lit the cauldron at the opening of the 2000 Olympic Games, both Rose and Goolagong appealed to many white observers who, ordinarily, had little contact with nor sympathy for

Aboriginal dissidents, such as those who fashioned the Aboriginal Tent Embassy in Canberra in 1972; [101] or, for that matter, Aborigines who took their protests about land rights to the streets during the Commonwealth Games of 1982. In the latter case the Queensland government was so 'spooked' by this Aboriginal assertiveness that it declared a state of emergency in order to constrain such public demonstrations. [102]

During the 1980s and 1990s increased numbers of Aborigines participated at the elite level in the country's two largest football codes – Australian Rules and rugby league. By the early twenty-first century players from Aboriginal or Torres Strait Islander heritage constituted around 10% of all professional players in both the Australian Football League (AFL) and the National Rugby League (NRL) – a staggering proportion given that the indigenous population of Australia is about 2% of the national total. [103] However, as scholars have shown, these footballers battled long and hard against racism on and off the field. Not until the late 1990s did football administrators have anti-vilification policies fully in place, and they were in effect pushed into doing so by outspoken and articulate players like Essendon's Michael Long. [104] The profile, status and remuneration of professional indigenous athletes has never been better, [105] but there remains more to be achieved – particularly in terms of career transition planning and retirement experiences of Aboriginal sportspeople. [106]

Issues of discrimination and stereotyping in sport have also been apparent among ethnic minority groups in Australia. While soccer, for example, was an important sport for the great flood of European migrants after World War II, the game was typecast as 'foreign' by comparison to the existing staples of the rugby codes and Australian Rules. [107] Soccer was commonly ridiculed as 'wogball' and a game for 'poofters'; this derision not only impacted upon so called 'New Australians' playing soccer, but residents of Anglo-Celtic heritage with a passion for the sport. [108] Ethnicity has, of course, been part of Australian sport since the nineteenth century. Scots were particularly noticeable in golf and lawn bowls, Irish Catholics were prominent as bookmakers in the racing industry, while the English were especially zealous about cricket and fox hunting. These practices were basically extensions of migrant cultural baggage in the Antipodes. [109] But it would be misleading to speak of ethnic enclaves among the Australian population or within the sporting culture of the late nineteenth and early twentieth centuries. Indeed, despite protracted Anglo-Irish tensions, most notably after the Easter Rising of 1916, which had local impacts upon Australian society, sport appears to have been less affected by sectarianism than education, party politics and the public service. [110] There have been suggestions that Irish-Catholic Test cricketers suffered discrimination at the hands of team mates and selectors, though there is debate among historians as to whether this was systematic persecution or merely a series of personality conflicts. [111]

In Australia, historical research into sport and ethnicity has focused principally on the second half of the twentieth century. [112] It was given impetus as a subject for inquiry by the emergence of a federal government policy of multiculturalism, first adopted by Labour in 1973. Previously, 'New Australians' were expected to assimilate into a dominant English-speaking, Anglo-Celtic culture. Now there was an emphasis on respect for group differences within a society that, as a consequence of mass migration – not only from Europe but increasingly Asia – had become more culturally diverse and ethnically cosmopolitan. [113] In terms of sport, however, little seemed to change. For example, although a promising nineteen year-old fast bowler, Len Durtanovich, played junior representative cricket for New South Wales, it was the pragmatically re-named Len Pascoe who played for Australia between 1977 and 1982. His parents' Yugoslavian origins were, however, still a source of derision for some cricket opponents. [114] Soccer, meanwhile, remained subject to discourses propounding it as a game for ethnic 'others' (minorities) and thus not 'true-blue' Australian. [115] Sport therefore remained a culturally conservative institution within which traditional forms and norms of physical activity dominated.

In the past two decades, however, there has been a greater emphasis on social inclusion and the engagement of various communities into sport – with a particular focus on attracting people from culturally and linguistically diverse backgrounds. [116] Yet this has coincided, ironically, with a move away from sports clubs dedicated to particular ethnic groups, and towards the 'cosmopolitanising' of Australian sport culture – within which people of all ancestries and skin colours are assumed to have a place. On the one hand this has represented loss. For example, sports clubs organised by and for Jews have a long lineage in Australia. [117] This includes the Monash Golf Club in Sydney, named after Australia's renowned Jewish military commander of World War I. However, demographic and socio-economic changes have in effect transformed Monash into a 'cosmopolitan' golf club, albeit with a Jewish past. [118]

This theme of loss has also been noticeable among soccer clubs that were originally formed to cater for the fraternal needs of ethnic groups from non-English speaking backgrounds – Italians, Greeks, Serbs, Croats, and so on. [119] The profile and status of such clubs has been denuded, since the mid-1990s, by a National Soccer League (NSL) decision to in effect 'de-ethnicise' elite-level club competition in Australia. [120] A key expectation was that club names be revamped in an attempt to garner fan support from beyond an 'ethnic' base. Greek club West Adelaide Hellas, for example, changed its name to the West Adelaide Sharks. This was part of an explicit effort to reinvent soccer as a game intended to appeal to 'mainstream' Australia, not just particular ethnic communities that many of the clubs appeared to represent. [121] At the elite level, club soccer faced protracted financial and administrative difficulties, as well as a perception (sometimes created by the media) that matches between Serbs and Croats, for example, were little more than occasions for historic, European-based inter-group hostilities to be played out in an Antipodean setting. [122] Intriguingly, NSL efforts to 'mainstream' soccer were a contrast to strategies by the AFL and the NRL, both of which actively courted players and supporters from CALD backgrounds and, though they did not put it this way, a more conspicuously 'cosmopolitan' following. [123]

However, no Australian sport has gone through more reform than soccer in recent decades; and, while this has involved loss it has also presented opportunity. The NSL has been supplanted by the A-League, which involves team franchises and single clubs representing cities or regions. It has received financial backing from Jewish-Australian property magnate Frank Lowy, while the long-overdue involvement of the 'Socceroos' in the World Cup (2006) gave the sport – renamed football in Australia – unprecedented profile and public following. Although it is early days, the 'mainstreaming' of football via the A-League and the expectation of the 'Socceroos' participating regularly in the World Cup, appears to have put the game in a sounder financial position. [124] What is more, preliminary research indicates that CALD fans of the NSL have, for the most part, not been isolated by the A-League, and that a new generation of football fans – from all sorts of backgrounds – are attending matches. [125] As with the Monash Golf Club there is both loss and opportunity; erosion of ethnic traditions, but opportunity to engage a wider range of followers. It is an example of the emerging cosmopolitanisation of Australian sport cultures. Of course sport and Australian nationalism persists, but for many people it is a hybrid sense of fan allegiance – Australian *and* Vietnamese, Australian *and* Serbian, and so on. Rather than a site of monolithic parochialism and patriotism, Australian sport – both in local and global contexts – appears to be moving towards a postmodern, cosmopolitan phase. [126]

'Re-visioning' and revisiting Australian sport history

As explained at the outset, there are very few career opportunities in Australia for academics aspiring to work as sport historians, and the vast majority of current practitioners are located in human movement, sports studies or business environments within which historical analysis tends to have a low priority. That said, there have been some important contributions by Australians to the practice of sport history. Murray Phillips and Douglas Booth have been at the forefront of global initiatives to make the sub-discipline more receptive to innovations within social and cultural history generally. They have encouraged researchers to explicitly situate themselves within a theoretical paradigm; they have urged scholars to be more conscious of archives as sources of power, not simply evidence; they have prompted writers to reflect upon their research methods and their positions, as investigators, within that process; and they have emphasised the constructed and contingent nature of 'findings'. [127] Their counsel has so far received mixed responses: sport historians familiar with the 'cultural' or 'linguistic' turn in the discipline of history are well placed to benefit from both the Phillips and Booth recommendations, but those limited to conventional social history face something of a challenge from deconstructionism and postmodernism. [128] Concepts like reflexivity and tropes, as well as methods of discourse analysis or semiotics are not grasped easily, in part because many who deploy them insist on highly specialised, even obtuse language. Thus the challenge for Phillips and Booth, world leaders in their own right, is to convey their arguments in a way that inspires others to follow.

While there has recently been important debate about a 're-visioning' of the craft of sport history, there are further priorities that need revisiting. First, remarkably little systematic research has been conducted into the economic history of Australian sport. [129] In Britain, by contrast, there is a wealth of knowledge about club ownership, profit and utility maximising behaviours, player salaries and unions, and so on. [130] Second, while there has been sustained research into the impact of the media on Australian sport since the late 1970s, the era when television became crucial to professionalisation and commercialisation, [131] too little is presently known about the role and significance of the print media and radio in the formative years of Australian sport. [132] Such conventional forms of mass mediated sport are less significant in the age of digital television and the Internet, but they are surely of major historical import. Third, there are distinctive aspects of Australian sport history that are well known but poorly understood. Why is it that professional clubs in the football codes and cricket have typically been member-based rather than, as with soccer and baseball in Britain and the USA, either owned by individuals or shareholders? [133] What values and aspirations have been associated with club membership in Australian sport history? [134] Why, in addition, is there no tradition (other than in soccer) of Australian sport spectators being formally segregated in stadia on the basis of team allegiance? What is more, given the passion typically associated with 'barracking' at Australian sport, why has the hard core 'hooligan' phenomenon been largely absent from the football codes Down Under? [135] In sum, a key problem with the state of Australian sports history is not simply a lack of theoretical or methodological vision, but also a need to systematically revisit historical archives – documentary, visual and oral. Revisionism can emerge from reforms to the academic craft of sport history; equally it can arise from painstaking reading and interpretation of primary sources – many of which are as yet untouched by scholars of sport. The latter message is not novel; it has long been propounded by Wray Vamplew. [136]

Notes

[1] Recently, though, there have been important efforts to try to revive Australian history as a school subject. This has also involved heated debate between conservatives and progressives about the content and delivery of such a subject. Department of Education, Employment and Workplace Relations, 'Teaching Australian history', available online at http://www.dest.gov.au/sectors/school_education/policy_initiatives_reviews/key_issues/australian_history/default.htm, accessed 4 Apr. 2009.

[2] D. Booth, 'Sports history: What can be done?', *Sport, Education and Society*, 2 (2) (1997), pp. 191–204; D. Adair, 'Location, location! Sports history and academic real estate', *Australian Society for Sports History Bulletin*, 36 (2002), pp. 11–14.

[3] C.M.H. Clark, *A history of Australia*, vols. 1–6 (Melbourne, 1962–1999), pp. 1963–87.

[4] G. Blainey, *A game of our own: The origins of Australian football* (Melbourne, 1990).

[5] D. Booth, ' "On the shoulders of a giant": W.F. Mandle and the foundations of sports history in Australia', *International Journal of the History of Sport*, 19 (1) (2002), pp. 151–8.

[6] W.F. Mandle, 'The professional cricketer in England in the nineteenth century', *Labour History*, 23 (1972), pp. 1–16; W.F. Mandle, 'Games people played: Cricket and football in England and Victoria in the late 19th century', *Historical Studies: Australia & New Zealand*, 15 (60) (1973), pp. 511–35; W.F. Mandle, 'Cricket and Australian nationalism in the nineteenth century', *Journal of the Royal Australian Historical Society*, 59 (4) (1973), pp. 225–46; and W.F. Mandle,

Going it alone: Australia's national identity in the twentieth century, (Ringwood, 1978).

[7] R. Cashman, 'A most memorable conference: The inaugural 1977 sporting traditions conference', *Sporting Traditions,* 23 (2) (2007), p. 2.

[8] R. Cashman and M. McKernan, eds, *Sport in history: The making of modern sporting history* (St Lucia, 1979).

[9] Key examples include W. Vamplew, *The turf: A social and economic history of horse racing* (London, 1976); and the NASSH prize-winning *Pay up and play the game: Professional sport in Britain, 1875–1914* (Cambridge, 1988).

[10] W. Vamplew, 'The history of horse racing in South Australia: A statistical approach', *Australian Historical Statistics,* 1, (1980), pp. 14–53; W. Vamplew, 'Sports crowd attendance in South Australia 1919–39: An economic interpretation', *Australian Historical Statistics,* 2 (1981), pp. 20–40; W. Vamplew, 'From sport to business: The first seventy-five years of horse racing in South Australia', *Journal of the Historical Society of South Australia,* 11 (1983), pp. 15–33; and W. Vamplew, R. Cashman and J. Daly, 'Sport and recreation. South Australian statistics', *Historical Statistics Monograph,* 3 (*South Australian historical statistics*), pp. 193–235.

[11] W. Vamplew, ed., *Australian historical statistics,* (*Australia 1788–1988: A bicentennial history* series) (Broadway, 1987).

[12] D. Adair and W. Vamplew, *Sport in Australian history* (Melbourne, 1997), p. v.

[13] T. Magdalinski, 'Recentring Anglo-Celtic males, decentring the other(s)', *Sporting Traditions,* 13 (2) (1997), pp. 101–8; and D. Booth, 'Descriptive history and passionless sport in contemporary Australian sports history', *Sporting Traditions,* 13 (2) (1997), pp. 111–16.

[14] D. Adair with W. Vamplew, 'Writing sports history for "non-specialists": A reply to the review symposium on Adair and Vamplew's *Sport in Australian history* and the state of Australian sports history', *Sporting Traditions,* 14 (1) (1997), pp. 111–34.

[15] D. Adair and W. Vamplew, 'Not so far from the madding crowd: Spectator violence in Britain and Australia – A review article', *Sporting Traditions* 7 (1) (1990), pp. 95–103; W. Vamplew, *Sports violence in Australia: Its extent and control* (Canberra, 1991); W. Vamplew, *Sports crowd disorder: An Australian survey,* (*ASSH Studies in Sports History* series) 7 (Sydney, 1994), pp. 79–111; W. Vamplew, *Violence in Australian soccer: The ethnic contribution,* (*ASSH Studies in Sports History* series) 10 (Sydney, 1994), pp. 1–15; and W. Vamplew, 'It's not cricket and perhaps it never was: An historical look at Australian crowd and player behaviour', *Sports Historian,* 14 (1994), pp. 1–7.

[16] T. Collins and W. Vamplew, *Mud, sweat and beers: A cultural history of sport and alcohol* (Oxford, 2002); and W. Vamplew, 'Alcohol and the sportsperson: An anomalous alliance', *Sport in History,* 25 (3) (2005), pp. 390–411.

[17] W. Vamplew, 'Artefacts, archives and analysis: Sports museums and sports historians', *La Comune Eredita Dello Sport in Europa,* (1996), pp. 43–8; and W. Vamplew, 'Facts and artefacts: Sports historians and sports museums', *Journal of Sport History,* 25 (2) (1998), pp. 268–82.

[18] J. Kay and W. Vamplew, *Weather beaten: Sport in the British climate* (Edinburgh, 2002); and J. Kay and W. Vamplew, 'Under the weather: Combating the climate in British sport', *Sport in Society,* 9 (1) (2006), pp. 94–107.

[19] W. Vamplew, 'Playing with the rules: Influences on the development of regulation in sport', *International Journal of the History of Sport*, 24 (7) (2007), pp. 843–71.

[20] This should not imply that Vamplew has taken his 'eye off the ball' in terms of Australian sport history. Since 2006 he has reviewed 22 books on Australian sport for the journal *Reviews in Australian Studies.* I doubt whether any Australian-based historian has even come close to that output in the same period.

[21] R. Cashman, *Paradise of sport: The rise of organised sport in Australia* (Melbourne, 1995); and D. Booth and C. Tatz, *One-eyed: A view of Australian sport* (Sydney, 2000).

[22] B. Stoddart, *Saturday afternoon fever: Sport in the Australian culture* (North Ryde, NSW, 1986); and P. Kell, *Good sports: Australian sport and the myth of the fair go* (Sydney, 2000).

[23] Adair and Vamplew, *Sport in Australian history*, p. 145.

[24] G. Blainey, *The tyranny of distance: How distance shaped Australia's history* (Melbourne, 1966).

[25] Cashman, *Paradise of sport*; and J.A. Daly, *Elysian fields: Sport, class and community in colonial south Australia, 1836–1890* (Adelaide, 1982).

[26] D. Adair, M. Phillips, and J. Nauright, 'Sporting manhood in Australia: Test cricket, rugby football, and the imperial connection, 1878–1918', *Sport History Review*, 28 (1) (1997), pp. 46–60; and D. Adair, 'Rowing and sculling', in W. Vamplew and B. Stoddart, eds, *Sport in Australia: A social history* (Melbourne, 1994), pp. 172–92.

[27] R. Cashman, 'Symbols of imperial unity: Anglo-Australian cricketers, 1877–1900', in J.A. Mangan, ed., *The cultural bond: Sport, empire, society* (London, 1992), pp. 129–41; and E. Nielsen, 'Australian nationalism and middle-class Britishness: Understanding Australian identity through amateur sport', Paper presented to the *27th Annual Conference of the British Society for Sports History*, 17–19 Aug. 2009, University of Stirling.

[28] J.B. Hirst, *Convict society and its enemies: A history of early New South Wales* (Sydney, 1983); and R. Hughes, *The fatal shore: A history of the transportation of convicts to Australia, 1787–1868* (New York, 1987).

[29] Mandle, 'Cricket and Australian nationalism', pp. 225–46.

[30] See R. Norris, *The emergent Commonwealth: Australian federation, expectations and fulfilment 1889–1910* (Melbourne, 1975).

[31] Mandle, 'Cricket and Australian nationalism', pp. 225–46.

[32] N. Meaney, 'Britishness and Australian identity: The problem of nationalism in Australian history and historiography', *Australian Historical Studies*, 32 (116) (2001), pp. 76–90; and R. McGregor, 'The necessity of Britishness: Ethno-cultural roots of Australian nationalism', *Nations and Nationalism*, 12 (3) (2006), pp. 493–511.

[33] M. McKernan, 'Sport, war and society: Australia, 1914–1918', in R. Cashman and M. McKernan, eds, *Sport in history: The making of modern sporting history* (St Lucia, 1979), pp. 1–20; D.J. Blair, ' "The greater game": Australian football and the army at home and on the front during World War I', *Sporting Traditions*, 11 (2) (1995), pp. 91–102; E. Jaggard, 'Forgotten heroes: The 1945 Australian services cricket team', *Sporting Traditions*, 12 (2) (1996), pp. 61–79;

M.G. Phillips, 'Football, class and war: The rugby codes in New South Wales, 1907–15', in J. Nauright and T.J.L. Chandler, eds, *Making men: Rugby and masculine identity* (London, 1996), pp. 158–80; M.G. Phillips, 'Sport, war and gender images: The Australian sportsmen's battalions and the first World War', *International Journal of the History of Sport*, 14 (1) (1997), pp. 78–96; G. Rodwell and J. Ramsland, 'Cecil Healy: A soldier of the surf', *Sporting Traditions*, 16 (2) (2000), pp. 3–16; M. Crotty, *Making the Australian male: Middle-class masculinity 1870–1920* (Melbourne, 2001); J. Ramsland, 'A remarkable life: Roden Cutler as sporting, military and local hero', *Sporting Traditions*, 20 (2) (2004), pp. 39–54; and P. Cohen, 'Behind barbed wire: Sport and Australian prisoners of war', *Sporting Traditions*, 23 (1) (2006), pp. 63–86.

[34] G. Seal, *Inventing ANZAC: The digger and national mythology* (St Lucia, 2004).

[35] This concentration of people in cities persists: Australia remains one of the most urbanised countries in the world, with the vast majority of its population living near the coastline. See P. Drew, *The coast dwellers: Australians living on the edge* (Ringwood, 1994).

[36] D. Adair, ' "Two dots in the distance": Professional sculling as a mass spectacle in New South Wales, 1876–1907', *Sporting Traditions*, 9 (1) (1992), pp. 52–83; and R. Cashman and T. Hickie, 'The divergent sporting cultures of Sydney and Melbourne', *Sporting Traditions*, 7 (1) (1987), pp. 24–46.

[37] K. Saunders, ' "Specimens of superb manhood": The lifesaver as national icon', *Journal of Australian Studies*, 56 (1998), pp. 96–105.

[38] D. Booth, *Australian beach cultures: The history of sun, sand, and surf* (London, 2001); E. Jaggard, ed., *Between the flags: One hundred summers of Australian surf lifesaving* (Sydney, 2006); and S. Brawley, *Vigilant and victorious: A community history of the Collaroy Surf Life Saving Club, 1911–1995* (Collaroy, 1995); and C. White, 'Picnicking, surf-bathing and middle-class morality on the beach in the eastern suburbs of Sydney, 1811–1912', *Journal of Australian Studies*, 80 (2004), pp. 101–10.

[39] M.G. Phillips, 'Public sports history, history and social memory: (Re)presenting swimming in Australia', *Sporting Traditions*, 15 (1) (1998), pp. 93–102; and M.-L. McDermott, 'Changing visions of baths and bathers: Desegregating ocean baths in Wollongong, Kiama and Gerringong', *Sporting Traditions*, 22 (1) (2005), pp. 1–19.

[40] D. Booth, 'Surf lifesaving: The development of an Australasian "sport" ', *International Journal of the History of Sport*, 17 (2) (2000), pp. 166–87; E. Jaggard, 'Tempering the testosterone: Masculinity, women and Australian surf lifesaving', *The International Journal of the History of Sport*, 18 (4) (2001), pp. 16–36; D. Booth, 'The dark side of surf lifesaving', *Journal of Sport History*, 29 (1) (2002), pp. 7–14; E. Jaggard, 'Writing Australian surf lifesaving's history', *Journal of Sport History*, 29 (1) (2002), pp. 15–24; M.G. Phillips, 'A critical appraisal of narrative in sport history: Reading the surf lifesaving debate', *Journal of Sport History*, 29 (1) (2002), pp. 25–40; and D. Booth, 'A tragic plot? A reply to Jaggard and Phillips', *Journal of Sport History*, 29 (1) (2002), pp. 41–8.

[41] D. Booth, 'From bikinis to boardshorts: Wahines and the paradoxes of surfing culture', *Journal of Sport History*, 28 (1) (2001), pp. 3–22. For some bathers, no swimwear was preferred. See C. Daley, 'From bush to beach: Nudism in Australasia', *Journal of Historical Geography*, 31 (1) (2005), pp. 149–67.

[42] D. Booth, ' "War off the water": The Australian Surf Lifesaving Association and the beach', *Sporting Traditions*, 7 (2) (1991), pp. 134–62; D. Booth, 'Surfing '60s: A case study in the history of pleasure and discipline', *Australian Historical Studies*, 26 (103) (1994), pp. 262–79; and D. Booth, 'Swimming, surfing and surf-lifesaving', in W. Vamplew and B. Stoddart, eds, *Sport in Australia: A social history* (Melbourne, 1994), pp. 231–54.

[43] D. Booth, 'Ambiguities in pleasure and discipline: The development of competitive surfing', *Journal of Sport History*, 22 (3) (Fall, 1995), pp. 189–206.

[44] C. Giles and J. Fitzgerald, 'Embracing cultural diversity in SLSA: "On the same wave"', Paper presented to the *12th National Conference on Volunteering*, Gold Coast, Queensland, 3–5 Sept. 2008, available online at www.volunteeringaustralia.org/files/ICIATN1SJ9/bn08020_VA8_Chris%20Giles.pdf, accessed 10 Nov. 2008.

[45] C. Forster, 'Sport, society and space: The changing geography of country cricket in South Australia 1836–1914', *Sporting Traditions*, 2 (2) (1986), pp. 23–47; Cashman and Hickie, 'The divergent sporting cultures of Sydney and Melbourne', pp. 24–46; S. Bennett, 'Regional sentiment and Australian sport', *Sporting Traditions*, 5 (1) (1988), pp. 98–111; J. O'Hara, 'The Jockey Club and the town in colonial Australia', *Journal of Gambling Studies*, 7 (3) (1991), pp. 207–15; J. O'Hara, *Big river racing: A history of the Clarence River Jockey Club 1861–2001* (Sydney, 2002); T. Magdalinksi, 'Cricket and regional development on the sunshine coast', *Sporting Traditions*, 18 (2) (2002), pp. 15–29; D. Topp and J. Nauright, 'Rugby league, community and identity in the Lockyer Valley, Queensland', *Sporting Traditions*, 21 (1) (2004), pp. 53–65; K. Atherley, 'Sport, localism and social capital in rural western Australia', *Geographical Research*, 44 (4) (2006), pp. 348–60; and P. Horton, 'Football, identity, place: The emergence of rugby football in Brisbane', *International Journal of the History of Sport*, 23 (8) (2006), pp. 1341–68.

[46] See J. Bale, *Landscapes of modern sport* (Leicester, 1994); and J. Bale, *Sports Geography* (London, 2003).

[47] J.B. Hirst, *Sense & nonsense in Australian history* (Melbourne, 2006).

[48] Stoddart, *Saturday afternoon fever*; G.A. Lawrence and D. Rowe, eds, *Power play: Essays in the sociology of Australian sport* (Sydney, 1986); D. Rowe and G. Lawrence, eds, *Sport and leisure: Trends in Australian popular culture* (Sydney, 1990); J. McKay, *No pain, no gain?: Sport and Australian culture* (Sydney, 1991).

[49] See Richard Holt's chapter 'Amateurism and the Victorians' in his *Sport and the British: A modern history* (Oxford, 1989); and Richard Cashman's chapter 'Amateur versus professional' in his *Paradise of sport.*

[50] C. Cunneen, 'The rugby war: The early history of rugby league in New South Wales', in R. Cashman and M. McKernan, eds, *Sport in history: The making of modern sport history* (St Lucia, Qld., 1979), pp. 293–306; P.A. Horton, 'Dominant ideologies and their role in the establishment of rugby union football in Victorian Queensland', *International Journal of the History of Sport*, 11 (1) (1994), pp. 115–28; T. Collins, 'From Bondi to Batley: Australian players in British Rugby League, 1907–1995', *Sporting Traditions*, 16 (2) (2000), pp. 71–86; T. Collins, 'Australian nationalism and working-class Britishness: The case of rugby league football', *History Compass*, 3 (1) (2005), pp. 1–19; and C. Little,

'The "hidden" history of the birth of rugby league in Australia: The significance of "local" factors in Sydney's rugby split', *Sport in History*, 27 (3) (2007), pp. 364–79.

[51] J. Ross, 'Pedestrianism and athletics in England and Australia in the nineteenth century: A case study in the development of sport' (Bachelor of Human Movement Studies (Hons.) thesis, University of Queensland, St. Lucia, 1984); P. Mason, *Professional athletics in Australia* (Adelaide, 1985); J.A. Daly, 'Track and field', in W. Vamplew and B. Stoddart, eds, *Sport in Australia: A social history* (Melbourne, 1994), pp. 255–68.

[52] R. Hess, 'A mania for bicycles: The impact of cycling on Australian rules football', *Sporting Traditions*, 14 (2) (1998), pp. 3–24; J. Weaver and J.T. Weaver, ' "We've had no punctures whatsoever": Dunlop, commerce and cycling in fin de siècle Australia', *International Journal of the History of Sport*, 16 (3) (1999), pp. 94–112; and C.S. Simpson, ed., *Scorchers, ramblers and rovers: Australasian cycling histories*, (*ASSH Studies in Sports History* series) 21 (Sydney, 2006).

[53] Adair, 'Two dots in the distance', pp. 52–83.

[54] Jobling, 'The making of a nation through sport: Australia and the Olympic Games from Athens to Berlin, 1898–1916', *Australian Journal of Politics & History*, 34 (2) (1988), pp. 160–72.

[55] E. Halladay, *Rowing in England: A social history: The amateur debate* (Manchester, 1990).

[56] Adair, 'Rowing and sculling', pp. 172–92; M. Crotty, ' "Separate and distinct"? The manual labour question in nineteenth-century Victorian rowing', *International Journal of the History of Sport*, 15 (2) (1998), pp. 152–63; and S. Ripley, 'The golden age of Australian professional sculling or skullduggery?', *International Journal of the History of Sport*, 22 (5) (2005), pp. 867–82.

[57] K. Moore and M.G. Phillips, 'The sporting career of Harold Hardwick: One example of the irony of the amateur-professional dichotomy', *Sporting Traditions*, 7 (1) (1990), pp. 61–76; Cashman, *Paradise of sport*, pp. 54–71; Adair and Vamplew, *Sport in Australian history*, pp. 37–40; M.G. Phillips, 'Diminishing contrasts and increasing varieties: Globalisation theory and "reading" amateurism in Australian sport', *Sporting Traditions*, 18 (1) (2001), pp. 19–32; J. Senyard, 'From gentleman to the manly: A large step for the amateur', *Sporting Traditions*, 18 (2) (2002), pp. 1–14; and E. Nielsen, ' "Oh error, ill-conceived": The New South Wales Amateur Sports Federation, rugby league and amateur athletics', Paper presented to *The Centenary Conference of Rugby League* in Australia, Powerhouse Museum, Sydney, 7–8 Nov. 2008.

[58] Senyard, 'From gentleman to the manly', pp. 1–14; Adair, 'Two dots in the distance', pp. 52–83; and Adair, 'Rowing and sculling', pp. 172–92.

[59] See S. Ripley, 'A social history of New South Wales professional sculling, 1876–1927' (unpublished PhD thesis, School of Arts and Humanities, University of Western Sydney, 2003); and Ripley, 'The golden age of Australian professional sculling or skullduggery?', pp. 867–82.

[60] As examples, see I. Harriss, 'Packer, cricket and postmodernism', in D. Rowe and G. Lawrence, eds, *Sport and leisure: Trends in Australian popular culture* (Sydney, 1990), pp. 109–21; R.K. (Bob) Stewart, ' "I heard it on the radio, I saw it on the television": The commercial and cultural development of Australian first class cricket: 1946–1985' (unpublished PhD thesis, School of History,

La Trobe University, Melbourne, 1995); and G. Haigh and R. Dundas, *The cricket war: The inside story of Kerry Packer's world series cricket* (Melbourne, 2001).

[61] There are, of course, numerous non-academic eulogies of Australian professional tennis. But analytical studies are rare. Fewster looks at the impact to Australian team tennis of the many Americans joining professional circuits in the 1950s. See K. Fewster, 'Advantage Australia: Davis Cup Tennis 1950–1959', *Sporting Traditions*, 2 (1) (1985), pp. 47–68. There is also a rather cursory discussion of professional tennis in G. Kinross-Smith, 'Lawn tennis', in W. Vamplew and B. Stoddart, eds, *Sport in Australia: A social history* (Melbourne, 1994), pp. 133–52.

[62] B. Stoddart, 'Golf' in W. Vamplew and B. Stoddart, eds, *Sport in Australia: A social History* (Melbourne, 1994), pp. 77–92.

[63] Key studies include G. Kinross-Smith, 'Privilege in tennis and lawn tennis: The Geelong and Royal South Yarra examples but not forgetting the story of the farmer's wrist', *Sporting Traditions*, 3 (2) (1997), pp. 189–216; B. Blashak, *'The ignorant labelled it a ladies' game': Masculinity in Australian tennis in the late nineteenth and early twentieth centuries*, (*ASSH Studies in Sports History* series) 16 (Sydney, 2004), pp. 1–59; C. Tatz and B. Stoddart, *The Royal Sydney Golf Club: The first hundred years* (Sydney, 1993); M.G. Phillips, 'Ethnicity and class at the Brisbane Golf Club', *Sporting Traditions*, 4 (2) (1988), pp. 201–13; and M.G. Phillips, 'Golf and Victorian sporting values', *Sporting Traditions*, 6 (2) (1990), pp. 120–34.

[64] Key studies include B. Griffen-Foley, 'Playing with princes and presidents: Sir Frank Packer and the 1962 challenge for the America's Cup', *Australian Journal of Politics & History*, 46 (1) (2000), pp. 51–66; C. Thompson, *Boats, Bondy and the boxing kangaroo: The 1983 America's Cup*, (*ASSH Studies in Sports History* series) 14 (Sydney, 2004), pp. 60–117; J. O'Hara, 'Horse racing and trotting', in W. Vamplew and B. Stoddart, eds, *Sport in Australia: A social history* (Melbourne, 1994), pp. 93–111; and J. O'Hara, 'Globalisation, historical consciousness and the Melbourne Cup', *Sporting Traditions*, 23 (2) (2007), pp. 33–46.

[65] Q. Beresford, 'The Melbourne Cup: Australia's first national day', *Hemisphere*, 27 (1982), pp. 180–4; K. Ahearne, 'The myth lives on. Cultural significance of the Melbourne Cup', *Australian Society*, 6 (12) (1987), pp. 52, 57–8; and R. White, 'National days and the national past in Australia', *Australian Cultural History*, 22 (2003), pp. 55–72.

[66] M. Cronin, 'Defenders of the nation? The Gaelic Athletic Association and Irish nationalist identity', *Irish Political Studies*, 11 (1) (1996), pp. 1–19; P.F. McDevitt, 'Muscular Catholicism: Nationalism, masculinity and Gaelic team sports, 1884–1916', *Gender and History*, 9 (2) (1997), pp. 262–84; I.D. Brice, 'Ethnic masculinities in Australian boys' schools: Scots and Irish secondary schools in late nineteenth-century Australia', *Paedagogica Historica*, 37 (1) (2001), pp.139–52; and N.J. Watson *et al.*, 'The development of muscular Christianity in Victorian Britain and beyond', *Journal of Religion and Society*, 7 (2005), pp. 1–21.

[67] Key publications include R. Crawford, *Athleticism, gentlemen and empire in Australian public schools: L.A. Adamson and Wesley College, Melbourne*, (*ASSH*

Studies in Sports History series) 1 (Sydney, 1986), pp. 42–64; D.W. Brown, 'Muscular Christianity in the Antipodes: Some observations on the diffusion and emergence of a Victorian ideal in Australian social theory', *Sporting Traditions*, 3 (2) (1987), pp. 173–87; M. Connellan, *The ideology of athleticism, its Antipodean impact, and its manifestation in two elite catholic schools*, (*ASSH Studies in Sports History* series) 5 (Sydney, 1988); B. Stewart, 'Athleticism revisited: Sport, character building and Protestant school education in nineteenth century Melbourne', *Sporting Traditions*, 9 (1) (1992), pp. 35–50; and M. Crotty, 'Manly and moral: The making of middle-class men in the Australian public school', *International Journal of the History of Sport*, 17 (2) (2000), pp. 10–30.

[68] B. Collins, M. Aitken and B. Cork, *One hundred years of public school sport in New South Wales 1889–1989* (Sydney, 1990); D. Kirk and K. Twigg, 'Civilising Australian bodies: The games ethic and sport in Victorian government schools, 1904–1945', *Sporting Traditions*, 11 (2) (1995), pp. 3–34; D. Kirk and K. Twigg, 'The militarization of school physical training in Australia: The rise and demise of the junior cadet training scheme, 1911–31', *History of Education*, 22 (4) (1993), pp. 391–414; and D. Kirk, 'Foucault and the limits of corporeal regulation: The emergence, consolidation and decline of school medical inspection and physical training in Australia, 1909–30', *International Journal of the History of Sport*, 13 (2) (1996), pp. 114–31; and I.R. Wilkinson, 'School sport and the amateur ideal: The formation of the Schools' Amateur Athletic Association of Victoria', *Sporting Traditions*, 15 (1) (1998), pp. 51–70.

[69] G. Sherington, 'Athleticism in the Antipodes: The Athletic Association of the Great Public Schools of New South Wales', *History of Education Review*, 12 (2) (1983), pp. 16–28.

[70] R. Light and D. Kirk, 'High school rugby, the body and the reproduction of hegemonic masculinity', *Sport, Education and Society*, 5 (2) (2000), pp. 163–76; and R. Light and D. Kirk, 'Australian cultural capital – Rugby's social meaning: Physical assets, social advantage and independent schools', *Culture, Sport, Society*, 4 (3) (2001), pp. 81–98.

[71] R. Crawford, 'Sport for young ladies: The Victorian independent schools 1875–1925', *Sporting Traditions*, 1 (1) (1984), pp. 61–82; B. Stewart, 'Athleticism revisited: Sport, character building, and Protestant school education in nineteenth century Melbourne', *Sporting Traditions*, 9 (1) (1992), pp. 52–83; and D. Kirk, 'Gender associations: Sport, state schools and Australian culture', *International Journal of the History of Sport*, 17 (2) (2000), pp. 49–64.

[72] J. Nauright and T.J.L. Chandler, eds, *Making men: Rugby and masculine identity* (London, 1996); Light and Kirk, 'High school rugby, the body and the reproduction of hegemonic masculinity', pp. 163–76; and C. Hickey, 'Physical education, sport and hyper-masculinity in schools', *Sport, Education and Society*, 13 (2) (2008), pp. 147–61.

[73] M. Treagus, 'Playing like ladies: Basketball, netball and feminine restraint', *International Journal of the History of Sport*, 22 (1) (2005), pp. 88–105; and T. Taylor, 'Gendering sport: The development of netball in Australia', *Sporting Traditions*, 22 (1) (2005), pp. 57–74.

[74] M.G. Phillips, *An illusory image: A report on the media coverage and portrayal of women's sport in Australia 1996* (Canberra, 1997); Adair and Vamplew, *Sport in*

Australian history, pp. 48–62; and R. Payne, 'Rethinking the status of female Olympians in the Australian press', *Media International Australia Incorporating Culture and Policy*, 110 (2004), pp. 120–31.

[75] A classic example of this approach is L.M. Randall, *A fair go?: Women in sport in South Australia, 1945–1965*, (*ASSH Studies in Sports History* series) 6 (Sydney, 1988).

[76] The quintessential example of this approach is M.K. Stell, *Half the race: A history of Australian women in sport* (North Ryde, 1991).

[77] D. Phillips, 'Australian women at the Olympics: Achievement and alienation', *Sporting Traditions*, 6 (2) (1990), pp. 181–200; and D. Phillips, *Australian women at the Olympic Games* (Sydney, 1996).

[78] R. Hess, 'Women and Australian rules football in colonial Melbourne', *International Journal of the History of Sport*, 13 (3) (1996), pp. 356–72; R. Hess, ' "Ladies are specially invited": Women in the culture of Australian rules football', *International Journal of the History of Sport*, 17 (2) (2000), pp. 111–41; and R. Hess, ' "For the love of sensation": Case studies in the early development of women's football in Victoria, 1921–1981', *Football Studies*, 8 (2) (2005), pp. 20–30.

[79] Exceptions include A. Burroughs and J. Nauright, 'Women's sports and embodiment in Australia and New Zealand', in J.A. Mangan and J. Nauright, eds, *Sport in Australasian society: Past and present* (London, 2000), pp. 188–205; M. Haig-Muir, 'Many a slip twixt cup and the lip: Equal opportunity and Victorian golf clubs', *Sporting Traditions*, 17 (1) (2000), pp. 19–38; T. Brabazon, 'Time for a change or more of the same? Les Mills and the masculinisation of aerobics', *Sporting Traditions*, 17 (1) (2000), pp. 97–112; Taylor, 'Gendering sport', pp. 57–74; A. Burroughs, 'Women, femininity and sport: The contribution of the "new woman" to nationhood', in R. Cashman, J. O'Hara and A. Honey, eds, *Sport, federation, nation* (Sydney, 2001), pp. 165–180; C. Little, ' "What a freak-show they made!" Women's rugby league in 1920s Sydney', *Football Studies*, 4 (2) (2001), pp. 25–40; R. Riddell, 'Wild women: Out of their corsets – A history of the Melbourne Women's Walking Club', *Australasian Parks and Leisure*, 4 (4) (2001), pp. 19–20; M. Haig-Muir, 'Handicapped from birth? Why women golfers are traditionally a fairway behind', *Sport History Review*, 35 (1) (2004), pp. 64–82.

[80] R.A. Howell and M.L. Howell, *The genesis of sport in Queensland* (St Lucia, 1992), pp. 7–16; and K. Edwards, *Choopadoo: Games from a dreamtime* (Brisbane, 1999).

[81] Smith, ed., 'Games from the dreamtime', interview with Ken Edwards in *The Sports Factor*, ABC Radio National, 10 Nov. 2000, http://www.abc.net.au/rh/talks/8.30/sports/stories/s210119.htm, accessed 4 Apr. 2008.

[82] Edwards, *Choopadoo.*

[83] K. Edwards with T. Meston, *Yulunga: Traditional Aboriginal games* (Canberra, 2008).

[84] See various books by Henry Reynolds, such as *Dispossession: Black Australians and white invaders* (Sydney, 1996); and *The other side of the frontier: Aboriginal resistance to the European invasion of Australia* (Sydney, 2006).

[85] C. Stevens, *White man's dreaming: Killalpaninna mission, 1866–1915* (Melbourne, 1994); and J. Mitchell, *Flesh, dreams and spirit: Life on Aboriginal mission stations, 1825–1850: A history of cross-cultural connections* (Canberra, 2005).

[86] J. Mulvaney and R. Harcourt, *Cricket walkabout: The Australian Aborigines in England* (Melbourne, 1988); and D. Sampson, 'Strangers in a strange land: The 1868 Aborigines and other indigenous performers in mid-Victorian Britain' (PhD thesis, Faculty of Humanities and Social Sciences, University of Technology Sydney, 2000), Australian Digital Thesis Repository, available online at http://hdl.handle.net/2100/314, accessed 4 Apr. 2009.

[87] See various studies by Bernard Whimpress, such as 'Few and far between: Prejudice and discrimination among Aborigines in Australian first class cricket 1869–1988', *Journal of the Anthropological Society of South Australia*, 30 (1–2) (1992), pp. 57–70; and *Passport to nowhere: Aborigines in Australian cricket, 1850–1939* (Sydney, 1999).

[88] B. Whimpress, 'The Marsh-Maclaren dispute at Bathurst, 1902, and the politics of selection', *Sporting Traditions*, 10 (2) (1994), pp. 45–58; M. Colman and K. Edwards, *Eddie Gilbert: The true story of an Aboriginal cricketing legend* (Sydney, 2002); and M. Bonnell, *How many more are coming? The short life of Jack Marsh* (Petersham, 2003).

[89] N. Newlin and C. Moran, 'Living cultures', in R. Craven, *Teaching Aboriginal studies* (Sydney, 1999), p. 35.

[90] See various publications by C. Tatz, such as *Aborigines in sport*, (*ASSH Studies in Sports History* series) 3 (1987); and *Obstacle race: Aborigines in sport* (Kensington, 1995).

[91] G.C. Blades, 'Australian Aborigines, cricket and pedestrianism: Culture and conflict, 1880–1910' (Honours thesis, Bachelor of Human Movement Studies, University of Queensland, 1985); R. Broome, 'Professional Aboriginal boxers in eastern Australia 1930–1979', *Aboriginal History*, 4 (1–2) (1980), pp. 49–71; R. Broome, 'Theatres of power: Tent boxing *circa* 1910–1970', *Aboriginal History*, 20 (1996), pp. 1–23; and C. Mooney and J. Ramsland, 'Dave Sands as local hero and international champion: Race, family and identity in an industrial working-class suburb', *Sport in History*, 28 (2) (2008), pp. 299–312.

[92] A. Honey, 'Sport, immigration restriction and race: The operation of the white Australia policy', in R. Cashman, J. O'Hara and A. Honey, eds, *Sport, federation, nation* (Sydney, 2001), pp. 26–46.

[93] R. Broome, 'The Australian reaction to Jack Johnson, black pugilist, 1907–09', in R. Cashman and M. McKernan, eds, *Sport in History* (St Lucia, 1979), pp. 343–63; and J. Wells, *Boxing day: The fight that changed the world* (Sydney, 1998).

[94] A. Ritchie, *Major Taylor: The extraordinary career of a champion bicycle racer* (Baltimore, 1996).

[95] G. Osmond, M. Phillips and M. O'Neil, ' "Putting up your dukes": Statues, social memory and Duke Paoa Kahanamoku', *International Journal of the History of Sport*, 23 (1) (2006), pp. 82–103.

[96] G. Osmond and M.G. Phillips, 'The bloke with a stroke', *Journal of Pacific History*, 39 (3) (2004), pp. 309–24; and G. Osmond and M.G. Phillips, ' "Look at that kid crawling" – Race, myth and the "crawl" stroke', *Australian Historical Studies*, 37 (127) (2006), pp. 43–62.

[97] G. Osmond, and M-L. McDermott, 'Mixing race: The Kong Sing brothers and Australian sport', *Australian Historical Studies*, 39 (3) (2008), pp. 338–55.

[98] S. Brawley, ' "They came, they saw, they conquered": The Takaishi/Saito tour of 1926–27 and Australian perceptions of Japan', Paper presented at the conference *Sport, Race and Ethnicity: Building a Global Understanding*, University of Technology Sydney, 30 Nov.–2 Dec. 2008; and N. Guoth, 'Kangaroos and dragons: The 1923 Chinese football tour of Australia', Paper presented at the *Biennial Conference of the Australian Society for Sports History: Sporting Traditions XVI*, Canberra, 27–30 June 2007.

[99] B. Whimpress, 'Absent Aborigines: The impact of federation on indigenous Sport', in R. Cashman, J. O'Hara and A. Honey, eds, *Sport, federation, nation* (Sydney, 2001), pp. 47–54.

[100] L. Rose and R. Humphries, *Lionel Rose Australian: The life story of a champion* [as told to Humphries by Rose] (Sydney, 1969).

[101] E. Goolagong Cawley and P. Jarratt, *Home! The Evonne Goolagong story* (East Roseville, 1993); T. Bruce and C. Hallinan, 'Cathy Freeman: The quest for Australian identity', in D. Andrews and S. Jackson, eds, *Sports stars: The cultural politics of sporting celebrity* (New York, 2001), pp. 257–70; and K. Lothian, 'Moving blackwards: Black power and the Aboriginal embassy', *Aboriginal History Monograph*, 16 (2007), pp. 19–34.

[102] C. Tatz, 'Aborigines and the Commonwealth Games', *Social Alternatives*, 3 (1) (1981), pp. 48–51; and C. Tatz, 'Race, politics and sport', *Sporting Traditions*, 1 (1) (1984), pp. 2–36; and N. Shannon, *The friendly games? Politics, protest and Aboriginal rights at the XII Commonwealth Games, Brisbane 1982*, (*ASSH Studies in Sports History* series) 14 (2004), pp. 1–59.

[103] J-U. Korff, 'Aboriginal indigenous sport', http://www.creativespirits.info/aboriginalculture/sport/, accessed 7 Jan. 2009.

[104] G. Gardiner, 'Racial abuse and football: The Australian Football League's racial vilification rule in review', *Sporting Traditions*, 14 (1) (1997), pp. 3–26; I. Warren, 'Racism and the law in Australian rules football: A critical analysis', *Sporting Traditions*, 14 (1) (1997), pp. 27–53; L. McNamara, 'Tackling racial hatred: Conciliation, reconciliation and football', *Australian Journal of Human Rights*, 6 (2) (2000), pp. 5–31; and I. Warren, 'Combating vilification: The AFL and NRL anti-vilification rules', *ANZSLA Commentator*, 9 (4) (2000), pp. 13–15.

[105] C. Tatz and P. Tatz, *Black diamonds: The Aboriginal and islander sports hall of fame* (St. Leonards, 1996); and C. Tatz and P. Tatz, *Black gold: The Aboriginal and islander sports hall of fame* (Canberra, 2000).

[106] G. Stocks and A. East, *Lewie, Lewie: Chris Lewis – An Aboriginal champion* (Perth, 2000); S. Gorman, *Brotherboys: The story of Jim and Phillip Krakouer* (Crows Nest, 2005); and M. Stronach and D. Adair, 'Retirement experiences of elite indigenous Australian athletes: Policies, programs and practices', Paper presented to the conference *Sport, Race and Ethnicity: Building a Global Understanding*, University of Technology Sydney, 30 Nov.–2 Dec. 2008.

[107] R. Hay, ' "Our wicked foreign game": Why has association football (soccer) not become the main code of football in Australia?', *Soccer and Society*, 7 (2) (2006), pp. 165–86.

[108] J. Warren, A. Harper and J. Whittington, *Sheilas, wogs and poofters: An incomplete biography of Johnny Warren and soccer in Australia* (Sydney, 2002).

[109] D. Adair, 'Conformity, diversity, and difference in Antipodean physical culture: The indelible influence of immigration, ethnicity, and race during the formative years of organised sport in Australia, *c.*1788–1918', in M. Cronin and D. Mayall, eds, *Sporting nationalisms: Identity, ethnicity, immigration, and assimilation* (London, 1998), pp. 14–48.

[110] M.C. Hogan, *The sectarian strand: Religion in Australian history* (Ringwood, 1987); and J. Kildea, *Tearing the fabric: Sectarianism in Australia, 1910 to 1925* (Sydney, 2002).

[111] For a summary, see A. Bairner, 'Wearing the baggie green: The Irish and Australian cricket', *Sport in Society*, 10 (3) (2007), pp. 457–75.

[112] P. Mosely *et al.*, eds, *Sporting immigrants: Sport and ethnicity in Australia* (Sydney, 1997).

[113] J. Jupp, 'One among many: The relative success of Australian multiculturalism', in D. Goodman, C. Wallace-Crabbe and D. O'Hearn, eds, *Multicultural Australia* (Newham, 1991), pp. 119–33.

[114] See G. Lawson, *Henry: The Geoff Lawson story* (Randwick, 1993); and G. Haig, 'Pascoe was like a bull at a batsman', *The Age*, (21 Feb. 2004).

[115] J. Hughson, 'Australian soccer: "Ethnic" or "Aussie". The search for an image', *Current Affairs Bulletin*, 68 (10) (1992), pp. 12–16; and L.M. Danforth, 'Is the "world game" an "ethnic game" or an "Aussie game"? Narrating the nation in Australian soccer', *American Ethnologist*, 28 (2) (2001), pp. 363–87.

[116] T. Taylor and K. Toohey, 'Negotiating cultural diversity for women in sport: From assimilation to multiculturalism', *Race, Ethnicity and Education*, 1 (1) (1998), pp. 75–90.

[117] A. Hughes, 'Muscular Judaism and the Jewish Rugby League competition in Sydney, 1924 to 1927', *Sporting Traditions*, 13 (1) (1996), pp. 61–80; and A. Hughes, 'Sport in the Australian Jewish community', *Journal of Sport History*, 26 (2) (1999), pp. 376–91.

[118] C. Tatz, *A course of history: Monash Country Club 1931–2001* (Sydney, 2002).

[119] P. Mosely, *Ethnic involvement in Australian soccer: A history 1950–1990*, (Canberra, 1995); and R. Hay, 'Croatia: Community, conflict and culture: The role of soccer clubs in migrant identity', *Immigrants and Minorities*, 17 (1) (1998), pp. 49–66.

[120] J. Hughson, 'Football, folk dancing and fascism: Diversity and difference in multicultural Australia', *Journal of Sociology*, 33 (2) (1997), pp. 167–86.

[121] H. Westerbeek *et al.*, 'De-ethnicization and Australian soccer: The strategic management dilemma', *International Journal of Sport Management*, 6 (3) (2005), pp. 270–88.

[122] J. Hughson, 'The boys are back in town: Soccer support and the social reproduction of masculinity', *Journal of Sport and Social Issues*, 24 (1) (2000), pp. 8–23; J. Hughson, ' "The wogs are at it again": The media reportage of Australian soccer "riots" ', *Football Studies*, 4 (1) (2001), pp. 40–55; and R. Hay, ' "Those bloody Croatians": Croatian soccer teams, ethnicity and violence in Australia, 1950–99', in G. Armstrong and R. Giulianotti, eds, *Fear and loathing in world football* (Oxford, 2001), pp. 77–90.

[123] For a comparison of the football codes in Australia, see B. Stewart, ed., *The games are not the same: The political economy of football in Australia* (Carlton, 2007).

[124] J. Skinner, 'Coming in from the margins: Ethnicity, community support and the rebranding of Australian soccer', *Soccer and Society*, 9 (3) (2008), pp. 394–404; and B. Dabscheck, 'Moving beyond ethnicity: Soccer's evolutionary progress', in B. Stewart, ed., *The games are not the same: The political economy of football in Australia* (Carlton, 2007), pp. 198–235.

[125] D. Lock, T. Taylor and S. Darcy, 'Soccer and social capital in Australia: Social networks in transition', in M. Nicholson and R. Hoye, eds, *Sport and social capital* (Oxford, 2008), pp. 317–38; and D. Lock, 'Fan perspectives of change in the A-League', *Soccer and Society*, 10 (1) (2009), pp. 109–23. For a dissenting view, see R. Hay, 'A victory for the fans? Melbourne's new football club in recent historical perspective', *Soccer and Society*, 8 (2) (2007), pp. 298–315.

[126] B. Bowden, 'Nationalism and cosmopolitanism: Irreconcilable differences or possible bedfellows?', *National Identities*, 5 (3) (2003), pp. 235–49.

[127] M.G. Phillips, 'Public sports history, history and social memory: (Re)presenting swimming in Australia', *Sporting Traditions*, 15 (1) (1998), pp. 93–102; M.G. Phillips, 'Deconstructing sport history: The postmodern challenge', *Journal of Sport History*, 28 (3) (2001), pp. 327–44; M.G. Phillips, ed., *Deconstructing sport history: A postmodern analysis* (New York, 2006); D. Booth, 'Escaping the past? The cultural turn and language in sport history', *Rethinking History*, 8 (1) (2004), pp. 103–25; D. Booth, 'Evidence revisited: Interpreting historical materials in sport history', *Rethinking History*, 9 (4) (2005), pp. 459–83; D. Booth, *The field: Truth and fiction in sport history* (London, 2005); and D. Booth, 'Sites of truth or metaphors of power? Refiguring the archive', *Sport in History*, 26 (1) (2006), pp. 91–109.

[128] For a range of responses, see R. Hay, 'Approaches to sports history: Theory and practice', *Sporting Traditions*, 22 (2) (2006), pp. 70–81; B. Stoddart, 'In search of meaning: Historians and their work', *Sporting Traditions*, 22 (2) (2006), pp. 82–7; M. Johnes, 'Archives, truths and the historian at work: A reply to Douglas Booth's "Refiguring the archive" ', *Sport in History*, 27 (1) (2007), pp. 127–35; and A. Guttmann, 'Review essay: The Ludic and the ludicrous', *International Journal of the History of Sport*, 25 (1) (2008), pp. 100–12.

[129] Important exceptions include B. Stewart, 'The economic development of the Victorian football league 1960–1984', *Sporting Traditions*, 1 (2) (1985), pp. 2–26; B. Dabscheck, 'The Professional Cricketers Association of Australia', *Sporting Traditions*, 8 (1) (1991), pp. 2–27; B. Dabscheck, 'Early attempts at forming soccer player unions in Australia', *Sporting Traditions*, 10 (2) (1994), pp. 25–40; R. Booth, 'History of player recruitment, transfer and payment rules in the Victorian and Australian Football League', *Australian Society for Sports History Bulletin*, 26 (1997), pp. 13–33; B. Dabscheck, 'Australian baseball's second unsuccessful attempt to establish a players' association', 14 (2) (1998), pp. 87–90; B. Stewart, 'The crisis of confidence in Australian first-class cricket in the 1950s', *Sporting Traditions*, 20 (1) (2003), pp. 43–62; R. Booth, 'The economics of achieving competitive balance in the Australian Football League, 1897–2004', *Economic Papers – Economic Society of Australia*, 23 (4) (2004), pp. 325–44; and Stewart, *The games are not the same*.

[130] Classic examples include W. Vamplew, *The turf: A social and economic history of horseracing* (London, 1976); W. Vamplew, *Pay up and play the game: Professional*

sport in Britain, 1875–1914 (Cambridge, 1988); and N. Tranter, *Sport, economy, and society in Britain, 1750–1914* (Cambridge, 1998).

[131] Key studies include D. Rowe, *Sport, culture and the media* (Buckingham, 1999); Lawrence and Rowe, *Power play*; B. Hutchins and M.G. Phillips, 'Selling permissible violence: The commodification of Australian Rugby League 1970–1995', *International Review for the Sociology of Sport*, 32 (2) (1997), pp. 161–76; and M.G. Phillips and B. Hutchins, 'Losing control of the ball: The political economy of football and the media in Australia', *Journal of Sport and Social Issues*, 27 (3) (2003), pp. 215–32.

[132] Exceptions include C. Cunneen, 'Elevating and recording the people's pastimes: Sydney sporting journalism 1886–1939', in R. Cashman and M. McKernan, eds, *Sport: Money, morality, and the media* (Sydney, 1981), pp. 162–76; R. Grow, 'Nineteenth century football and the Melbourne press', *Sporting Traditions*, 3 (1) (1986), pp. 23–37; S.R. Wenn, 'Lights, camera, little action: Television, Avery Brundage and the 1956 Melbourne Olympics', *Sporting Traditions*, 10 (1) (1993), pp. 38–53; P. Brown, 'Gender, the press and history: Coverage of women's sport in the *Newcastle Herald*, 1890–1990', *Media Information Australia*, 75 (1995), pp. 24–34; and B. Stewart, 'Radio's changing relationship with Australian cricket: 1932–1950', *Sporting Traditions*, 19 (1) (2002), pp. 49–64.

[133] J. Nauright and M. Phillips, 'A fair go for the fans?: Super leagues, sports ownership and fans in Australia', *Social Alternatives*, 15 (4) (1996), pp. 43–45; M.G. Phillips and J. Nauright, 'Sports fan movements to save suburban-based football teams threatened with amalgamation in different football codes in Australia', *International Sports Studies*, 21 (1) (1999), pp.16–38; J. Nauright and M. Phillips, 'Us and them: Australian professional sport and resistance to North American ownership and marketing models', *Sport Marketing Quarterly*, 6 (1) (1997), pp. 33–39.

[134] Significant academic studies thus far include, R. Stremski, *Kill for Collingwood* (Sydney, 1986); A. Moore, *The mighty bears!: A social history of North Sydney Rugby league* (Sydney, 1996); M.G. Phillips, 'Rugby league and club loyalty', in D. Headon and L. Marinos, eds, *League of a nation* (Melbourne, 1996), pp. 106–11; and Lock, Taylor and Darcy, 'Soccer and social capital in Australia'.

[135] I. Warren, *Football, crowds and cultures. Comparing English and Australian law and enforcement trends*, (*ASSH Studies in Sports History* series) 13 (2003).

[136] Vamplew, 'Facts and artefacts', pp. 268–82.

The Tyranny of Deference: Anglo–Australian Relations and Rugby Union before World War II

Tony Collins

Historians have traditionally viewed sport in Australia as a vehicle for nationalist sentiment. This paper explores the history of Australian rugby union and its relationship with Britain in the first half of the twentieth century to argue against that assumption that sporting rivalry automatically means national rivalry at a cultural or political level. It suggests that the reality is much more complex and that, for rugby union at least, Australians were far more deferential to Britain than has hitherto been believed.

It is a widely accepted axiom among historians that sport was an indicator of popular nationalist sentiment in the white Dominions of the British Empire. Partly derived from C.L.R James's observations about the role of cricket in West Indian society in *Beyond a Boundary*, this apparent truism is especially common in works dealing with the role of sport in Australian society from the late Victorian period. First articulated by W.F. Mandle in 'Cricket and Australian Nationalism in the Nineteenth Century' in 1973, the proposition now has the standing of an accepted truth. In *A Nation at Last?* Stephen Alomes writes that 'sport brought a sense of shared Australianness'. [1] Richard Cashman in *Sport in the National Imagination* argues that 'sport has been closely linked to the representation of Australia and to promoting Australianness'. This assumption is so strong that in

---

Tony Collins, Leeds Metropolitan University.

2001 John Rickard, writing in *Australian Historical Studies*, criticised Neville Meaney for dismissing sport as a 'test of nationalism', implying that Meaney was not taking seriously something that was self-evidently an expression of nationalism. The idea that Australia 'came to nationhood' during the First World War and that this evolving nationalism was reflected by sport in the interwar period is widespread, most notably in the standard assessment of the 1932–33 Bodyline cricket tour. [2]

This approach to Australian history and its relationship to the British Empire has recently been subject to sustained criticism, most notably by many of the contributors to *Australia's Empire*, one of the companion volumes to the *Oxford History of the British Empire*. [3] This article will use the example of rugby union football to look at how a major Australian sport viewed the imperial relationship and to question the assumption that Anglo–Australian sporting rivalry necessarily meant national antagonism at a political level. As I have argued in the case of Australian rugby league, the historical relationship between sport and Australian nationalism is not so straightforward that it will allow one to 'read off' nationalist feelings from sporting rivalry. [4] Until well into the second half of the twentieth century, sport was seen as a means of strengthening Australia's links with its fellow members of the British Empire, most importantly with Britain itself. Considering oneself as Australian was not at all counterposed to feelings of Britishness nor did it imply, for the vast majority of the population, a desire to separate oneself from the British Empire. Indeed, one could argue that Australian identity during the first half of the twentieth century was a subset of a 'Greater British' identity.

Historians seeking to address the apparent contradiction between the intensity of Anglo–Australian sporting contests and the Britishness of much of Australian sport have argued that Australian nationalism operated alongside imperial loyalty, implying that nationalist ideas were somehow incubated within this framework. This paper will argue that there is almost no evidence to support the contention that nationalist ideas were articulated or pursued in Australian rugby union in the first half of the twentieth century. It will argue that levels of deference towards Britain in Australian rugby actually increased in the decades following the First World War, that disputes with the British rugby authorities were based largely on Australians's sense of thwarted Britishness, rather than incipient nationalism, and that when faced with a choice between challenging the British link or reaffirming their loyalty towards the empire, the Australians invariably chose the latter. In short, this article will seek to place a question mark over the widespread belief that sport was an expression of nationalism in interwar Australia.

Rugby before 1914: Bodyline foreshadowed

Although in the 1850s the founders of Victorian (later Australian) rules football took their inspiration from the football that was played at Rugby School in England, it wasn't until 1863 that a club which actually played the Rugby School code of football was founded in Australia, Sydney University Football Club. Over the next three decades New South Wales and eventually Queensland adopted rugby football as their primary football code. In 1874 the Southern Rugby Union (SRU) was formed in Sydney as the governing body of the rugby code in Australia. From its inception, the sport was closely associated with the universities and the Great Public Schools. [5] By the late 1890s, however, rugby had become a mass-spectator sport for all classes in the eastern states, attracting considerable crowds, press coverage and public interest.

Part of the game's appeal was the opportunity it offered for competition between different countries of the empire. As with cricket, the growth of rugby brought with it regular tours from teams representing New Zealand and, most importantly, Britain. In 1888 an unofficial British rugby tour organised by the sporting entrepreneurs Alfred Shaw and Arthur Shrewsbury had given added impetus to the popularity of the game. Rugby also presented an important form of cultural exchange, as young middle-class Australian males took up studentships at Oxford, Cambridge or the London and Edinburgh medical schools. Indeed, a number, such as C.G. Wade and S.M.J. Woods, even represented England or Scotland at international level. Rugby thus became an important part of the imperial sporting network that included cricket, rowing and athletics. Welcoming the 1904 British rugby team to Australia, J.C. Davis, Sydney's leading sports journalist of the time, encapsulated this when he wrote that sporting tours created 'an extended feeling of appreciation and racial sympathy. They have incidentally shown to the muscular Britisher at home that the Britisher abroad and his sinewy colonial descendents are not aliens because thousands of miles of sea intervene.' [6] Rowland Hill, English rugby union's key administrator in the early part of the twentieth century, believed that international tours were 'of great Imperial importance in binding together the Mother Country with the Overseas Dominions'. [7]

It was in this spirit that the governing body of English rugby, the Rugby Football Union (RFU), organised the first official rugby tour to Australia by a British representative side in 1899. Captained and managed by the Reverend Matthew Mullineux, the tour proved to be unexpectedly controversial. Mullineux was disappointed with the spirit in which the

Australians played the game. Most of all, he was horrified by the widespread, and well-founded, rumours that players received money for playing, contrary to the amateur regulations of the sport. For their part, the Australians felt let down because, contrary to expectations, the British team was not truly representative; only seven of the 21 players in the side had ever appeared in an international before. [8] Most importantly, they were somewhat shocked at the highly competitive manner in which the British played the game. Much to their hosts's surprise, the British tourists appeared to go all out to win, rather then to play the game for its own enjoyment, as would be expected by representatives of the home of 'fair play'. The contrast between the rhetoric and the reality of British play was highlighted in a newspaper cartoon published during the tour, in which a British Lion confronted a Kangaroo:

> Lion: 'Look here, you don't play fair!'
> Kangaroo: 'What do you call fair?'
> Lion: 'Well-er-you see, I didn't come out here to get licked.' [9]

Far from being temporary hiccough in international rugby relations, these problems were exacerbated during the next British tour of Australia in 1904. Captained by Scottish forward David Bedell-Sivright, the side departed Australia unbeaten before going on to face sterner opposition in New Zealand, but left a trail of controversy behind them. Foreshadowing Douglas Jardine, the captain of the 1932–33 English cricket tourists, much of the ill-feeling of the tour was generated by the behaviour of Bedell-Sivright, about whom it was said 'his conception of football was one of trained violence.' [10] Two of the three test matches were punctuated by brawling between the British captain and his Australian adversaries and a match in Newcastle against Northern Districts was interrupted when he led his men off the field in protest against the dismissal of British forward Denys Dobson. The referee alleged that Dobson had sworn at him after being penalised at a scrum. Bedell-Sivright denied that one of his men would do anything so low and promptly marched his side off the pitch. [11] Eventually they were persuaded to return, but the incident became notorious as another example of the ease with which the British dispensed with their principles of fair play when it suited them.

The relationship deteriorated further during the first Australian rugby union tour of Britain in 1908. Following in the wake of successful tours 'home' by the New Zealand and South African national sides, the tourists – known as the Wallabies – were dogged by controversy and deteriorating relations with their British hosts. The Scottish and Irish rugby unions refused to play them because of suspicions that the Australians were professionals. On the pitch, the tourists were accused of being violent and playing solely for the purpose of winning. Unprecedentedly, three players were sent off during the tour, including one, Syd Middleton, against Oxford University, the very embodiment of the amateur 'rugger' tradition. For many in Britain, the tour demonstrated the moral deficiencies of the typical Australian. Scottish rugby writer Hamish Stuart claimed that 'custom and the national idea have so blunted their moral sense that they are sublimely unconscious of their delinquency and are sincerely surprised when accused of unfair practice'. [12] The Australians were reciprocally less than enamoured by their treatment in Britain. Returning home, James McMahon, the tour manager, complained that 'as visitors to the Mother Country, as representatives of part of the British nation, [the players] could not understand and were certainly not prepared for such hostility as was shown them by a section of the press.' [13]

In many ways these rugby disputes anticipated the 1932–33 Bodyline cricket controversy. Like the Bodyline events, the disputes were not caused by any Australian proto-nationalism but by the injustice felt by Australians when British sides did not abide by the supposedly British sporting values of 'fair play' or refused to accept their opponents as equally as British as they. This was precisely the basis of much of the anger of Australians during Bodyline. It was not so much that the English cricket captain Douglas Jardine was engaging in intimidatory tactics but that he appeared to have departed from the ethical code of the British gentleman and was using such tactics against fellow Britons. This feeling of betrayed loyalty was captured by an anonymous 'Man in the Street' who published a pamphlet in Sydney titled *The Sporting English*, a scathing attack on the English in response to the 1932–33 cricket tour and its aftermath:

> We Australians are at a loss to understand why we, alone of all the Empire, are singled out for these continual attacks. We claim to be loyal to the throne, and to uphold the traditions of the British race. Also we pay our debts and are England's very best customer within the Empire. When danger threatened, we were of the first to respond to the call to arms by the Motherland. [14]

The underlying imperial loyalty of such complaints was made explicit by Wallaby captain H.M. Moran who, despite noting that his fellow tourists had 'developed a dislike for everything English', also pointed out that 'there is one symbol of [Australian] unity with the nation of nations. It is the monarchy.'

> An Australian will often express himself rudely about a visiting Englishman who behaves superciliously. That is common. He will frequently hurl angry criticisms at a British government. That, he considers his right. He will even in a pet be disrespectful to a British government, though this is rare. But to the King, no man with impunity may offer insult. [15]

Thus what was being expressed by Australians in these sporting disputes was not an embryonic form of nationalism but a thwarted imperial loyalty. And in attempting to deal with this frustration over the next three decades, far from being driven to greater hostility towards Britain, the Australian rugby union authorities sought to bend over backwards in an attempt to appease their tormentors.

Rugby before and after World War I

Part of the reason for the rise in the level of the Australian rugby authorities' deference to Britain can be found in the rugby split that led to the establishment of rugby league in Australia. In 1907 and 1908 a significant section of Australian rugby clubs and players broke away from rugby union to play the semi-professional and predominantly working-class game of rugby league. Indeed, at the same time as the Wallabies were touring Britain, the Australian rugby league tourists, the Kangaroos, were also on tour there. On their return home, fourteen of the Wallabies immediately announced their affiliation to the rebel rugby organisation. The new game, with its streamlined rules, open play and rejection of amateurism, quickly overtook rugby union in players and spectators and by 1912 had established itself as the leading football code in New South Wales. [16]

The rugby union authorities took a stance of unremitting hostility to the rival game. Following the split in English rugby and the foundation of rugby league in the north of England in August 1895 the RFU had decreed that anyone who had played or been involved with rugby league, regardless of whether they had been paid for doing so, would receive an automatic life-ban from rugby union. At root this reflected the class prejudices of that section of the English middle-classes that ran the RFU and their desire to be free of pressures from working-class players and spectators which they felt would undermine the moral character of rugby. Intrinsic to this conception of rugby was the belief that its moral role was bound up with an imperial purpose. Rugby union football, claimed the *Times*, was 'a most practical means of continuing and strengthening the bonds of interest between us and our relations scattered over the world ... Often in the past the ties between this country and the colonies have been slender, and the strongest of them is the common interest in British games'. [17]

This indivisibility of rugby union and the British Empire – or at least the Dominions, the sport never being terribly keen to play with those of a darker skin – was an article of faith among its supporters. Although no less loyal to the empire, rugby league was at variance with the middle-class ethos of rugby union, and the dominance of the game by players and spectators from the working classes was profoundly at odds with the rigid social hierarchy desired by the leaders of rugby union. [18] Thus rugby league was the 'other' for rugby union, to be feared and despised in equal measure (even in places, such as South Africa, where it had no presence). Its rapid rise to sporting dominance over Australian rugby union thus seemed to confirm the anti-Australian prejudices of the British rugby union authorities that had been voiced on the 1908 tour, forcing Australian rugby union to feel obligated to demonstrate a higher level of loyalty to Britain and the RFU.

As with rugby union in the other countries of the empire, the outbreak of World War I in August 1914 saw Australian rugby union players and officials rush to join the colours. Australian rugby clubs ceased playing for the duration of the war and effectively turned themselves into auxiliaries of the recruitment campaign. H.Y. Braddon, the president of the NSW Rugby Union was the chairman of the Sportsman's Recruiting Committee. Half of those who joined its Sportman's Battalion were rugby union players. [19] In Sydney, the Manly club declared that its purpose was 'to prepare the members for active service when they came of military age'. [20] The NSW Rugby Union set up its own drill and rifle clubs 'for the purpose of providing military training for members before joining the armed forces'. [21] By April 1916 the NSWRU had seen 109 of its registered players killed in action. [22] By the end of the war, the Eastern Suburbs Club reported, of its 82 members who 'went to the help of the Motherland, twenty have made the supreme sacrifice'. [23]

However, the social upheaval of the war also had an impact on rugby. In 1916, in response to the huge influx of rugby players of both codes into the British forces, the RFU lifted its ban on rugby league players being involved with rugby for the duration of the war. The commingling of the two codes, together with the debates about the future of rugby that had been going on immediately before the war, led to a questioning within rugby union of aspects of its conservatism. Even in England, there were calls for rugby union to adopt league-style rule changes to make it more open and attractive. [24] But in Australia and New Zealand, similar ideas for changes to the rules were already being implemented, such as a ban on kicking the ball directly into touch, something that had been introduced by league in 1902. [25] Writing from England, the rugby correspondent of the authoritative *Athletic News*, W.L. Sinclair, confidently predicted that, 'in very little while we may expect to see Union and League united' in the southern hemisphere. [26] In March 1920 the NSWRU (effectively Australian rugby union's governing body at that time) voted to support a New Zealand proposal for changes to the laws of the game and to relax the code's strict amateurism. It also decided to press the RFU for representation on the game's International Board (IB), which was dominated by the RFU and comprised only England, Ireland, Scotland and Wales. [27] Consequently the Australian and New Zealand rugby unions submitted to the IB a joint document proposing 13 rule changes, many of which were modeled on rugby league rules. On all substantive issues the IB voted to reject the proposals but a 'dispensation' was granted to the Australasian unions to allow them to ban direct kicking into touch from outside the kicking team's 25 yard line. [28] Beyond this, the IB was not prepared to go.

More to the point, it was determined to roll back what it saw as a dangerous backsliding over the central tenets of the rugby game. For the RFU and its supporters, the war, and especially the huge toll of death among rugby union players, had been a powerful vindication of their belief in the moral and patriotic role of rugby. As RFU president Arthur Hartley declared in 1919, 'we are proud of the race that give us Rugby football at its best, and we would hold to the fine traditions now handed down to us by the fallen ... Their supreme sacrifice will not have been in vain if we live nobly and carry into the game their spirit.' [29] In the eyes of the RFU, the debate of the sport's rules and the apparent softness towards rugby league from the southern hemisphere placed this heritage in danger. The blood sacrifice that had been made during the war became the ultimate answer to those who questioned the sport's leadership. Thus the response of the RFU's supporters to calls for change was not primarily to argue the merits of any proposed changes but to use its moral authority to question the patriotism of its critics. This can be seen with stunning clarity in a letter to the Sydney *Referee* in early 1921 that signaled the end of meaningful discussion about change within the rugby union world:

> I believe that there are still some people in Australia and New Zealand who want to see rugby played ... I believe the Great Public Schools of Sydney will never desert the rugger game – a beautiful edifice, built up by years of patient labour, and over which is shed the lustre of a tradition that will live as long as red blood flows in Australian veins – this tradition (I quote from the 1919–20 *Rugby Football Annual*):

> 'On the last Saturday of the 1913–14 season the London Scottish [rugby club] placed four teams in the field, of these sixty players, forty-five have been killed. Altogether the club had seventy of three hundred members killed and fifty-two wounded. Some of the smaller clubs have lost almost all of the playing members.'
>
> Now, Billy Hill [the Australian official who had called for rule changes], old friend, that's the sort of game whose fortunes are entrusted to your (amongst other) hands. You know the record of the New South Wales and New Zealand rugby unions in the terrible but wonderful years of Armageddon.
>
> Before you and your friends, in this sudden, new found zeal of yours for 'improving the rules' destroy that edifice – think!
>
> And think again!
>
> In England it is imperishable and indestructible. [30]

The message could not be clearer: the RFU and its supporters were warning dissidents that there could be no compromise. Faced with the possibility of a question mark being placed over their British patriotism, the leaders of Australian rugby union had no difficulty falling in behind the RFU and turning their backs on those who sought to reform rugby union. [31]

Interwar rugby imperial relations

This is not to say that the Australian authorities were completely at one with the RFU about the way the rugby union was played and organised. Australian society did not fully replicate the harsh social rigidity of the British class structure which allowed the RFU to impose its unbending amateurism on the English game and pursue an unremitting vendetta on transgressors. Thus the official amateur regulations of the sport were never implemented as rigorously in Australia as they were in Britain. [32] The Australians were also less conservative in their attitude to rule changes. This was due in part to rugby union's eclipse by league in NSW and in Queensland – where the union code had collapsed during the war and would not be played seriously again there until 1927 – which compelled the sport to make itself attractive to spectators used to the faster, more open, league game. Thus in 1924 and 1926 the NSWRU proposed or supported rule changes that were submitted to the IB, which, needless to say, failed to meet the approval of the RFU-led IB and were dismissed with little discussion. [33] At no time did the Australians seek to force the issue or campaign for their proposals, indicating that when confronted with a choice between seriously opposing the British leadership of the sport or deferring to it, Australian rugby always chose the latter.

Although controversies over the rules would flare up during the interwar years – usually when the British found something objectionable in the play of Dominion sides, such as on the 1930 British isles team's tour of New Zealand and Australia when the British objected so much to the tactics of New Zealand sides that they returned home and changed the rules relating to scrums – the main focus for discussions between the Australians (and New Zealanders) and rugby's British leadership centred on representation on the IB. The board had been founded in 1886 as an attempt by the non-English home nations to appropriate some of the power of the RFU. Even so, the RFU had traditionally dominated the board, partly through the weight of its authority but also because the constitution of the IB gave it three permanent delegates while the other countries had two each. In the mid-1900s the success of their touring sides to Britain had led to calls for Australia, New Zealand and South Africa to be represented on the IB. This was dismissed at the time, but the joint sacrifices of the First World War and the continuing success of Antipodean sides in the 1920s led to increasing pressure from the Dominions to have delegates of their own on the IB. In recognition of this, in 1923 the IB decided to agree to convene a conference 'with the Unions in the Colonies' for 1924.

To some extent this reflected the changing post-war relationship between Britain and the Dominions in the wider political sphere, and, of course, the idea of an imperial rugby conference paralleled the series of Imperial Conferences that were held between the leaders of the major nations of the empire in the interwar years. The discussions which led to the declaration of the 1926 Imperial Conference that the Dominions and Britain were self-governing nations of equal status could not fail to have found a sympathetic response from rugby administrators in the southern hemisphere. However, the IB's terms for the 1924 conference harked back to the empire's pre-1907 Colonial Conferences which were only held when visiting statesmen happened to be in London for other events. The IB specified that the conference had to be in London and that it would not pay for delegates to travel to the conference. The gathering was eventually held in December 1924 during the New Zealand tour of the UK and served only to emphasise the complete resistance to reform on the part of the leaders of the British game. The IB proved to be less amenable to the idea of Dominion equality than British politicians, vetoing any discussion on relaxing the amateur regulations and voting against any Dominion representation on the IB. As a concession, it was agreed to hold an Imperial Conference every five years at which the IB would meet with Dominion representatives. However, its decisions would not be binding on any party, it would always be held in London and the IB would not pay travel costs. Needless to say, the resulting conference was a damp squib, with the Australian game being represented by two Australians resident in the UK. [34]

The New Zealand delegates to the conference had suggested the formation of an Imperial Rugby Advisory Board, the 'advisory' being carefully chosen so as not to alarm the IB. But at its meeting in March 1925 the IB still found this formulation too strong and voted instead to organise an Imperial Rugby Conference to be held every three years in London. The issue was debated again the following year and the RFU delegates this time proposed that a conference should be held to establish an Imperial Advisory Board, comprising two delegates each from the four home countries and the three rugby-playing Dominions. When the conference was held in November 1926 it yet again proved to be highly resistant to change. The NSWRU and the South African Rugby Union both submitted suggestions for amendments to the rules, with the NSWRU proposing that the Imperial Advisory Board should provide 'uniform international government' for rugby union. However, the IB ruled these proposals out of order and they were not formally discussed at the conference. In the report of the conference in the 1927 NSW *Rugby Annual*, the NSWRU sought to cover its embarrassment at the summary dismissal of its ideas by claiming that 'although not on the agenda for the conference . . . the Dominion unions' views [were] informally placed before the assembled delegates'. [35]

This was about as far as they would get in the interwar years – there was to be no equivalent of the 1931 Statute of Westminster – which introduced legislative equality between the Dominions – for rugby. The RFU maneuvered effectively between the Dominions and the other home countries, playing on the latter's fear that they would be reduced to third place in the rugby hierarchy below the RFU and the stronger overseas governing bodies. It also continued to dangle the carrot of consultation in front of the Australians and New Zealanders if they would abandon the rule 'dispensations' granted to them. 'Now the game is played throughout the British Empire,' wrote Sydney Coopper, the RFU secretary, in 1930, 'there should be no exceptions anywhere. We have found the particular dispensations once granted to you, of late a growing embarrassment to other Dominions and are desirous of checking a growing tendency to take advantage of a special arrangement made with you.' [36] In exchange for ending the dispensations, the RFU proposed the setting up of a Rugby Football Commission representing the home countries and the Dominions which would 'consider the laws of the game with the view of uniformity around the world'. But this would not be a decision-making body, being able only to submit suggestions to the IB which would accept or decline them as it saw fit. Even so, the NSWRU (and the New Zealand Rugby Union) agreed to end their use of the dispensations, despite the RFU proposal falling far short of their demand for direct representation on the IB. [37]

Why were the Australians so deferent and afraid of confronting the RFU in pursuit of their own interests, even in seemingly minor matters? The answer lies in the fact that the Australian rugby union authorities shared the same British imperial framework as the RFU. Their wish to be represented on the IB came from a desire to develop the sport's imperial character, not to challenge the British. Dominion representation on the IB, wrote the editor of *Rugby News* in 1931, would be 'a great day for rugby. Its Empire aspect will have been strengthened and its status as a world's game established.' [38] The fear of offending the British, and particularly the RFU, ran very deep within the psyche of rugby union officials, especially given the difficulties of the pre-1914 tours and the disaster of the 1908 rugby league split. In short, imperial loyalty overrode their own self-interest.

Touring the 'Mother Country'

In keeping with its British patriotism, the ultimate goal of the NSWRU was to be invited to tour the UK. The 1908 tour had left a deep stain that they had long wished to remove, and the success of the 1924 New Zealand tour to the UK had raised their hopes that the RFU was prepared to partake of the new imperial spirit of co-operation between the mother country and the Dominions. When the invitation for NSW to tour Britain finally arrived in June 1926, after some prevarication by the Scottish Rugby Union, the NSWRU was jubilant: 'the invitation must indeed be gratifying to those who have worked unceasingly to obtain this recognition'. [39] The NSWRU set out to make sure that none of the mistakes of the 1908 tour would be repeated and that nothing could occur which might embarrass their British hosts. It was determined to be *plus royaliste que le roi* when it came to professionalism and introduced a set of stringent regulations that forbade players from writing for the press or endorsing products. This resulted in the not-so-mysterious removal of the photograph of Ted Thorn, the NSW captain, from the advertisement for

Macmur football boots that appeared regularly in *Rugby News* (although the hypocrisy of the amateur regulations did allow his endorsement to be replaced by that of NSWRU official Tom Griffen). [40] Anxious to avoid British complaints of Australian arrogance, the tour party stated that they were going to Britain 'with our minds turned towards an attitude of learning rather than teaching'. It was in this spirit that on their return home the players were congratulated for their 'general tact', the lack of which had been a major criticism made by their hosts in 1908. [41] On the departure of the team, which was known as the Waratahs, an editorial in *Rugby News* highlighted the greater purpose of the tour: 'their mission does not end on the playing fields of other countries, for they are looking to strengthen the ties that bind the Mother Country with the Dominions – a duty which our players are well able to perform'. [42]

The tour itself was conducted with all the solemnity of a state visit, with the playing of rugby often appearing to take second place to the endless procession of visits, lunches and receptions. As tourist Syd Malcolm later remembered, 'we had entrée into places few private travellers were privileged to enter'. [43] As well as numerous visits to military bases, various gentlemen's clubs and the sights of London and the major cities, the tourists attended a reception in their honour hosted by the Lord Mayor of London, had dinner with Lord Lonsdale, enjoyed afternoon tea with the Duke and Duchess of Devonshire and met the Prince of Wales and the King, the latter presenting each member of the side with a freshly shot grouse before entertaining them with tea at Sandringham. In their report to the NSWRU on their return home, the manager and captain of the side E.G. Shaw and A.C. Wallace recorded with pride how the team had 'been entertained by members of the Royal Family in their own homes, and have been accepted in friendship by the Empire's statesmen and sportsmen'. [44] The care and attention that the NSWRU had taken in ensuring that nothing could offend their hosts was vindicated when, at the farewell reception for the tourists, RFU president Admiral Sir Percy Royds declared that they were 'the greatest band of sportsmen that has ever visited us'. [45]

The impact of the tour provided the impetus for the renewed growth of Australian rugby union. Since the end of the war it had been much to the chagrin of its supporters that the imperial football link with the mother country had been maintained exclusively by rugby league, which had hosted two tours by British teams and toured Britain itself in 1921. But the prospect of the re-establishment of an imperial rugby union link helped to affirm the sport's self-identity as the 'Empire game'. The game was restarted in the private and grammar schools of Queensland and universities in Brisbane and Melbourne switched from league to union. [46] It was this connection to Britain, and ultimately Australian rugby union's subservience to the mother country, together with its middle-class exclusivity, which now more than anything defined the sport, as *Rugby News* laid bare in 1928:

> In all and to the furthermost ends of the British Empire the great Rugby game is played and all owe allegiance to the great controller of the game, the English Rugby Union. It is the tradition of the rugby union game that makes us stand behind that great body to which the game owes its origin.
>
> They gave us the game and we believe that its destinies can safely be left in their hands. At all times they have been willing to allow us to adopt modes of play and rules which are more suitable for the advancement of the game in Australia. At all times [Australian] rugby union stands behind its Alma Mater, not only because it believes and trusts in it, but also because it feels that by so doing the bonds of Empire are through the brotherhood of sport more closely knit. [47]

In confirmation that the Australians were now a trusted member of the RFU's imperial family, it was announced in June 1928 that a side representing the British Isles would tour Australia and New Zealand in 1930. Underlining the balance of power within British rugby, the tour was organised entirely by the English RFU. [48] Its captain, Doug Prentice, spelt out the purpose of the tour in familiar terms: 'Each member of the side is an ambassador from the Mother Country, and if, by these, visits, the bond of friendship between parents and children is more firmly tightened, then that alone would be sufficient reason for sending out touring teams to the Dominions'. [49]

As with the invitation to tour Britain in 1927, the NSWRU council took a series of measures to avoid upsetting its 'parents'. In May 1930 it sent a circular to all its clubs expressing 'grave concern the rough tactics evident in recent games, particularly in view of the approaching visit of the British team' and the council also became engulfed in a huge debate over what to do about players who had played rugby league but who now wanted to play union. The dominance of the league game meant that traditionally the Australian rugby union authorities had turned a blind eye to league players in their game, in contrast to the strict RFU rules on the matter, but the approach of the British tourists brought panic because of fears that this attitude may endanger the relationship with Britain. The NSWRU council eventually decided by one vote to allow former league players to continue playing union but appointed a committee to look at the rules relating to professionalism, which governed the stance towards rugby league, in view of 'local conditions and the development of the game throughout Australia'. [50] The tour itself turned out to be something of a flop, recording a profit of just £91. [51]

Throughout the 1930s the sport showed no sign that it saw itself as anything but dutiful British servants of the empire and loyal subjects of the Crown. Indeed, it was effusive in its Britishness, most notably when it concerned the Royal family. *Rugby News* printed full-page photographs of King George VI during the week of his coronation and subsequent birthdays. To mark the departure to Britain of the 1939 Australian touring side the magazine carried two photographs of the former King Edward VIII with the 1927 tourists. That these attitudes were sincerely held and not merely a public stance can be seen from the unpublished report and diary of the manager of the 1939 tour W.F. Matthews. 'We were greatly impressed by the King's appearance. He looked strong and healthy, and was full of confidence and assurance, and the Queen was graciousness itself – all the boys agreed on this – she is very very beautiful,' he wrote after a reception hosted by the monarch. [52] When the tourists had left for Britain, the rugby union correspondent of the Sydney *Referee* had written that 'the trip should send them back to Australia remarkably well-fitted to take a hand in the destiny of their own country and the Empire as a whole', a sentiment that was amply confirmed by Matthews in his own diary entry two days after the declaration of war when he recorded that he was:

> very struck with feeling which is universal that a serious war is in front of Empire and everyone ready to make any sacrifice that may be necessary. Saw Mr Hay [the NSW Agent General] again this morning and told him I am ready to remain for any special duty if wanted. [53]

Conclusion

In 1948 Australia, together with New Zealand and South Africa, finally achieved its goal of representation on the International Board. Even then, the Dominions only received one representative each, in contrast to the two allocated to each home country. In exchange, Australia and New Zealand once again had to relinquish the rule dispensations that had been restored to them in 1936. [54] It was not until the 1960s, following the embarrassment of Suez, the dismantling of the empire and Britain's abrupt redefinition of its relationship with Australia and New Zealand, that the traditional deference towards the RFU and the British rugby authorities began to crumble. Even today, however, echoes of the old relationship remain: in 1998 the trophy for series between Australia and Scotland was named the Lord Hopetoun Cup by the Australian Rugby Union, in honour of the Scottish first governor-general of Australia.

To a large extent, none of the above should come as a surprise. Imperial loyalty and British self-identity ran deep in interwar Australia and sport reflected this. Of course, it must also be asked how representative of Australian society were the people who played, watched and administered rugby union? After all, clearly they were drawn largely from the middle-classes and could therefore reasonably be expected to be strongly pro-British. But in this, rugby did not differ substantially from the leadership of Australian cricket, which also came from the same social strata. And the attitude of the leadership of Australian cricket to the Bodyline crisis, which resulted in the Australians backing down in the face of threats from England to break the relationship, parallels that of rugby. As Syd Smith, the former secretary of cricket's Australian Board of Control, argued in 1933, 'we cannot afford, from an Empire point of view, to allow the Tests to be abandoned. They mean more than cricket. They mean friendships between England, Australia, South Africa, New Zealand and the West Indies.' [55]

Richard Cashman has argued that Sydney's sporting culture was 'more derivative and pro-British' than that of Melbourne's 'more independent and indigenous sporting culture', but cricket, the quintessentially British game, was no less popular in Victoria than in NSW. [56] Indeed, rugby union itself underwent considerable expansion in Melbourne in the interwar years, so much so that Victoria became the sport's second state in Australia, defeating NSW four times between 1929 and 1938, and supplying players to the Australian national side, including four members of the 1939 Wallaby side. But the implication of Cashman's thesis is that it was Australian rules football, the only major difference in the sporting culture of the two cities, that was more 'indigenous'. Historians of Australian rules have paid little attention to its relationship with Britain (although this paper is part of a broader project looking at Australian national identity and the football codes) other than to assume that it is a signifier of Australian nationalism. However, its origins clearly lie in the British public school codes of football and it fully shared the British concepts of 'fair play', amateurism and the moral value of sport. Moreover, the idea that 'football' as a generic game was integral to British masculinity was a common idea throughout the empire.

But the assumption that sporting differences necessarily indicate a deeper political divergence also illustrates a common methodological mistake among historians who have looked at sport. This is the supposition that hostility in the sports arena is equivalent to political, social or national hostility, something which is particularly easy to do because of the importance of competition to sporting activity. But this is not automatically the case, especially when looking at sport in the countries of the British Empire, for whom the playing of games was a means of demonstrating their Britishness. Indeed, the intense rivalry between the Dominions and British sporting sides flowed largely from the shared desire to demonstrate which was the best representative of imperial manhood. As this paper has sought to demonstrate, Australian rugby union saw itself as no less British than those born in the 'mother country' and its greatest frustrations and disappointments occurred when those at home refused to fully acknowledge this. It was impossible for them to conceive of an existence separate from Britain, and the danger of that happening led them to become more deferential to the British rulers of rugby in the two decades following the First World War than had been the case before the war.

Although often misunderstood by modern historians, the underlying Britishness of imperial sports did not go unnoticed by nations outside of the empire. It was captured in the 1920s by the acting Japanese consul general in Australia, S. Yamasaki, after he had watched a game of rugby union in Sydney: 'this game seems to singularly reflect the true spirit of the British people. Its encouragement, therefore, in my country will help to bring about a better understanding of that spirit by the Japanese people.' [57] To those involved in Australian rugby union in the interwar years, this was the greatest compliment that they could wish to be paid.

Acknowledgements

I am grateful to the Council of Australian State Libraries for providing me with a fellowship in 2004 during which much of the research for this paper was carried out.

Notes

[1] C.L.R James, *Beyond a boundary* (London, 1963); Stephen Alomes, *A nation at last? The changing character of Australian nationalism 1880–1988*, (NSW, 1988), p. 16; Richard Cashman, *Sport in the national imagination: Australian sport in the Federation decades*, (Sydney, 2002), p. 15; W.F. Mandle, 'Cricket and Australian nationalism in the nineteenth century' *Journal of the Royal Australian Historical Society*, 59 (4) (1973), pp. 225–46; John Rickard 'Imagining the unimaginable?' *Australian Historical Studies*, 116 (2001), pp. 128–131. A critique of Mandle can be found in K.S. Inglis, 'Imperial cricket: Test matches between Australia and England, 1877–1900', in Richard Cashman and Michael

McKernan, eds, *Sport in history: The making of modern sporting history* (St Lucia, 1979), pp. 149–79.

[2] The quote is from W.F. Mandle, *Going it alone. Australia's national identity in the twentieth century* (Melbourne, 1978), p. 23, and is perhaps the clearest expression of this idea. For Bodyline, see Ric Sissons and Brian Stoddart, *Cricket and empire: The 1932–33 Bodyline tour of Australia* (London, 1984).

[3] Deryck M. Schreuder and Stuart Ward, eds, *Australia's empire* (Oxford, 2008). See also Neville Meaney's 'Britishness and Australia: Some reflections', *Journal of Imperial and Commonwealth History*, 31 (2) (2003), p. 122–35 and Stuart Ward, *Australia and the British embrace: The demise of the imperial ideal* (Melbourne, 2001). The March 2005 issue of the *Journal of Australian Politics and History*, 51 (1) is also a collection of articles dealing with similar issues.

[4] See Tony Collins 'Australian nationalism and working-class Britishness: The case of rugby league football', *History Compass*, 3 (142) (2005), pp. 1–19.

[5] For the origins of rugby in Australia see Tom Hickie *They ran with the ball* (Melbourne, 1993) pp. 120–9. The influence of Rugby School on Victorian rules is highlighted in G.M. Hibbins, 'The Cambridge connection: The English origins of Australian rules football', in J.A. Mangan, ed., *The cultural bond. Sport, empire, society* (London, 1993), pp. 108–127.

[6] J.C. Davis, *Official souvenir – English team of rugby football players* (Sydney, 1904), p. 3.

[7] G.R. Hill quoted in *Rugby football: A weekly record of the game*, 17 Nov. 1923, p. 273.

[8] Matthew Mullineux's views are reported in great detail in the *Australian Field*, 26 Aug. 1899.

[9] *Brisbane Courier*, 29 June 1899.

[10] H.M. Moran, *Viewless winds. Being the recollections and digressions of an Australian surgeon* (London, 1939), p. 46.

[11] *Sydney Morning Herald*, 7 July 1904.

[12] Hamish Stuart quoted in Greg Ryan, 'A lack of *esprit de corps*': The 1908 Wallaby tour of Britain', *Sporting Traditions*, 17 (1) (2000), p. 45.

[13] James McMahon in *Referee*, 31 Mar. 1909.

[14] Anon., *The sporting English? A commentary by a 'Man in the Street'* (Sydney, undated, *c.*1933), p. 18, pamphlet in Box 379, ES Marks Collection, Mitchell Library, Sydney.

[15] Moran, *Viewless winds*, pp. 29, 69.

[16] See Chris Cunneen, 'The rugby war. The early history of rugby league in NSW, 1907–1915', in Richard Cashman and Michael McKernan, eds, *Sport in History* (Queensland, 1979), p. 303.

[17] *Times*, 22 Mar. 1919.

[18] For example, the encouragement of Maori involvement by the New Zealand Rugby Union 'had as much to do with countering the perceived negative of rugby league than with any positive desire to advance the Maori game', according to Greg Ryan, 'The paradox of Maori rugby', in Greg Ryan, ed., *Tackling rugby myths* (Otago, 2005), p. 103. On Australian rugby league and its relationship to Britain, see Collins 'Australian nationalism and working-class Britishness', pp. 1–19.

[19] Murray Phillips, 'Football, class and war: The rugby codes in New South Wales 1907–18', in John Nauright and Timothy J.L. Chandler, eds. *Making men: Rugby and masculine identity* (London, 1996), pp. 158–80. Michael McKernan. 'Sport, war and Australia', in Richard Cashman and Michael McKernan, eds, *Sport in History* (Brisbane, 1979), p. 3.

[20] Manly District Rugby Union Football Club (RUFC), *10th Annual Report and Balance Sheet for Season 1915*, p. 3.

[21] NSW Rugby Union, *Annual Report 1915*, p. 3.

[22] NSWRU, *Annual Report 1916*, p. 3.

[23] Eastern Suburbs District Football Club (FC), *16th Annual Report and Balance Sheet 1915–19*, p. 3.

[24] See, for example, a letter from 'An Old International', in *Times*, 30 Dec. 1918, p. 12.

[25] *Referee*, 11 May 1921.

[26] *Athletic News*, 5 Feb. 1919.

[27] RFU committee minutes, 17 Oct. 1919. NSWRU management committee minutes, 29 Mar. 1920. NSWRU *Annual Report 1920*, p. 3.

[28] International Board minutes, 19 Mar. and 23 July 1920. See also NSWRU *Annual Report 1921*, p. 3.

[29] *Yorkshire Rugby Football Union commemoration book 1914–1919 & official handbook, 1919–1920* (Leeds, 1920), p. 272. See also Tony Collins 'English rugby union and the First World War', *The Historical Journal*, 45 (4) (2002), pp. 797–817.

[30] John Hughes, 'Stands rugger yet', *Referee*, 5 Jan. 1921.

[31] See, for example, the first issue of *Rugby News*, 5 May 1923, p. 2.

[32] For the contrasting zealotry of the RFU's rulemakers, see Tony Collins, 'The ambiguities of amateurism: English rugby in the Edwardian era' in *Sport in History*, 26 (3) (2006), pp. 390–411.

[33] IB minutes, 14 Mar. 1924 and 22 Oct. 1926.

[34] IB minutes, 30 Nov. 1923, 14 Mar., 11 Oct. 1924; *Times*, 13 Dec. 1924.

[35] NSWRU, *Rugby Annual 1927* (Sydney, 1927), p. 21.

[36] Letter from S.F Coopper to A.E. Neilson, 2 Jan. 1931 (RFU Archives, Twickenham). The idea of removing the dispensation had been raised as early as 1929, see IB minutes, 15 Mar. 1929.

[37] IB minutes, 29 July 1931. NSWRU *Annual Report*, 1931, p. 3. The RFU agreed to restore the 'dispensation' on kicking directly into touch to counter rugby league's appeal, see RFU committee minutes, 20 Mar. 1936. The IB eventually brought in the 'dispensation' for the entire game in 1968.

[38] *Rugby News*, 9 May 1931, p. 3.

[39] IB minutes 19 Mar. 1926. NSWRU council minutes, 21 June 1926; *NSW Rugby Annual 1927*, p. 11.

[40] See *Rugby News*, 14 May 1927, p. 4 for the regulations.

[41] E.G. Shaw and A.C. Wallace, *Report of the tour of the NSWRU representative team The Waratahs 1927–28*, 27 Mar. 1928, pp. 6, 9.

[42] *Rugby News*, 16 July 1927, p. 3.

[43] *Rugby News*, 12 May 1937, p. 17.

[44] E.G. Shaw and A.C. Wallace, *Report*, p. 8.

[45] E.G. Shaw and A.C. Wallace, *Report*, p. 18.

[46] For Queensland, see Ian Diehm, *Red, red, red. The story of Queensland rugby* (NSW, 1997), pp. 43–47 and *Rugby News*, 12 May 1928, p. 15. For Melbourne, see June Senyard, *The ties that bind. A history of sport at the University of Melbourne* (Petersham, 2004), p. 134.

[47] 'Editorial', *Rugby News*, 12 May 1928, p. 4.

[48] RFU New Zealand and Australia tour committee minutes, 7 Dec. 1929.

[49] F.D. Prentice 'Australasia 1930', in HBT Wakelam, ed., *The game goes on* (London 1954), p. 154.

[50] NSWRU council minutes, 28 May, 16 June and 16 July 1930.

[51] NSWRU management committee report, 15 October 1930, p. 3.

[52] W.F. Matthews, *Manager's Report of the Australian Rugby Union Team's Tour 1939 to the Presidents of the Australian Rugby Unions*, undated, un-paginated MSS, Australian Rugby Union archives, Sydney. I am grateful for the help of Australian Rugby Union (ARU) archivist Judy MacArthur for her help locating these materials.

[53] *Referee*, 29 June 1939. W.F. Matthews, *Report of 1939 Australian Rugby Union's Tour of Great Britain* undated diary MSS, entry for 5 Sept. 1939. ARU archives, Sydney.

[54] IB minutes, 19 Mar. 1948. The dispensations were once again allowed in 1951; see IB minutes 17 Mar. 1951.

[55] Quoted in Chris Harte, *A history of Australian cricket* (London, 1993), p. 348.

[56] Cashman, *Sport in the national imagination*, p. 57.

[57] Letter reprinted in *Rugby News*, 3 Sept. 1927.

Boxers United: Trade Unionism in British Boxing in the 1930s

Matthew Taylor

Historians have been slow to follow the lead provided by Wray Vamplew's pioneering work on trade unionism in the British sports industry. The attention paid to permanent unions in sports such as golf and football has led to a neglect of those bodies which failed to make a lasting impact. This paper focuses on the history of one of those forgotten organisations, the National Union of Boxers (NUB). It argues that, despite organisational and financial difficulties, the NUB became an influential voice in the politics of British professional boxing during the 1930s.

The development of trade unionism is an under-researched topic in the historiography of British sport. Attention has, perhaps not surprisingly, been drawn to the most successful and influential unions or professional associations, such as the Professional Golfers' Association (PGA) and the Professional Footballers' Association (PFA). The latter has easily attracted the most scholarship, with a number of book sections, chapters and journal articles devoted to examining its origins, growth and contribution to the emergence of labour relations in professional soccer. [1] Alongside John Harding's meticulous centenary history of the PFA we now also have Richard Holt, Peter N. Lewis and Wray Vamplew's scholarly centenary of the PGA. [2] Yet with one or two notable exceptions, the absence of permanent union organisation seems to have discouraged investigation into other sports or research into the comparative history of trade unionism in sport. [3] Set against the wealth of historical writing on labour relations

Matthew Taylor, De Montfort University.

and sports unions in the United States, in particular, we know relatively little about the labour history of British sport. [4]

The fortunes of the trade union movement in Britain fluctuated significantly –over time and across industries – between the wars. From an overall membership peak of 8,348,000 in 1920, numbers dipped to 4,919,000 in 1927, in the aftermath of the General Strike, and then to an interwar low of 4,392,000 in 1933. [5] Membership grew as the economy recovered during the rest of the decade, reaching 6,298,000 by 1939. The traditional picture of the decade or so after the General Strike had been of a period in which trade unionism was 'on the retreat, toothless and passive'. [6] But the years after 1933 also demonstrated the resilience of the trade union movement and its ability to recover and consolidate its position in relation to employers, the government and the public. In a period marked by 'relative industrial tranquillity' [7] and a decline in strike activity, one sector of the economy that witnessed particular union growth was entertainment and sport. Stephen G. Jones has traced the rise of trade unionism in the cinema industry between the wars, with a myriad of organisations such as the National Association of Theatrical Employees (NATE) and the Association of Cine-technicians (ACT) catering for backstage workers. These developed alongside established organisations for performers, such as the Musicians' Union (MU) and the Variety Artists' Association (VAA), and new bodies such as the actors' union, Equity, formed in 1929. [8]

Although it is rarely acknowledged, trade unions were also created in a number of professional sports. Most were neither as permanent nor as successful as the established unions catering for footballers and golfers but it would be a mistake to ignore them simply because they failed. The Northern Rugby Union Players' Union (NRUPU), for example, was founded in November 1920 but was unable to achieve its aims to reform the sport's transfer and benefit regulations, and was dissolved in May 1923. [9] A Speedway Riders' Association (SRA) was launched in the early 1930s and claimed to represent 'the majority of riders' in the south, with a sister body covering the north of England. [10] By 1937, it had developed sufficient support to launch industrial action in protest against the importation of American riders and convince the Ministry of Labour to modify its policy relating to work permits. [11] In horse racing, meanwhile, there was 'significant industrial unrest', despite most trainers' opposition to unionisation. Discontent among stable lads over pay increased from the mid-1930s. Strikes across a number of courses were eventually settled by conciliation and a Stable Lads' Union secured modest pay increases. [12]

Trade unionism also emerged as an important facet of the internal politics and industrial relations of professional boxing in the 1930s. Formed in July 1934, the National Union of Boxers (NUB) has tended to be marginalised or else ignored entirely by boxing historians. [13] It was not the first boxers' union. A union had been created in 1910 under the guidance of welterweight champion Young Joseph, journalist John Murray and honorary secretary Frank Ward but does not seem to have lasted more than a few years. [14] Nor was it to be the last. Two separate bodies with an identical name – the Professional Boxers' Association (PBA) – were formed in 1949 and in 1993 respectively and have arguably made a more lasting impression on public memory. [15] Yet although it lasted only a handful of years, the NUB was undoubtedly an organisation of some significance in the chaotic British boxing industry of the 1930s. If it was first and foremost the representative of a particular occupational group, the NUB undoubtedly punched above its weight and came to assume a wider and pivotal role in discussions over the organisation and future direction of professional boxing. Its story not only highlights the significance of trade unionism in the production of British sport but also reveals the importance of examining sports organisations that struggled and 'failed' as well as those that succeeded.

Professional boxing in 1930s Britain

First of all, some sort of background is needed if we are to understand the environment within which trade unionism in boxing emerged. What follows is necessarily a brief sweep of more complicated developments but it is crucial to be aware of the state of professional boxing at this time as a sport, a business and a spectacle.

At the forefront of the development of professional boxing in its modern form was the National Sporting Club (NSC). Founded in 1891, the NSC was a private club based in Covent Garden, presided over by the Earl of Lonsdale and John Fleming and A.F. 'Peggy' Bettinson. It established its own set of rules – a modified version of the Queensberry Rules – and from 1909 began to present title belts to the winner of any British title-fight held at its premises. [16] Before the interwar years, it thus effectively held a monopoly over the sanctioning and promoting of title fights in Britain. In June 1918, a British Boxing Board of Control (BBBC) was established by members of the NSC to serve as the 'sole governing body for the professional sport'. [17] Its aims included the encouragement of boxing in the UK, raising the standard of the sport, controlling and regulating professional boxing and acting as a central board of appeal. A self-appointed body, it remained dominated by representatives of the NSC and the Inter-services Boxing Association (ISBA) but also included members of the Amateur Boxing Association (ABA), the Referees' Association and three boxers' representatives drawn from past and present Lonsdale Belt holders. [18]

By early 1929, a reconstituted BBBC had been formed. It was composed of a president, two vice-presidents and six stewards, none of whom had a financial interest in the sport. Other sections of the 'boxing community' included on the board were promoters and referees (three representatives each), boxers and boxers' managers (two representatives each) as well as other ring officials and the NSC (one representative apiece). [19] Some commentators regarded this as a considerable improvement on the constitution of its predecessor. The *Times* considered that the stewards occupied a position of 'undisputed authority without fear and above reproach' and cautiously welcomed the new BBBC as 'the rulers and protectors of a great sport fast going wrong'. [20] For others, the power still rested in the hands of those associated directly or indirectly with the NSC. *Boxing, Racing and Football* regarded the new BBBC as 'even more a "Club Body" than it was when it first presented itself for criticism' and thought it 'impossible for any Board to exercise real and acceptable authority until one gets constituted on a really representative basis'. [21]

The power of the BBBC lay partly in its system of licensing. It licensed promoters, managers, trainers, ring officials (including referees, seconds, timekeepers and MCs) as well as boxers. All had to apply annually and pay a registration fee to be licensed. By December 1929, over 1,000 licences had been issued. [22] The withdrawal of a licence became a powerful sanction and ensured, in theory at least, that licence holders bowed to the authority of the board and kept in line with its regulations. The other major weapon in the BBBC's armoury was its authority – inherited from the NSC – to sanction major fights, particularly elimination and title bouts. [23] Through its edicts, which were widely circulated and published in the press, the BBBC decided who was worthy to challenge for area, national and international titles in each weight division. The procedure was that the BBBC (or a regional branch thereof in the case of area championships) would announce that a bout had to take place between boxer A and boxer B before a specified date, and give the respective managers a designated time period in which to arrange a promoter, venue, date and purse money. If arrangements could not be made in time, or the respective managers could not reach agreement, the BBBC put the bout out to promoters for tender. [24] Although relatively straightforward in theory, the sanctioning of title fights was among the most controversial issues in boxing.

To some extent, the popularity of British boxing depended on the success of its leading fighters. Eminent boxing historian Stan Shipley identified the years 1929 to 1939 as a peak period, associated particularly with flyweights Jackie Brown of Manchester and Benny Lynch of Glasgow, who between them held the world title from October 1932 until June 1938. [25] In the higher and more prestigious weight classes, British boxers made less impact on the international stage. Few British fighters, for instance, were good enough to seriously challenge the best American and continental European boxers who were coming to dominate the heavyweight division. [26] In the staging and promotion of title fights, Britain also followed where America led. Jack Dempsey's great world title fights of the 1920s, orchestrated by manager Jack Kearns and promoter Tex Rickard, set a precedent for the boxing 'spectacular' that few British-based promoters attempted to match. [27] From his headquarters in Paris, the American impresario Jeff Dickson staged a series of high-profile international programmes at a number of British venues, including the Royal Albert Hall. [28] Boxing was staged at large sporting arenas throughout the 1930s – such as Manchester's Belle Vue, the Liverpool Stadium, Glasgow's Shawfield Park and, in London, Olympia, Wembley's Empire Pool and Stadium, White City Stadium and Harringay Arena – but British promotions tended to be more modest than their American equivalents.

Indeed boxing's health as a spectator sport was based less on major championship contests and more on small hall boxing. In cities such as Manchester, Glasgow, Newcastle, Liverpool and, above all, London, boxing shows offered a new regular form of entertainment. In many cities shows were put on at least twice weekly (in London there was usually a programme every night of the week), with each bill featuring a main event and a supporting under-card of preliminary bouts. [29] All this relied on the existence of a substantial labour force. Exactly how substantial is difficult to tell. There were estimated to be a thousand registered professional boxers in Britain during the 1940s, which was the peak decade of boxing popularity in the twentieth century. [30] But even a figure such as this almost certainly underestimates the actual number who called themselves 'boxers' and fought at one time or another for money. The NUB itself estimated that in 1934 there were some 5,000 professional boxers in the country, although other suggestions of 3,000 or 4,000 may have been more realistic. [31] The majority of these would have been a casualised form of boxing labour, unregistered with the BBBC, and fighting from time to time when circumstances demanded it. Even the more regular performers were almost all part-timers. Only at the very highest level could boxers afford not to do any other paid work. It was the poor conditions experienced by boxing's rank-and-file – the so-called preliminary fighters – which provided the impetus for the emergence of trade union organisation in the 1930s.

The National Union of Boxers: Origins and organisation

The origins of the NUB lay in a letter sent to the weekly trade paper, *Boxing*, in June 1934 by a journalist calling himself 'Amateur'. A consistent critic of the sport's ruling body, *Boxing* had for some years been publishing reports and letters concerned with the poor treatment and meagre payment of preliminary boxers across the country. In response to a recent flurry of articles, 'Amateur' advocated the creation of a trade union. [32] His idea received widespread press support over the following weeks and months, particularly in the pages of *Boxing*, which quickly set itself up as the semi-official organ of the union. Within a month an inaugural meeting had taken place and a provisional committee had been established. [33]

The first committee included a number of individuals who were to become key figures in the development of the NUB. The first, the mysterious 'Amateur' who had set the ball rolling, turned out to be Harry Flower, a journalist who regarded himself as a 'supporter' of boxing. From his base in Fleet Street and then the National Trade Union Club on New Oxford Street, Flower took up the unpaid position of honorary general secretary and was instrumental in the day-to-day running of the union. He allegedly spent six or seven hours a day on union business, later claiming that his commitment to the role had cost him his savings and his health. [34] Most important of all, Flower was responsible for publicising the work of the union through a weekly column in *Boxing* called 'National Union News'.

The president of the union throughout its existence was Jimmy Wilde. Born in Rhondda, south Wales, Wilde was one of Britain's greatest ever professional boxers. He had won the world flyweight title in December 1916 and retained it until June 1923, when defeat in New York to Pancho Villa led to his retirement. By this time he had fought around 864 bouts in a 13-year career and amassed a sum of £70,000. Like so many boxers before and after him, he then proceeded to squander the money, in his case on investments in London musicals, Welsh cinemas and other business ventures. [35] Wilde was from a mining background and continued to work underground during his early boxing career, only turning full-time in 1913 after years of fighting in the booths and working down the pits. As world champion, he had boxed in a charity exhibition for the miners during their 1921 lockout and came from a background where union organisation was strong. [36] By the time the NBU was formed, Wilde was in his forties but was still a well-known character in the boxing world. He was certainly more than a mere figurehead. In May and June 1935, for example, Wilde undertook a five-week provincial tour to Glasgow, Newcastle, Manchester, Liverpool and Leeds, in which he visited boxing halls and lectured on cinema stages. He also produced a short promotional film on the NUB to be shown in cinemas and publicised the union in his weekly *News of the World* boxing column. [37]

The vice-president of the NUB was Len Harvey. Like Wilde, Harvey was an internationally renowned boxer; unlike the Welshman, however, he was still active. He came originally from Cornwall and boxed out of Plymouth as a teenager but, like many talented provincial fighters, was drawn to the greater opportunities which existed in London's flourishing boxing scene. Harvey's career was a perfect illustration of how hard and gruelling boxing could be as a form of work. In the two years after his arrival in London – 1924 and 1925 – he was said to have fought in 31 contests, mostly at The Ring in Blackfriars. [38] In a 20-year career, Harvey progressed in weight and ability, from a teenage eight-stone preliminary fighter to a middle-weight, light-heavyweight and ultimately a heavyweight. He won a series of British and British Empire titles and was involved in a number of memorable championship bouts – with Jack Petersen, Jock McAvoy, Larry Gains as well as the American John Henry Lewis for the world light-heavyweight title – during his involvement with the NUB. [39] Like Wilde, Harvey was a respected sportsman and a valuable spokesman for the union. Charlie Rose, a former manager and boxing journalist, considered him 'an omnivorous reader' and an excellent public speaker. [40]

The NUB also garnered significant support from the wider trade union movement. Its most famous supporter was Ben Tillett, one of the most important labour leaders of the late nineteenth and early twentieth centuries. Tillett had, of course, led the Dockers' Strike of 1889 and been instrumental in the establishment of the 'New Unionism' of the 1890s. [41] By the 1930s, he was an old man who had not been active in serious politics or union struggle for a number of years. He was said to have been a keen boxer in his youth. *Boxing* described him as a 'hero of many knuckle battles in the "good old days", and always a fighter for the underdog'. [42] Tillett was in fact 75 years old when he wrote to Harry Flower to pledge his support for the NUB in August 1934. He was made a trustee and played a critical role in securing practical support from trade unionists in different parts of Britain. [43] Within the labour movement, Arthur Gilliam of the Chemical Workers' Union, Jack Tanner of the Amalgamated Engineering Union and George Hicks MP of the Amalgamated Union of Building Trade Workers also took an active role on the NUB executive. An all-party group of MPs led by Tom Graves of Stratford also committed itself 'to assist boxers to organise' and put the union's case in parliament. [44]

By April 1935, a National Council comprising twelve boxer-members and twelve supporter-members had been established. Three months later the NUB's constitution and rules were approved and it became legally registered as a trade union. The membership stood at just 400 but it was hoped that the setting up of provincial branches would soon swell the numbers. [45] In September, *Boxing* reported that union committees 'from Glasgow to Bournemouth, and Belfast to Lowestoft – all over Britain and the Irish Free State – are now busy arranging branch meetings . . . in their respective areas'. [46] Fourteen branches were set up but progress in many areas was slow. Only in Glasgow, Birmingham and London (which divided into six sections in 1936) did regional branches thrive. [47] As we can see from Table 1, overall membership had risen to more than 1,000 by the end of 1937 and hit a recorded peak of 1,344 by 1939, although leaders claimed a significantly higher figure of over 2,000. [48] This was broadly comparable with the more established Association Football Players' and Trainers' Union (AFPTU), although significantly lower than Equity, which operated a closed shop throughout the 1930s.

A number of the factors put forward by Vamplew as hindering the development of unionism among sports labourers affected the growth of the NUB. One of the chief problems was the creation of 'a community of interest amongst professionals' in an occupation which was fundamentally competitive and individualistic. [49] At the 1936 annual general meeting, Wilde could record 'an infusion of the Union spirit in unlikely places' alongside an increased membership 'recruited from all ranks of the game. Men whose

Table 1 Membership of boxers', footballers' and actors' unions, 1935–39

	NUB/ NBA*	AFPTU**	Equity*
1935	430	1,314	4,055
1936	528	1,291	4,078
1937	1,081	1,359	4,599
1938	1,267	1,720	3,469
1939	1,344	1,931	

Sources: National Boxing Association, Form AR21, Annual Returns, National Archives, Kew: FS 27/269; Note on Union Membership in the 1930s, Professional Footballers' Association (PFA), Manchester: File 35; Michael Sanderson, *From Irving to Olivier: A Social History of the Acting Profession in England, 1880–1983*, London, 1984, p. 249.

* As at 31 December of each year.

** As at end of each football season.

names are household words have joined forces in the Union with humble, but ambitious six-rounders.' [50] The NUB did indeed secure the support of many of boxing's stars from the beginning. Among its early recruits were Jimmy Walsh, Nel Tarleton, Ernie Roderick, Benny Caplan, Harry Mizler and world flyweight champion Benny Lynch. [51] Along with Jack Hyams and Tommy Farr, Lynch publicised the union by wearing the initials 'NUB' on his boxing shorts in major championship contests. [52] However, Wilde's concern that there existed 'a "leave-it-to-the-other-fellow" air on the part of too many boxers' was to prove a significant obstacle. [53] Organisers feared that boxers were too selfish and individualistic to make good trade unionists. The secretary admitted in the *Boxers' Bulletin* that the NUB had had 'to break through suspicion and consequent apathy'. [54]

Equally problematic was the geographical dispersal of boxing's labour force. [55] Stewards were appointed by branch committees to recruit members and collect membership fees but it proved difficult to cover more than a small proportion of gymnasiums and boxing venues. [56] In a letter to the Trades Union Congress (TUC) general secretary Sir Walter Citrine, Flower complained that

> the job of organising boxers is one of the most difficult imaginable. No boxer works (boxes) in the same hall twice in succession, and until we can extend our corps of voluntary collectors (who act in the manner of shop stewards) to cover a majority of boxing halls, we simply do not get the members' contributions. [57]

This, in turn, had an effect on the finances of the union. The difficulty of collecting regular members' dues left the NUB reliant on 'donations and other forms of outside help to keep going'. [58] Planned affiliation to the TUC was delayed and then abandoned in October 1936 because 'the NUB is still a struggling organization, and none too strong financially'. [59] It was able to affiliate to the powerful London Trades Council, and the TUC encouraged the assistance of local trades councils in line with its policy to 'get Trade Unionism introduced into the amusement industries'. [60] Yet for this all, the NUB's 'scattered potential membership' [61] remained a crucial factor in limiting its growth and defining it as a weak and marginal body within the wider labour movement.

Wages, welfare and power: The objectives and policy of the NUB

What, then, were the aims and objectives of the NUB? What did it hope to achieve? The first draft of its rules, published in the pages of *Boxing* in November 1934, specified four main goals:

- a 'rock bottom' minimum of £1, without deductions, for every boxer in the country
- abolition of deductions from boxers' pay for seconds and whips
- provision for members of legal aid, disablement pay, dispute pay and death payment
- provision of 'better encouragement and opportunities for preliminary boxers to rise to the top' [62]

Its first set of rules in the summer of 1935 clarified and broadened its objectives to include regulating employment relations between boxers on the one hand, and managers and promoters on the other and raising the status 'of all employed in professional boxing'. [63] The goals to raise purse money, prevent deductions from wages, create a Benevolent Fund and procure legal aid for members, however, remained high on the list. In certain respects, these were standard policies for any trade union. Relations with employers, levels of pay and welfare provision were key union prerogatives. As with unions in the film and football industries, the primary aims were industrial and involved improving the pay and working conditions of members. [64] Significantly, however, a number of its objectives hinted at a broader involvement in the administration of professional boxing. From the beginning, many union leaders and agitators had envisaged the NUB as a vehicle to 'clean up' the sport as well as a body to protect the interests of boxing workers. [65] The exploitation of boxers was, in this view, fundamentally connected to the decline and degeneration of the sport as a whole. Pay and conditions were only a starting-point. In its initial objectives, the NUB signalled a wider intention to influence the actual competitive structure and operation of the boxing industry, which was to become increasingly prominent throughout its short history.

The issue of boxers' earnings, or more specifically what was deducted from their earnings, was at the forefront of early union agitation. Deductions had in many respects become conventional practice within the sport. The relatively large purses received by the top-of-the-bill or championship boxer never went straight into his pocket. Expenses were always incurred. These would include the manager's cut, training expenses and gymnasium fees but also fees to sparring partners, the trainer, seconds, and so on. [66] At the top level, this was accepted practice; at the lower end of the scale, it was increasingly coming to be viewed as a form of exploitation. The BBBC had laid down a rule in the 1920s that ensured a minimum of £1 for any fight and also that no manager could deduct commission on boxers' fees below £5. [67] The problem was that these rules were being widely ignored by managers and promoters and no attempt was being made to enforce them by the governing body.

It was not low pay in general, or the managers' commission, which aroused the most anger, but the issue of 'seconds money' (sic.). This became the rallying cry of the NUB in its first year or two. Seconds were important figures in boxing. Their role was vital: most commentators agreed that they could win or lose a bout for a fighter. In basic terms, their job was to look after the boxer in the interval between rounds: to sponge him down, give him water, treat cuts, and the like. The chief second was also expected to advise the boxers 'as to the best methods to use to beat his opponent'. [68] In the big fights, the seconds would be part of the boxer's entourage, possibly his trainer and manager. But the fighter engaged in a six-round preliminary bout in a small hall had no such support. He would generally be attended by staff seconds, who were employees of the venue or the promoter. Poorly paid themselves, these seconds would often expect a cut of the boxers' earnings, even if these amounted to little more than the BBBC minimum. [69] Most boxers felt they had little choice but to accept the situation. To complain would be to 'court disaster' and minimise the likelihood of further fights at those halls where the practice was carried out. [70]

The NUB campaigned hard to stamp out 'seconds money'. It launched a powerful attack on the practice through the pages of *Boxing* and via commissioned articles and sympathetic journalists in the popular press. One typically sensational article published in *Boxing* in February 1935 was titled 'The Boxer's Nightmare: Scandal of Underpaid Six-Round Boxers who have to Part with Half Their Earnings'. It depicted the boxers as 'half-starved boys', battered and bruised and taking home only five shillings a night. 'The villainy', according to the author, 'lies at the door of the dressing-room hangers on. They are blood-suckers of the worst description because they batten on the poor'. [71] Another union spokesman regarded 'seconds money' as 'one of the greatest evils of professional boxing', explaining why under such conditions six-round lads might be forced to 'take a dive' for a 'few extra shillings'. Stepney flyweight and NUB member Johnny Hicks referred to it simply as 'blood money'. [72] Flower concentrated his attack on the system itself, which amounted to little more than 'begging' and was 'degrading to the seconds and unfair to the boxers'. [73] The NUB's main target was the promoters themselves, who may well have been unaware of the practice but inadvertently encouraged it through meagre wages to their own staff. [74] Some headway was certainly made. A number of promoters, including influential names such as Arthur Elvin at Wembley and John Harding of the NSC, signed declarations with the union that 'seconds money' would be prohibited in future at their promotions. [75]

It was never likely, however, that such an embedded practice could be stamped out quickly or easily. This became evident in March 1937 when London representatives of the NUB announced that they were in dispute over 'seconds money' with Jack Solomons's Devonshire Club in Hackney. The so-called 'NSC of the East End', the Devonshire had ironically been the first club to come out in support of the union and had even staged a fund-raising NUB show two years earlier. Union members began to picket the club on fight nights, carrying posters proclaiming 'Our Fight for Justice' and leafleting the audience. [76] It also publicly refuted a counter-claim that it had targeted Solomons and the Devonshire as a result of 'an anti-Jewish bias'. [77] Solomons responded to the picketing by claiming that he paid the £1 minimum to six-round contestants and had never demanded the payment of 'seconds money'. After a month of picketing, the pressure finally told and he signed an agreement not to pay 'seconds money'. [78]

More generally, much of the NUB's propaganda work was designed to persuade the promoters to pay the minimum rate of wages. Initially, a 'black list' of low-paying promoters in each area was suggested but persuasion proved to be a more fruitful tactic. In London, early enthusiasm for the union idea convinced some promoters not only to pay the stipulated minimum but also to hire union members exclusively for preliminary bouts. [79] The NUB also agitated to enforce a standard scale of minimum payments for six-round, eight-round and ten-round contests respectively. By the summer of 1938, it was even suggesting an end to the tradition of paying the same purse to the loser as the winner of supporting bouts. [80] But beyond 'seconds money', there is little evidence of lasting success in any of its pay demands. Small hall promoters, in particular, continued to pay below the minimum, to reduce the purse if the audience were smaller than anticipated, or simply not to pay the boxer at all if he had been judged not to have put on a 'good show'. [81]

The union's welfare arm was surprisingly limited. The initial objective to provide legal aid to boxers seems to have been fulfilled, in the short term at least. The NUB did win its first legal case in April 1935 against a Southampton promoter who retained a member's £4 purse because he felt the boxer 'did not try' against a larger opponent, but seems not to have taken on many more. In addition, members who were brought before a BBBC hearing were entitled to union representation, a benefit directed mainly at the more successful boxers who stood to gain less from the union's pay demands. [82]

One might also expect a boxers' union to regard medical provision as a priority. The physical dangers of boxing were certainly well known. The symptoms of what became known as 'punch drunk' syndrome had been identified by doctors in 1928 and were regularly discussed in the boxing press. [83] Yet it was not until 1946 that the BBBC appointed a medical officer and a medical committee was not formed until 1950. [84] Medical arrangements during the 1930s were haphazard, if they existed at all. Neither was there much in the way of compensation for boxers who suffered injury in the ring. A Boxers' Benevolent Fund had been established back in the early 1920s by the BBBC. It granted funds 'to old boxers of renown who had fallen on bad times, and to active boxers who have been temporarily incapacitated from following their professions owing to accidents and ill-health'. [85] As in horse racing and cricket, this partial assumption of welfare provision by the governing body may have weakened the union's own benevolent policies. [86] Yet BBBC provision was regarded as inadequate by many. Johnny Hicks, for one, received a lump sum payment of just £3 in 1936 for losing an eye: 'A benevolent fund cannot pay out money to a boxer week after week . . . [and] the fact remains that my right eye was worth a great deal more to me than £3'. [87] There were certainly still many stories of boxers blinded or otherwise seriously injured and relying on collections from boxing crowds. When the former British heavyweight champion Jack Petersen was forced to retire in 1937 at the age of 25 due to eye injury, one correspondent pointed out that other fighters who could not afford the services of an eye specialist would have had to continue fighting despite the risks to their health. [88]

Financial difficulties meant that the union took some time to establish a scheme of insurance for its members. Appeals for assistance to the TUC to help fund the scheme were declined but by June 1936 an insurance policy covering 'ring injury' had been arranged with Lloyds. [89] It allowed a boxer to draw £1 a week for 13 consecutive weeks' disablement on the basis of an annual payment of 28 shillings, with correspondingly larger premiums and benefits for fighters 'in the higher grades'. [90] A year later the National Boxers' Insurance Association was formed and a new 'Champions Policy' created which covered sickness and injury *outside* the ring as well as inside. The secretary reported a moderate take-up of the policy but there is no evidence that it was a great success. [91] By late 1939, when the union announced a nine-point plan for reform, medical provision had risen to the top of the agenda. Proposals included age limits for boxers, stipulated time periods between fights, and a medical officer to examine a boxer before he entered the ring and be on duty at all tournaments. [92] The outbreak of war prevented the implementation of the plan but it is noteworthy that health, welfare and insurance re-emerged as central elements in the post-war PBA's policy objectives. [93]

'A power in the boxing world' [94]: The NUB and the BBBC

It is important to remember that the union's relations with the direct employers of boxing labour – that is, the promoters and managers – were not necessarily adversarial. In fact, managers and promoters were included from the beginning in the membership of the NUB (as 'supporter-members' under Class B of its membership) [95] and some became active on branch and national committees. The relationship with the BBBC, however, was more difficult. Initially relations were relatively cordial, with both bodies making noises about cooperation and joint action. Sir Noel Curtis-Bennett, for example, a leading figure in the BBBC and chairman of the Wembley Competition Committee (a tournament for novice boxers), not only joined the NUB but also became a member of the provisional committee and actively campaigned for its pay demands. [96] For its part, the union's founders were careful to state that the NUB had not been created 'as an instrument to rival the Board of Control'. [97] By the autumn of 1935, however, a breach had emerged between the two bodies. In October, Curtis-Bennett wrote to the union and the press announcing his resignation on the grounds that the NUB had 'departed a very long way from their original ideals' and was in danger of 'undermining the Board's authority'. In response, Flower outlined the NUB's attempts to secure official recognition and joint consultation with the governing body and accused the BBBC of ignoring widespread abuse of its own regulations. [98] The NUB soon abandoned attempts at reconciliation and decided in May 1936 to 'act as an independent body'. [99]

The main source of conflict, it turned out, was the union's strike clause. As a governing body, the BBBC claimed that it could not accept union rules which were in 'direct conflict' with its own. [100] The NUB, meanwhile, announced that it was not prepared to forego 'the same right which workmen in all other unions have enjoyed by law for a century'. [101] Incensed by the board's refusal to recognise it as a legitimate representative of the interests of boxers, the NUB launched a series of public attacks in the pages of the popular and sporting press and its own *Boxers' Bulletin.* A particular target was the unrepresentative composition of the board, which included very few active boxers or ex-professionals in its membership. *Boxing* thought that most people regarded it as 'an employer's body', while Flower claimed it was widely accepted within the industry that 'the Boxers have no power in it'. [102] In his presidential address in 1938, Jimmy Wilde described the board as 'a dictatorship'. 'British people', he added, 'do not like dictatorships'. [103]

On the surface, this might seem like the typical cut and thrust of industrial relations but it could be suggested that there was more to it than this. Increasingly from the summer of 1936, it seemed that influential elements within the NUB were no longer content to confine it to the role of a mere union. From the start, there had been calls for the NUB to ultimately replace the BBBC but from this point on the union seemed to be manoeuvring itself into position for a more fundamental challenge to the governing authority of the Board of Control. This was not as unrealistic as it might first appear. The BBBC, of course, was a fairly young organisation which lacked the authority of older and more established sporting bodies. The *Times* referred to it as 'a belated Jockey Club' and a body whose birth 'came about in tumult, an argumentative tumult that bordered on the farcical, for sober debate is not professional boxing's strong point'. [104] It was also deeply unpopular, in the national press as well as in boxing and sporting journals. It was unpopular also among promoters and managers, even those who were represented on the board. Leading promoters such as Sydney Hulls and John Harding, for example, openly considered defying the regulation requiring them to pay 5% of gate receipts to the BBBC. [105] One writer felt that a 'real revolt' had been started against the board's failure to negotiate and compromise with the leading promoters. [106] There was even discussion of a widespread 'boxing rebellion', involving an alliance of boxers, managers and promoters, and the creation of a rival governing body similar to the short-lived British Boxing Alliance of the 1920s. [107]

In the midst of all this, at its annual meeting in December 1937, the union changed its name. The National Union of Boxers became the National Boxing Association (NBA). This was more than a cosmetic change. One of the motivations was to open membership to amateur boxers who were not adequately represented by the Amateur Boxing Association (ABA). The executive claimed that its policies had not significantly altered and that it remained committed to improving the lot of 'the Cinderellas of boxing' but it is clear that its main focus had now shifted beyond pay and conditions. [108] Some of its objectives now clearly overlapped with those of the governing body. New clauses were inserted into the rules which concerned increasing public interest in boxing, maintaining 'the general conduct of the sport', improving facilities and ensuring that boxers had 'equal opportunities of rising to the top'. [109] Issues concerning employment relations and remuneration were dropped down the list. The name itself also suggested a change of purpose and a new focus. It was not uncommon to drop the 'union' and take on 'association', as the footballers did in the late 1950s. Perhaps more significant was the use of 'Boxing' rather than 'Boxers', suggesting a body with a broader scope than the representation of boxers; and sounding, of course, like a governing body. Equally significant, and something which could not have escaped the notice of boxing enthusiasts at the time, the National Boxing Association was also the name of one of the two bodies (along with the New York State Athletic Commission) which controlled professional boxing in the United States.

More than ever before, the new NBA began to concern itself with the *competitive* structure of boxing. This was an important change in priorities. The union had always railed against the incompetence of the BBBC in designating title fights, accusing its representatives of knowing little about the intricacies of the sport. In July 1936, it had intervened when the promoter of the heavyweight contest between Jack Petersen and Ben Foord forgot to apply for the fight to be recognised as a British as well as an empire title bout. [110] But it went a step further in relation to the fight between Welshman Tommy Farr and world heavyweight champion Joe Louis in New York in August 1937. The American authorities had designated the contest as a world title fight but the BBBC, conscious of the claims of Germany's Max Schmeling to be considered the official world champion, ruled it to be a fight merely between title contenders. In the wake of the controversy sparked by the decision, the union publicly took the Americans' side and announced that it too recognised the fight as being for 'the heavyweight championship of the world'. [111] Such willingness to challenge the authority of the governing body led one newspaper to predict that the union 'may soon be fighting for control of British boxing'. [112]

In the summer of 1938, the NBA launched its most ambitious scheme of all – the so-called 'Ladder Plan'. In essence, this was a formal ranking system. Boxers were placed in a particular position on area and national 'ladders' in each weight category. They could then move up or down the 'ladder' depending on results until, after a designated period, the man at the top was declared the challenger and fought the champion in a title fight. The NBA promoted it as a means of drawing crowds (because every bout would mean something) and ensuring that the best fighters reached the top. [113] The intention was for all 'ladder' contests to be 'needle fights', providing value for money for spectators and eventually becoming 'as exciting as a Football

League Table'. [114] It is important to note how novel this idea was. There had been no previous attempt to organise competition and match fighters according to such a formal structure. Initial reaction to the scheme was positive, although the practical problems involved in obtaining records of every fighter in the country was always going to make it difficult to operate. [115] The BBBC, however, dismissed the 'Ladder Plan' as 'cumbersome, involved and unworkable' and would have nothing to do with it. [116] The NBA continued regardless, sending its 'ladders' to members and publishing them in the press over the next couple of years. It may have had limited impact on the decisions of the BBBC but what the scheme did represent was the emergence of an alternative competitive structure for professional boxing that chipped away further at the governing body's authority.

Conclusion

The success rate of unions for sports professionals in Britain has never been good. The NUB, however, emerged at a time when unionisation in sport was making tentative progress. Boxing was a part of this yet also apart from it. It was subject to many of the obstacles to unionisation common in all sports, such as inherent competition, the discrepancy between the elite and the rank-and-file, the paternalism of governing bodies, and the geographical scattering of potential members. Yet boxers also looked to models outside sport. In particular, they were influenced by the recent successes of Equity, which had quickly established control over the acting profession through a closed shop and a series of disputes during the early and mid-1930s. [117] Boxing, as a highly commercialised industry, with a casualised labour force and links with the worlds of theatre and entertainment, probably had as much in common with acting as it did with football.

Like many small voluntary organisations, the NBA struggled to cope with the outbreak of war. Most boxers who joined the forces were not immediately interested in competing, much less in continuing union activity. Engaged in national service and scattered across the globe, its officials had little time to attend to union affairs. In 1942, the NBA's solicitors informed the Registrar of Friendly Societies that until the war had ended 'it would be impossible for the Association to carry out its work as there is practically no Boxing and it does not deal with the "stars"'. [118] From a position of influence and strength at the end of the 1930s, the NBA simply atrophied during the war. A dynamic organisation capable of challenging the authority of boxing's governing body had long been killed off by the time its trade union registration was officially cancelled in 1948.

[119] It is surprising, however, that its history has been so completely forgotten. The NUB/NBA may not have lasted long but it would be wrong to define it in terms of failure. In an industry in which professionals literally stood alone in opposition to one another, the unionisation of the 1930s was a significant achievement.

Notes

[1] See Braham Dabscheck's ' "Defensive Manchester": A history of the Professional Footballers' Association', in Richard Cashman and Michael McKernan, eds, *Sport in History* (Brisbane, 1979), pp. 227–57; and ' "A man or a puppet?": The Football Association's 1909 attempt to destroy the Association Football Players' Union', *International Journal of the History of Sport*, 8 (2) (1991), pp. 221–38; Tony Mason, *Association football and English society, 1863–1915* (Brighton, 1980), pp. 110–17; Nicholas Fishwick, *English football and society, 1910–1950* (Manchester, 1989), pp. 86–91; Matthew Taylor's *The leaguers: The making of professional football in England, 1900–1939* (Liverpool, 2005), pp. 137–47; and 'Labour relations and managerial control in English professional football, 1890–1939', *Sport History Review*, 31 (2) (2000), pp. 80–99.

[2] John Harding, *For the good of the game: The official history of the Professional Footballers' Association* (London, 1991); Richard Holt, Peter N. Lewis and Wray Vamplew, *The Professional Golfers' Association, 1901–2001* (Droitwich, 2002).

[3] The main exceptions are Wray Vamplew's 'Not playing the game: Unionism in British professional sport, 1870–1914', *International Journal of the History of Sport*, 2 (3) (1985), pp. 232–47; *Pay up and play the game: Professional sport in Britain, 1875–1914* (Cambridge, 1988), pp. 239–53; and 'Successful workers or exploited labour?: Golf professionals and professional golfers in Britain, 1888–1914', *Economic History Review*, 61 (1) (2008), pp. 54–79. See also Tony Collins, *Rugby league in twentieth century Britain: A social and cultural history* (Abingdon, 2006), pp. 50–2, 87–9, 148–9.

[4] See Lee Lowenfish, *The imperfect diamond: A history of baseball's labor wars* (New York, 1980); David Q. Voigt, 'Serfs versus magnates: A century of labor strife in major league baseball', in Paul D. Staudohar and James A. Mangan, eds, *The business of professional sports* (Urbana, 1991), pp. 95–114; Paul D. Staudohar, *Playing for dollars: Labor relations and the sports business* (Ithaca, 1996); Robert F. Burk, *Never just a game: Players, owners and American baseball to 1920* (Chapel Hill, 1994); Robert F. Burk, *Much more than a game: Players, owners and American baseball since 1921* (Chapel Hill, 2001); Charles P. Korr, *The end of baseball as we knew it: The players union, 1960–81* (Urbana, 2002).

[5] Chris Wrigley, 'The trade unions between the wars', in Chris Wrigley, ed., *A history of British industrial relations*, vol. 2: *1914–1939* (Brighton, 1987), pp. 71–2.

[6] Keith Laybourn, *A history of British trade unionism* (Stroud, 1992), p. 143.

[7] W. Hamish Fraser, *A history of British trade unionism, 1700–1998* (Basingstoke, 1999), p. 177.

[8] Stephen G. Jones, *The British labour movement and film, 1918–1939* (London, 1987), pp. 67–88; Michael Sanderson, *From Irving to Olivier: A social history of the acting profession, 1880–1983* (London, 1984), pp. 233–51.

[9] Collins, *Rugby league*, pp. 50–2.

[10] *Speedway News*, 17 Apr. 1930.

[11] *Speedway News*, Feb. 1937 (Winter bulletin), 7 Aug. 1937, 14 May 1938. See also Jack Williams, ' "A wild orgy of speed": Responses to speedway in Britain before the Second World War', *The Sports Historian*, 19 (1) (1999), p. 5.

[12] Mike Huggins, *Horseracing and the British, 1919–39* (Manchester, 2003), p. 178 (quotation); Stephen G. Jones, *Sport, politics and the working class: Organised labour and sport in interwar Britain* (Manchester, 1988), p. 49.

[13] Stan Shipley, 'Boxing', in Tony Mason, ed., *Sport in Britain: A social history* (Cambridge, 1989), p. 98, makes only a general reference to boxers' unions that 'have been started but . . . have always failed in this individualistic occupation.' There is a brief mention of the NUB in Jones, *Sport, politics and the working class*, p. 49.

[14] John Harding, *Lonsdale's Belt: The story of boxing's greatest prize* (London, 1994), pp. 19, 21; *Times*, 21 Sept. 1911.

[15] On the earlier PBA, see Leslie Bell, *Inside the fight game* (London, 1952), pp. 13–25; *Boxing news*, 29 June 1949.

[16] Guy Deghy, *Noble and manly: The history of the national sporting club* (London, 1956); Harding, *Lonsdale's Belt.*

[17] Harding, *Lonsdale's Belt*, p. 72.

[18] British Boxing Board of Control (BBBC) Rules and Regulations, n.d.; *Annual Report of BBBC 1924*, National Archives (NA) Kew: HO 45/18745.

[19] *Sporting Life*, 7 Dec. 1929.

[20] *Times*, 24 Dec. 1928.

[21] *Boxing, Racing and Football*, 2 Jan. 1929.

[22] *Sporting Life*, 7 Dec. 1929.

[23] Shipley, 'Boxing', p. 97.

[24] W. Barrington Dalby, *Come on Barry!* (London, 1961), p. 116.

[25] Shipley, 'Boxing', p. 105. On Brown, see Denis Fleming, *The Manchester fighters* (Manchester, 1986). On Lynch, see John Burrowes, *Benny: The life and times of a fighting legend* (Edinburgh, 1982).

[26] Jeffrey T. Sammons, *Beyond the ring: The role of boxing in American society* (Urbana, 1990), pp. 79–91.

[27] Randy Roberts, *Jack Dempsey: The Manassa mauler* (London, 1987).

[28] Ted Broadribb, *Fighting is my life* (London, 1951), pp. 55–6; *Daily Express*, 26 Oct. 1934.

[29] Shipley, 'Boxing', p. 91; Matthew Taylor, 'Round the London ring: Boxing, class and community in interwar London', *London Journal*, 34 (2) (2009), pp. 140–63.

[30] Richard Holt, *Sport and the British: A modern history* (Oxford, 1989), p. 301.

[31] *Boxing*, 1 Aug. 1934, 21 Aug. 1935, 1 Jan. 1936.

[32] *Boxing*, 27 June 1934.

[33] *Daily Worker*, 24 July 1934; *Boxing*, 25 July 1934.

[34] *Boxing*, 5 Jan. 1938; Letter from H. Flower to G. Woodcock, 7 November 1957, Modern Records Centre (MRC), Warwick University: TUC Files on Boxers: MSS/91/30.

[35] Peter Wilson, *Ringside seat* (London, 1949), p. 156; Holt, *Sport and the British*, p. 302; Dai Smith, 'Focal heroes: A Welsh fighting class', in Richard Holt, ed., *Sport and the working class in modern Britain* (Manchester, 1990), p. 207.
[36] Gareth Williams, 'Jimmy Wilde, the "Tylorstown Terror" ', in Peter Stead and Gareth Williams, eds, *Wales and its boxers: The fighting tradition* (Cardiff, 2008), p. 60; Smith, 'Focal heroes', p. 207.
[37] *Boxing*, 8 May 1935.
[38] Shipley, 'Boxing', p. 93; Leslie Bell, *Bella of Blackfriars* (London, 1961), pp. 186–91.
[39] Trevor Wignall, *Ringside* (London, 1941), pp. 145–52.
[40] Charlie Rose, 'My trio of British heavyweight champs', *Weekly Sporting Review* (Xmas and New Year, 1948–9), p. 24. One reporter at an early NUB meeting noted that Harvey spoke with passion but was 'hesitant in talking from written notes'. *Daily Express*, 10 Oct. 1934.
[41] Jonathan Schneer, *Ben Tillett: Portrait of a labour leader* (London, 1982).
[42] *Boxing*, 8 Apr. 1936.
[43] *Boxing*, 8 Aug. 1934, 4 Dec. 1935; Letter from S. Gatley to I. Mackay, 23 Jan. 1951, MRC: Tillett Papers: MSS 74/6/2/31.
[44] National Union of Boxers, Titles and Names of Officers, 29 July 1935, NA: FS 27/269; *Boxing*, 22 Jan. 1936, 21 Nov. 1934.
[45] *Boxing*, 3, 10 Apr., 10 July 1935.
[46] *Boxing*, 25 Sept. 1935.
[47] *Boxing*, 20 Feb. 1935, 23 Sept. 1936; National Boxing Association, Form AR21, Annual Returns, NA: FS 27/269.
[48] Bob Lonkhurst, 'Jimmy Wilde led the way', *Boxing News*, 26 July 1991, p. 21.
[49] Vamplew, *Pay up and play the game*, p. 252.
[50] *Boxing*, 8 Apr. 1936.
[51] *Boxing*, 19 Sept., 10 Oct. 1934; List of National Council members on NUB notepaper, Letter from H.A. Flower to Registrar of Friendly Societies, 15 Dec. 1934, NA: FS 27/269.
[52] *Times*, 9 Nov. 1937; *Boxing*, 23 Sept. 1936; Lonkhurst, 'Jimmy Wilde led the way', p. 20.
[53] *Boxing*, 8 Apr. 1936.
[54] *Boxing*, 1 Jan. 1936; *Boxers' Bulletin* quoted in *Boxing*, 22 July 1936.
[55] Vamplew, *Pay up and play the game*, p. 252.
[56] Rules of The National Union of Boxers, 1935, NA: FS 27/269; *Boxing*, 8 May 1935, 4 Sept. 1935.
[57] Letter from H.A. Flower to W. Citrine, 12 June 1936, MRC: TUC Files on Boxers: MSS 292/91/30.
[58] Letter from H.A. Flower to W. Citrine, 12 June 1936, MRC: TUC Files on Boxers: MSS 292/91/30.
[59] Letter from D. Beech to W. Citrine, 13 Oct. 1936, MRC: TUC Files on Boxers: MSS 292/91/30.
[60] *Boxing*, 1 July 1936; Letter from Secretary of TUC Organisation Department to W. Shaw, Glasgow Trades Council, 29 January 1937, MRC: TUC Files on Boxers: MSS 292/91/30.
[61] Letter from H.V. Tewson to J.P. Roe, Bolton and District Trades Council, 17 Sept. 1936, MRC: TUC Files on Boxers: MSS 292/91/30.

[62] *Boxing*, 28 Nov. 1934.
[63] Rules of The National Union of Boxers, 1935, NA: FS 27/269.
[64] Jones, *British labour movement and film*, p. 75; Taylor, *The leaguers*, p. 137.
[65] See *Boxing*, 17 Oct. 1934, 20 Nov. 1935.
[66] M. Connolly letter, printed in *Boxing*, 6 Feb. 1935; *Topical Times*, 8 Sept. 1934.
[67] *Boxing, Racing and Football*, 29 July 1931.
[68] Dalby, *Come on Barry*, p. 118. See also Bell, *Inside the fight game*, pp. 85–7.
[69] *Boxing, Racing and Football*, 18 Nov., 9 Dec. 1931.
[70] *Topical Times*, 8 Sep. 1934.
[71] *Boxing*, 6 Feb. 1935.
[72] *Topical Times*, 8 Sept. 1934; J. Hicks letter, printed in *East London Advsertiser*, 8 May 1937.
[73] *Boxing*, 30 Oct. 1935.
[74] *Boxing*, 31 July 1935.
[75] *Boxing*, 27 Jan. 1937.
[76] *Boxing*, 24 Mar. 1937; J. Hicks letter, printed in *East London Advertiser*, 3 Apr. 1937.
[77] *Weekly Sporting Review*, 27 Mar. 1937.
[78] J. Solomons letter, printed in *East London Advsertiser*, 8 May 1937; *Boxing*, 21 Apr. 1937. Emerys Llewellyn, London organiser of the NUB, commented that though Solomons had never demanded 'seconds money', 'another official at his club had'. *Boxing*, 26 May 1937.
[79] *Boxing*, 17, 24 Oct., 14 Nov. 1934, 9 Jan. 1935.
[80] *Boxing*, 8, 15 Apr. 1936, 13 July 1938.
[81] *Boxing*, passim.
[82] *Boxing*, 3 Apr. 1935, 15 Apr. 1936.
[83] K.G. Sheard, ' "Brutal and degrading": The medical profession and boxing, 1838–1984', *International Journal of the History of Sport*, 15 (3) (1998), p. 79; *Boxing*, 2 June 1937; *Times*, 17, 18 Jan. 1939; Neil Carter, 'Boxing: A medical history', forthcoming.
[84] John Welshman, 'Only connect: The history of sport, medicine and society', *International Journal of the History of Sport*, 15 (2) (1998), p. 7.
[85] *Annual Report of BBBC 1924*, p. 8, NA: HO 45/18745.
[86] Vamplew, *Pay up and play the game*, pp. 251–3.
[87] *Boxing*, 22 Apr. 1936.
[88] *Boxing*, 14 Apr. 1937.
[89] Letter from H.A. Flower to W. Citrine, 26 September 1935, MRC: TUC Files on Boxers: MSS 292/91/30.
[90] *Boxing*, 17 June 1936.
[91] *Boxing*, 28 Apr., 30 June 1937; *Weekly Sporting Review*, 19 June 1937.
[92] Lonkhurst, 'Jimmy Wilde', p. 21.
[93] See Bell, *Inside the fight game*, pp. 13–20
[94] *Topical Times*, 8 January 1938.
[95] Rules of National Union of Boxers, 1935, NA: FS 27/269.
[96] See *Boxing*, 10, 17 Oct. 1934.
[97] *Boxing*, 25 July 1934.
[98] N. Curtis–Bennett letter, printed in *Boxing*, 9 Oct. 1935; H. Flower letter, printed in *Boxing*, 16 Oct. 1935. See also *Times*, 16 Oct. 1935.

[99] *Boxing*, 20 May 1936.

[100] C.F. Donmall letter, printed in *Boxing*, 27 May 1936 (quotation); *Sporting Chronicle*, 22 May 1936.

[101] *Boxing*, 3 June 1936.

[102] *Boxing*, 11 Nov. 1936; Letter from H.A. Flower to W. Citrine, 3 May 1937, MRC: TUC Files on Boxers: MSS 292/91/30.

[103] *Boxing*, 14 Dec. 1938.

[104] *Times*, 7 Jan. 1938.

[105] *Boxing*, 7 Sept. 1938. The levy was extended in 1939 to include receipts from 'television, broadcast, film, and still picture photography'. *Times*, 10 June 1939.

[106] *Topical Times*, 8 Jan. 1938.

[107] *Boxing*, 12 Jan. 1938. On the British Boxing Alliance, see Harding, *Lonsdale's Belt*, pp. 111–15.

[108] *Boxing*, 8 Dec. 1937 (quotation); *The Times*, 14 Dec. 1937.

[109] See Rules of The National Boxing Association, 1939, NA: FS 27/269.

[110] *Boxing*, 15 July 1936.

[111] *Boxing*, 18 Aug. 1937.

[112] *The People*, 25 July 1937.

[113] *Boxing*, 27 July 1938. One of the advantages suggested by the NBA in support of the plan was that 'no colour bar' would operate, a reference to the BBBC's exclusion of black boxers from fighting for championship titles in Britain. Under its scheme, excluded fighters such as Tommy Martin and Manuel Abrew would be open to compete for British titles. See *Boxing*, 24 Aug. 1938. On the colour bar more generally, see P.F. McDevitt, *May the best man win: Sport, masculinity and nationalism in Great Britain and the empire, 1880–1935* (New York, 2004), pp. 58–80; Harding, *Lonsdale's Belt*, pp. 117–22.

[114] *Topical Times*, 25 Mar. 1939.

[115] *Boxing*, 3, 17 Aug. 1938.

[116] *Boxing*, 5 Oct. 1938.

[117] On discussions of the possibilities of a closed shop in boxing, see *Boxing*, 27 Feb. 1935, 8 Apr. 1936.

[118] Letter from Pattinson and Brewer (solicitors) to Registrar of Friendly Societies, 17 July 1942, NA: FS 27/269.

[119] Letter from E. Davies to H.V. Tewson, 3 Apr. 1947, MRC: TUC Files on Boxers: MSS 292/91/30; Letter from Registrar of Friendly Societies to Chief Inspector of Taxes, 30 Nov. 1948, NA: FS 27/269.

Deeply Honoured: The Rise and Significance of the British Sporting Award, 1945–*c.*1970. [1]

Dave Russell

Focusing on four awards, the Sporting Record/Daily Express *'Sportsman/Sportswoman of the Year', the 'Footballer of the Year', the* Sportswriters's *'Sportsman/Sportswoman of the Year' and the BBC's 'Sports Personality of the Year', this study examines the general factors impacting upon the establishment of a sporting 'honours system' in the 1940s and the specific commercial and political reasons behind the foundation of these individual awards. It argues that while such awards can have an 'objective' value in helping us identify contemporary sporting pantheons, they are best seen as cultural rituals designed to elevate particular models of sporting behaviour, encourage a belief in the expert status of sports journalists, and to allow sporting stars and the sports media to show themselves to the public in the kindest possible light.*

Given that most sporting events have clear victors who have won more games or run or ridden faster than their rivals, the sporting award based upon such subjective criteria as 'service', 'contribution', 'personality' or 'sportsmanship', might seem entirely superfluous. Yet, in the twentieth-first century, these awards are so common that we rarely consider their origins, even if, when faced with the volume of trophies on offer, we might sometimes question their value and significance. The emergence of the sporting award from the mid-twentieth century is thus a topic well worthy of consideration, and this exploratory study seeks to examine the role of

Dave Russell, Leeds Metropolitan University.

sport's 'honours system' in articulating and constructing the complex network of relationships between elite sportsmen and women, the sports media and the public. This study focuses on the four highest profile awards: the *Sporting Record/Daily Express* 'Sportsman/Sportswoman of the Year', the (English) Football Writers' Association's 'Footballer of the Year', the Sports Writers' Association of Great Britain's 'Sportsman/Sportswoman of the Year' and the BBC's 'Sports Personality of the Year', and, although some aspects of the analysis are taken to 1970, it is especially concerned with the formative period of the 1940s and 1950s. [2]

The emergence and development of the sporting award

Sporting awards given for factors other than, or as well as, objective performance alone, certainly existed before the 1940s. It has been suggested, albeit by the publication itself, that the *Wisden Cricketers' Almanack*'s listing of the 'Five Cricketers of the Year', established in 1889, is likely to be 'the oldest individual award in cricket' and it may indeed be the oldest in any sport. [3] No trophies, formal presentations or dinners were associated with this selection, but it presumably conferred at least some prestige on recipients and provided a possible foundation for later ventures. *Gamages Association Football Annual* included a similar feature from 1909–10 through its selection of 'The Player of the Year'. The choice was made by Football Association Vice-President Alfred Davis and, perhaps significantly, H.R. McDonald of the *Football Evening News*, and eventually a founder member of an organisation central to the honouring of sportsmen and women, the Sports Writers' Association of Great Britain. [4] There were, too, a number of newspaper-based public ballots. Trevor Wignall recalled organising a 'very local . . . plebiscite' when 'I was no more than a hesitant starter in my trade', which would probably place the event in the early 1900s. [5] Awards certainly existed in other countries including the USA and Australia, where the 'Best and Fairest' medal tradition was established within Australian rules football from as early as 1898. In these awards, expert judges, usually match umpires, graded player performance and awarded points across a season. However, any player receiving significant disciplinary punishment was automatically discounted. [6] Again, in 1936, a boxing prize was inaugurated in honour of London-born amateur heavyweight, Val Barker, in recognition of his administrative work with its awarding body, the Federation Internationale de Boxe Amateur. The Val Barker Trophy was (and still is) given to the 'most stylish' boxer at the Olympic Games. [7] There was, finally, a very powerful model from another sector of the entertainment industry in the form of Cinema's Academy Awards, or 'Oscars', first presented in 1929. [8] More than one organisation was later to refer to its trophies as 'the sporting Oscars'.

Overall, however, for all these nascent developments and international examples the British award tradition remained thin, beginning only in earnest in 1946 with the establishment of Rugby League's Lance Todd Trophy and the *Sporting Record* newspaper's 'Sportsman of the Year'. The 'Lance Todd' admittedly falls outside the tradition of awards examined here. Named in honour of an outstanding New Zealand-born Wigan and Dewsbury player turned Salford manager and BBC commentator, who was killed in a car crash in 1942, it was presented to the 'man of the match' in the annual Rugby League Challenge Cup Final. [9] However, it does deserve mention as a symptom of this new appetite for awards within sport and a possible stimulus to it. These two prizes were closely followed by the establishment of the Football Writers' Association's

Table 1 Sporting awards, 1946–*c*.1970

Year	Award	Awarding body
1946	Lance Todd Trophy	Journalists present at Rugby League Challenge Cup final, later by Rugby League Writers' Association
1946	Sportsman of the Year	*Sporting Record** via readers's ballot
1948	Footballer of the Year	Football Writers' Association
1949	Sportsman of the Year	Sports Writers' Association of Great Britain
1950	Young Cricketer of the Year	Cricket Writers's Club
1954	BBC Sports Personality of the Year	BBC via viewers's ballot
1955	Yachtsman of the Year	Sir Max Aitken, Chairman of Express Newspapers, later by Guild of Yachting Writers
1959	Sportswoman of the Year	Sports Writers's Association of Great Britain
1960	BBC Overseas Sports Personality of the Year	BBC via viewers's ballot
1960	BBC Sports Personality Team of the Year Award	BBC via viewers's ballot
1963	Disabled Sports Personality of the Year	Sports Writers's Association of Great Britain, in memory of ex-chairman, W.K. 'Bill' McGowran
1966	Rugby League Writers' Player of the Year	Rugby League Writers's Association
1974	J.L. Manning Award	Sports Writers's Association of Great Britain

*This award was taken over by the *Daily Express* in 1956.

'Footballer of the Year' award in 1948, the Sports Writers' Association of Great Britain's 'Sportsman of the Year' in 1949 and the Cricket Writers' Club's 'Young Cricketer of the Year' in 1950. Table 1 lists these and other significant prizes founded in the period to 1970, the most important of which was undoubtedly the 'BBC Sports Personality of the Year' which commenced in 1954.

At the simplest level, this enthusiasm for conferring honours can be seen as part of the wider contemporary explosion of interest in sport. Long denied access to regular, high-quality sporting activity and seeing its return as symbolic of a return to normality, sports fans flooded to venues in unprecedented numbers. The late 1940s saw record attendances in sports including association football, cricket, rugby league, greyhound racing and speedway. [10] It is not surprising that, in such a climate, a variety of institutions should initiate new ways of engaging with the sporting world. At the same time, a new or, at least, substantially enlarged market for sports publications emerged, reflecting but also further stimulating this contemporary surge of interest in sport. Crucially, this material often allowed for a particular focus on individual lives and achievements. Association football, for example, saw the publication from the mid-1940s of the first book-length player autobiography, as well as a number of boys' annuals and the magazines, notably *Charles Buchan's Football Monthly* (1951) and *Soccer Star* (1952), that were often centred on personalities. [11] The emergence of the sporting award sat well in this context.

Public ballots

While a broad sporting and social setting formed a common ground for the sporting award in general, individual ones were shaped, in both their origins and subsequent development, by more specific factors. These are perhaps best examined by proceeding thematically rather than chronologically and looking in turn at the two broad categories of award, those decided by public vote and those by the votes of sportswriters. Commencing with the former, the *Sporting Record*'s 'Sportsman of the Year' award (a 'Sportswoman of the Year' followed in 1952, as will be discussed later) appears to have been Britain's first ever major national sporting ballot. It was ultimately a commercial venture rooted in the attempt by the London-based weekly sports paper to re-launch itself after its wartime reduction to a single-page sheet. Readers were invited to help produce 'a true reflection of the sporting mind of Britain by voting ('one person, one vote') for the individual 'who has done most this year to raise the prestige of British sport'. [12] With the looseness that so typified attitudes to the terms of reference governing these competitions, 'prestige' was left for the readers to define and 32,500 responded in a way that saw British and empire heavyweight boxing champion, Bruce Woodcock, narrowly defeat middle-distance runner, Sydney Wooderson.

Whether it echoed a popular, democrat mood drawing from the rhetoric and experience of the 'people's war' or simply represented a well-marketed novelty in an age of limited consumer choice, the award clearly captured the public imagination in the immediate post-war years, with the number of votes cast rising rapidly to a peak of 244,000 in 1950. While the paper may have found ways of inflating these figures, they are probably a reasonably accurate record of interest. Moreover, the *Record* was able to generate, and benefit from, a high level of more general awareness of its prize. The annual awards ceremony and dinner at London's Savoy Hotel was certainly a high-profile event. Health Minister Aneurin Bevan presented the trophy for its first four years and his successors included the Lords Aberdare and Brabazon. Media interest in the ceremony was strong, with the BBC covering the inaugural event on Light Programme and televising it as part of *Sportsview*'s 'Review of the Year' in 1954 and 1955, while a number of newsreel companies were invariably present. [13] The paper was also increasingly able to attract a substantial body of advertising specifically connected to the competition: the double-page spread announcing motorcyclist Geoff Duke's success in 1951, included adverts for five products carrying his endorsement. [14] The *Sporting Record* was suitably hyperbolic in its self-coverage. After only three awards it could claim that 'the vote has so captured the public imagination that it is now a national institution'. Vote-checking staff were invariably depicted as cheerfully overwhelmed and readers were told to place orders for the results edition well in advance to avoid disappointment. [15] For all the inevitable self-congratulation and commercially driven overstatement, the *Record*'s trophy was nevertheless clearly a significant addition to the post-war sporting ecology.

Although almost 200,000 voters were claimed in 1954, the fact that the next year saw the paper record the percentage rather than the number of votes received by each individual, suggests an attempt to disguise a significant fall in public participation. [16] Such a fall might explain why the paper passed the competition to the *Daily Express* in late 1956, 'by mutual agreement ... so that the ballot is projected from as wide a platform as possible'. [17] The *Daily Express* certainly saw the award as a highly suitable vehicle through which to publicise its talents and was to continue an enthusiastic sponsorship into the 1970s. In 1958, it pointed out that those watching the presentations on the previous night's *Sportsview* 'will have realised once again how completely the *Express* dominates the world of sports reporting and commentating in newspapers'. [18] The *Record's* decision to withdraw must also have been heavily influenced, however, by the launch in 1954 of the second major public ballot, the '*Sportsview* Personality of the Year', eventually the 'BBC Sports Personality of the Year'. The paper's editor, Cecil Bear, was certainly concerned that the new award would undermine what he claimed to be 'nationally recognised, in the press and the BBC, as *the ballot*.' [19] Peter Dimmock, the BBC's assistant head of outside broadcasting, tried to persuade him otherwise by pointing out that the BBC's 'little trophy' was only available to those who had appeared on the *Sportsview* (a rubric rapidly abandoned), but the prospect of a specialist weekly paper indulging in successful competition with the rapidly emerging vehicle of television, must have seemed daunting.

Dimmock's 'little award', while owing much to the initial cluster of post-war competitions, was essentially the product of a new and distinct environment. It was rooted in the particular needs of a newly established programme seeking its own identity but also in the context of the wider politics of broadcasting that had been so radically altered by the establishment of commercial television under the 1954 Television Act. [20] *Sportsview* had begun in April 1954 and rapidly became the BBC's major sports magazine programme. Although Dimmock was its main presenter and his political skills were critical to its establishment and subsequent health, its creative drive came from its editor, Paul Fox. In a memo to Dimmock in October 1954, Fox referred to 'our ballot for the Sportsman and Sportswoman of the Year' – his use of the phrase 'our ballot' clearly demonstrating that the idea had been under consideration for some time – and suggested that the award of a trophy for this competition might form part of a *Sportsview* end-of-year review that he sought to introduce. [21]

The award was indeed inaugurated as the finale to the resultant *Sportsview* 'Review' on 30 December 1954, with a modest postal electorate of 14,000 selecting athlete Chris Chataway as its first winner. [22] It actually received less space in the programme than its *Sporting Record* counterpart and Fox missed few opportunities to push for exclusive coverage in future editions, arguing that the only advantage in including both events lay in the fact that 'a crowd of sporting celebrities will be brought together and wined at the *Sporting Record*'s expense'. [23] In 1959, the BBC took the decision to focus exclusively on its own award ceremony, an action made easier by a *Daily Express* executive's blatant disregard of the programme's strict advertising code. [24] 'Personality' was never really defined and the call for people to choose their 'outstanding British sports star of the past 12 months' kept the criteria suitably general. [25] Records of voting figures were only infrequently kept but participation, although still very modest in comparison with the *Record*'s figures, appears to have increased with 44,000 votes having arrived days before the 1963 ceremony. [26] The annual 'Review' drew both good audiences – 25% of the potential adult viewing audience watched in 1963, for example – and an enthusiastic reaction, and the award build-up and ceremony clearly added a key dimension to the programme. Asa Briggs has described the sharp and topical *Sportsview* as 'a main weapon' in the BBC's battle over sporting matters with commercial television and the 'Personality of the Year' undoubtedly enhanced the programme's democratic, populist tone. Dimmock and Fox appear to have had an intuitive understanding of this requirement. When discussing the possibility of broadcasting the 1954 Sports Writers' Association of Great Britain's award dinner, Fox argued that 'it would make the ideal trailer for our own presentation – on the lines "the sports writers have chosen their man – now let the public have their say" '. Dimmock's scripts were suitably laced with references to 'your choice', 'your vote' and 'your personality' and, at least in the early years, with updates on the broad voting patterns thus far, designed to stimulate further interest. [27] The BBC had clearly found a most useful vehicle for engaging with and holding its audience.

Sportswriters' awards

The second major category of honour was that awarded on the basis of a vote taken by members of a particular sports writers' association. The establishment of such bodies is a critical and, as yet, understudied moment in the history of the professionalisation of British sporting journalism and utterly central to the development of the national system of sporting honours. An international body, the Association Internationale de la Presse Sportive had existed in the interwar period and the first purely British body was probably the Association of Golf Writers, founded in 1938. However, it was the post-war period that saw their real emergence. 1947 witnessed the birth of both the Cricket Writers' Club, initially rooted in an informal body of English and Australian journalists who played cricket for charitable purposes while awaiting the delayed start of the 1946–7 Ashes tour, and the Football Writers Association (FWA). [28] The Lawn Tennis Writers' Association followed in 1951 and by 1968

10 such bodies existed. Perhaps the most noteworthy, however, was the Sports Writers' Association of Great Britain (SWA), founded as an overarching body for writers across the whole sporting range in April 1948. [29] Twenty-one journalists joined at the inaugural meeting, with membership rising to over 60 by 1949 and eventually reaching about 500 by the end of the 1960s.

These organisations were ultimately pressure groups founded to effect improvement in working conditions. The FWA stemmed from the realisation by a group of English journalists that the impressive facilities they encountered in Belgium in 1947 resulted partly from pressure exerted by a recently formed Belgian Journalists' Association. [30] The SWA's foundation aims stressed a desire to improve facilities so that the 'reporting of sporting events shall be reliable, speedy and accurate'. [31] Very quickly, however, this desire to be able do their job more professionally became enjoined with an aspiration to a greater degree of professional status. Nothing suited this purpose better than the claim to specialist expertise engendered by the process of awarding sporting prizes. The first such award was 'Footballer of the Year', created in 1948 by the FWA and to be given to the player who 'by precept and example' had made the greatest contribution to the English game; Stanley Matthews was its first recipient. [32] This was closely followed in 1949 by SWA's establishment of 'Sportsman of the Year' award. The first recipients chosen were actually the seven British sportsmen then holding world championships and it was not until October 1950 that a formal ballot asking members to choose who had 'contributed most to Britain's international sporting prestige' was inaugurated. [33]

There were certainly other factors at play. There is little doubt that the vast majority of writers cared deeply about sport and saw the awards as a way of honouring those who had made their occupation both possible and, usually, pleasurable. This is a fundamental point and should not be lost in the wider commentary that follows. More prosaically, writers' associations were social bodies with the annual dinner (almost always held in London) as a key event. The award ceremony was a natural centrepiece for such occasions, and the 'Footballer of the Year' presentation was specifically suggested by the *Daily Mail*'s Roy Peskett for this very purpose. [34] Again, the associations eventually used awards to memorialise their own members. The SWA in particular built up a substantial roster of prizes, beginning with the 'Disabled Sports Personality of the Year', founded in 1963 in honour of Bill McGowran, a founder member and key activist. [35] The desire to demonstrate expert status was, however, never far away. The wish to display fine judgement, to play a role in the building of sporting pantheons and to influence both the public's view of sportsmen and sportsmen's view of themselves, was obviously not new. It was long at the core of journalistic activity, at least amongst leading practitioners. However, the bestowing of awards provided an altogether greater level of formality, a quasi-scientific quality conferred on the donors an ever-greater authority as the individual honours became more firmly established. This process was further aided in some instances by the gap between 'expert' and 'popular' opinion as exemplified by differing results between writers' and public ballots. Although footballers rarely won the latter – Johnny Haynes was the first to win the *Record/ Express* competition in 1961, Bobby Moore the BBC award in 1966 – those who polled well were infrequently those who headed the FWA's vote. Journalists appeared to have a more nuanced view.

One striking feature of the writers' selections was the extent to which they were governed by essentially moral definitions of what constituted sporting excellence. The FWA's emphasis on 'precept and example' is striking in this context. Joyce Woolridge has talked of an 'elevatory project' within professional football in the immediate post-war period through which leading players, taking advantage of the social democratic discourses that had emerged during the 'people's war', sought to raise 'the status of the professional both as an admirable figure as well as a national hero'. [36] The FWA played its role in this by constructing the year's leading player, both at the ceremonies and the reports of them as a 'gentleman', model professionals who were also model sportsmen. There was thus an air of inevitability about the choice of Stanley Matthews as the first winner in 1948, his seasonal award effectively standing as reward for a virtuous career. Amos Brook Hirst, chairman of the Football Association, set the tone for many speeches that followed in the decades beyond when informing his audience that Matthews, 'does not know how to foul. He is a perfect example for all the thousands of boys who watch soccer'. The next year, a press report termed Manchester United's Johnny Carey, 'gentlemanly', while, in 1951, Blackpool captain Harry Johnston was described as 'a model professional footballer – scrupulously clean, loyal to his Blackpool club'. [37] The choice of Johnson was an interesting one. Although his attractive Blackpool side finished third in the first division that season and they were about to contest a second FA Cup final in three years, there may well have been stronger candidates. Roy Peskett's description of him as a player who, until his award, had only 'one England cap and Cup Final loser's medals' to show for his career, suggests a decision based on recognition of faithful and model service to the game. [38] The choice of Luton Town's captain, Syd Owen, in 1959 had a similar ring. [39]

It was, then, as one contemporary journalist noted 'not enough just to be a good footballer to gain this highly prized award. Conduct both *on* and *off* the field is the guiding factor and, because of this, quite a number of possible candidates have not been elected – though wild horses would not drag their names from me.' [40] There are suggestions that some writers felt that the disciplinary record of the 1956 winner, Manchester City's German goalkeeper, Bert Trautmann, should have barred him from the honour. [41] In a game against Charlton at Maine Road, Manchester in 1954 he had refused to defend a penalty awarded against his team, he had given his name as 'Stanley Matthews' when booked, and he had appeared to jostle the referee and strike him with his cap at the end of the game. In March 1956 (by which time the votes were probably counted) a blatant foul on Tottenham Hotspur forward George Robb in an FA Cup quarterfinal tie became a source of major controversy. [42] A degree of latitude was clearly allowed in Trautmann's case but further research would probably identify others who were deemed to have fallen on the wrong side of the moral line.

Evidence of ethical policing can certainly be found within the SWA's management of the 'Sportsman of the Year' awards. What appears to be a calculated attempt to ignore the achievements of athlete Gordon Pirie will be returned to later, but the clearest example occurred in 1967 when the committee altered the result of the ballot in order to avoid an outcome which they felt compromised the underlying values of the competition. Glasgow Celtic's victory in the 1967 European Cup final led to heavy voting both for the team as a whole and its captain, Billy McNeil. The previous year had witnessed a similar situation involving the England football team and its captain, Bobby Moore, resulting in a decision to amalgamate the votes and award the prize to 'Bobby Moore and the World Cup winning XI'. In 1967, this precedent was followed and the combined vote took McNeil and Celtic into first place. However, the week before the award ceremony, Celtic were involved in a notoriously violent World Club Championship play-off game with Argentinean side, Racing Club. Three Celtic players (and two from Racing Club) were sent off and a fourth Celtic player, also dismissed, managed to stay on the field in the ensuing chaos. [43] After much anxious discussion within the SWA committee, it was agreed to expunge the entire Celtic-related vote and the trophy passed to motorcyclist Mike Hailwood. [44] Unsurprisingly, the wider public was kept in ignorance of these machinations.

The moral mindset was not immutable. Shifting attitudes within society combined with journalists' appreciation of changed sporting contexts eventually led to the appreciation of new skills and mentalities at the expense of older ones, particularly from the mid-1960s. The award of 'Footballer of the Year' to the Leeds United triumvirate of Bobby Collins in 1965, Jack Charlton in 1967 and Billy Bremner in 1971 certainly suggests a revised notion of the 'model professional' that made allowances for a certain physicality and possible lapses in discipline provided these remained aligned to high levels of skill and footballing intelligence. George Best's brilliance in Manchester United's European Cup winning year of 1968 made him a popular winner, but, even though his most problematic years lay largely ahead of him, he may not have earned the title if he had begun his career even a few years earlier. Nevertheless, a particular concept of sporting worth remained intact for much of the period studied here.

Being honoured

The emphasis so far has fallen on the donor, but the importance of the sporting award to the recipient is also highly important. Winners were often pleased enough – and certain enough of the *kudos* generated – to use their success for publicity purposes. A picture of Bolton Wanderers and England centre-forward Nat Lofthouse as 1953 'Footballer of the Year' served both as front cover and frontispiece illustration to his 1954 autobiography, while the strapline 'Footballer of the Year 1956' adorned the front cover of Bert Trautmann's *Steppes to Wembley.* Celebration and pleasure, however, were always tempered by modesty, humility and expressions of surprise, variously articulated; 'you're kidding mate. Cor, stone the crows! That's a right turn-up for the book' are the words reputedly used by Henry Cooper on discovering his success in the 1970 *Daily Express* competition. [45] Many chose to depict the honour as reward for either their team-mates or for their sport more generally. 1955 'Footballer of the Year', Manchester City captain Don Revie, captured a familiar refrain when seeing the trophy as 'an award to the team as much as me'. [46] The dedication of awards to fellow athletes was probably strongest in sports, particularly amateur ones, which tended to gain only limited media recognition. Cyclist Beryl Burton made this abundantly clear in accepting the 1967 'Sportswoman of the Year' award.

> It is not just for myself I am so pleased, it is also on behalf of the tens of thousands of cyclists in this country, be it the tourist or racing type, potterer or mile-eater, they all add up in my book to the greatest international sport in the world ... [I am] thanking you all for your reception, and for considering me and the sport of cycling worthy of the honour of voting me your Sportswoman of the Year. [47]

Award-winners also showed an acute sense of having been placed in a lineage in which the stature of previous winners made their own achievement all the more worthy. Staying simply within football, Nat Lofthouse claimed that his election as 'Footballer of the Year' in 1953 helped him 'forget my disappointment at missing a Cup Medal. There are 11 winners' medals every season – only one soccerman gets the honour of being "Footballer of the Year"'. Bert Trautmann, dumbfounded that I, an alien, should be thus honoured', also saw the award as highly prized and reported that he had 'heard some players say they'd rather win it than a Cup Medal'. [48] Bobby Charlton felt 'humble' about his success in 1966 and listed the winners whose number he had joined and, in later years, Leicester City, Stoke City and England goalkeeper, Gordon Banks, recalled a pride in being the first goalkeeper selected since his boyhood hero Trautmann. [49] Numerous similar examples could be found in other sporting fields. Especially in the earlier years of the awards, codes of expected public behaviour admittedly made it highly unlikely that recipients could have responded with anything other than the utmost graciousness but it would be unduly cynical to perceive too great a degree of artifice at work. Being 'honoured' clearly mattered.

The cultural function of the sporting award

It is within the discourses of modesty, decency and humility that some of the sporting award's greatest cultural significance can be found. Crucially, they were deployed not only by the winners but by other key parties. Journalists were always anxious to comment favourably on those honoured at their events. In 1949 Trevor Wignall used his *Sporting Record* column to commend boxer Freddie Mills, who had polled heavily, for the improvement in his public demeanour. On previous meetings, Wignall claimed 'the aura of fairgrounds and boxing booths was still with him' and he appeared 'rather crude in demeanour and speech'. At the awards dinner he was now 'a very different person ... a delight'. [50] More specifically, however, a media narrative was rapidly established which demanded an emphasis on the unassuming and self-effacing nature of recipients. By the 1960s, readers would have been surprised if the *Express*'s Desmond Hackett had not described walker Don Thompson as 'the most modest and certainly the most astonished winner', golfer Tony Jacklin as 'a quiet chap [with] simple charm', or noted that tennis star Ann Jones was 'oddly shy off her beloved tennis court'. [51] Perhaps the most important commendations, however, were those that came to sport from outsiders, from the distinguished guests who presented prizes and conferred status. This was especially the case for professional sportsmen whose reputation and social position was still sometimes uncertain, especially in the 1940s and early 1950s. Bevan was certainly always generous in his speeches for the *Sporting Record*, invariably stressing the links between sporting prowess and a wider moral compass. 'It is a most interesting fact that the men who reach the top of their profession in the sporting world are usually men of good character: they are also gentle', he informed the Savoy audience in 1947. Two years later he described Denis Compton as possessing 'modesty and charm' and called for aspiring sportsmen to 'emulate his achievements and remember his modesty'. [52] Cyclist Reg Harris was, in his turn, not only a great champion but 'a complete man'. [53]

In all its component parts, then, the sporting award became a ritual in which the sports world literally and metaphorically appeared dressed in its best clothes and showed itself to the public in the kindest possible light. The not infrequent tensions between sportsmen and the press could be glossed over and cordial relations established. Lofthouse told readers of his autobiography that, while journalists could be hurtful, they are generally a force for the good. 'How fortunate it is for soccer they do so much to foster and further soccer. What a boost it is for soccermen, too, that the Football Writers' Association annually award their Footballer of the Year trophy. This is soccer's own Oscar'. [54] Chris Brasher, in receipt of the *Daily Express*'s first award in 1956–7, thanked both the press and television for their efforts in raising sport's profile and similar expressions were the hallmark of most presentations. [55] Unsurprisingly ceremonies and other related activities were largely uncontentious. Unthreatening ideas for the improvement of the sporting infrastructure might be proffered, as when Reg Harris called for greater investment in facilities for aspiring athletes and the odd personal grievance might be elicited by a skilled interviewer. [56] In 1957, *Daily Express* award winner, middle-distance runner Derek Ibbotson, thus told Hackett during a post-ceremony interview that, while 'I have never groused before' the public should know that the ruling Amateur Athletics Association had failed to thus far to ratify his world mile record set earlier that year. [57] This was, however, controversy of the mildest sort.

The one significant exception was provided by athlete Gordon Pirie. Pirie was an outstanding middle-distance runner and a popular figure amongst the wider sporting public. He had won both the SWA's and the *Sporting Record*'s awards in 1953 and the BBC and the *Record*'s polls in 1955. However, he failed even to appear on the SWA's shortlist in that year and took the opportunity of his televised speech on receipt of the *Record*'s trophy to query how he might win two awards but fall so far short in another and, to settle scores with a sports press that he felt had become hostile to him. He told viewers that 'a few unkind words will inflict more damage than they (the sports writers) realise. I hope they will be kinder in future'. [58] The *Sporting Record* appears to have been slightly embarrassed, noting that he made a 'frank speech', which 'created something of a sensation' but the battle was fully joined by most national newspapers. [59] The *Daily Mirror*'s Peter Wilson, a leading figure in the SWA, was especially savage. Under the heading 'The Poison in the Heart of Gordon Pirie', he claimed that the athlete had made,

> what I consider to be one of the most unpleasant, ungracious and utterly outrageous speeches it has ever been my misfortune to listen to . . . I for one am sick and tired of trying to cover up his arrogance when he wins and his excuses when he loses. [60]

The *Express* gave Pirie space to expand his argument – he excluded his 'good friend' Desmond Hackett, from his strictures – and he took the opportunity to complain about the press claims that he exaggerated the extent of his injuries and was 'yellow'. [61]

Even in later years when elite athletes were less hidebound by certain notions of public behaviour, probably only athlete Steve Ovett's boycott of the SWA's ceremony in 1978 (he accepted the BBC's 'Sports Personality of the Year' trophy the next evening) matched Pirie's action. [62] However, although Pirie's action was a noteworthy break from tradition, that very untypicality merely draws attention to the essential rules governing the relationship between the press and elite athletes as enshrined within the rituals of the sporting honour and its accompanying activities. The sporting award created a series of spaces, sites where any tensions were to be ignored in favour of a mutually beneficial celebration of the modest sportsperson in grateful and fruitful partnership with a benign media. In this regard, it was, and still remains for all its frequent blandness, a potent mechanism.

Although there is not space here to develop the point, the designation to, and performance by, award winners of a specific public persona, genuine or contrived, also represents an important contribution to the historical process through which sporting 'stardom' has been constructed. [63] The press, newsreel, radio and a variety of material objects such as collectable cards and children's games had already established clear and widely accepted notions of sporting stardom long before the 1940s. [64] Nevertheless, the emergent sporting award gave significant reinforcement and refinement, adding both expert sanction and an, albeit highly qualified, sense of objective public endorsement to the procedure. However, particular individuals were given special status and shown to be able to respond to the honour with suitable dignity and the 'ordinariness' that is so much a hallmark of star quality. The process of speech-making is interesting in this regard. Previous generations of stars had undoubtedly addressed public gatherings such as annual general meetings, civic dinners and post-event celebrations and the radio and newsreel interview was established by the 1930s. The acceptance speech, however, especially when radio and/or television were present, was essentially a new element that demanded the honing of new skills of presentation and self-representation. While the often intense 'nervousness' that so many speakers claimed on facing their audience was, for some, part of a conscious display of the modesty they knew was expected, for some it must have genuinely captured a response to a situation infrequently or never before encountered. The amateur, or, at least, the middle-class one, was expected to be competent in this arena but the working-class professional engendered lower expectations. The fact that some comfortably exceeded them played a role in raising their status and that of their colleagues. Journalist Graham Selkirk commented that a 'notable feature of these ['Footballer of the Year'] dinners has been the remarkably high standard of speech-making shown by the chosen footballers. It is a nerve-wracking occasion, but their sincerity and delight at receiving the honour always shines through.' [65] While the formal processes of media management were still some way in the future, the efforts of these earlier sportsmen and women of the year gave some valuable pointers to future generations.

The woman sports star was arguably a particular beneficiary of the awards system. The *Sporting Record* encouraged voters to nominate women as 'Sportsman of the Year' from the outset but few did so. Kay Stammers, tennis player and the paper's women's sports correspondent, was the highest placed women in 1947, but gained less than 1% of the vote, clear testimony to Martin Polley's argument that 'coming out of the Second World War, women's sporting roles were heavily constrained by norms that had been established during the nineteenth-century debates over medicine and anatomy'. [66] Although the paper's motives were unclear, as already noted, it nevertheless inaugurated a 'Sportswoman of the Year' award in 1952, giving the prize to the highest placed woman in the poll; the first winner was skier, Jeanette Altwegg. The *Daily Express* added a specific 'sportswoman' category to the ballot paper in 1956 and the SWA introduced its equivalent award in 1959. Three years later, the BBC trophy was won by a woman, swimmer Anita Lonsbrough, for the first time. Indeed, all three top places went to women in 1962 and Dorothy Hyman and Mary Rand won the award in the next two years.

The extent and impact of these developments should not be exaggerated. While attitudes to women in sport were shifting in the period to 1970, the pace was slow and old assumptions and stereotypes deeply rooted. The SWA's award dinners were initially strictly men-only, unsurprisingly perhaps, given contemporary social *mores* and the almost exclusively male membership. In October 1949, Millie Hudson, the swimming editor of the *London Evening Standard*, became the first woman member and her involvement caused a certain degree of operational embarrassment. In 1954, for example, the organising committee slightly shame-facedly offered her two theatre tickets as compensation for her exclusion; she politely returned them. Although the 'Sportswoman of the Year' was instigated in 1959, it was not until 1963 that opponents of a mixed gathering, led by Bill McGowran and Frank Butler of the *Daily Express* and *News of the World* respectively, were persuaded to turn the event into a dinner dance and for the two sets of awards to be made at the same event. [67] Moreover, from Lord Brabazon's favourable comments on the attractiveness of show jumper Pat Smythe during his awards speech for the *Sporting Record* in 1955, to Desmond Hackett's many hymns to feminine beauty – swimmer Judy Grinham was 'a luscious mermaid', Britain's leading performers in general 'disprove that all [sports]women have legs like billiard tables and faces only mother could love' – the award ceremony and its coverage was hardly a site of major challenges to gender relationships within sport. [68] However, the very existence of awards that consciously acknowledged women's sporting achievements represented an important punctuation mark in the often hesitant and partial enlargement of women's place within the national sporting culture.

Measuring stardom?

The sporting award has largely been treated in this study as a cultural construct designed to serve a variety of discursive and performative functions within the fields of both media and sport. It is, however, worth a brief consideration of the extent to which it can be viewed in more 'objective' terms as a record of sporting achievement or index of popularity. Can we see the various lists of names as any more than the products of specific historical conjunctions? In many senses it is easier to find arguments against the possibility, or even validity, of taking such an approach than to undertake the task. The very terms of reference used could be interpreted differently even by a small and specialist constituency, with words such as 'outstanding' or 'prestige' capable of be related to actual results but also to the nature and style of performance; heroic failure could be valued as highly as comfortable dominance. Without attempting to bring too serious a tone to events that were hardly intended to be exact democratic exercises, it is certainly the case that public ballots are especially hard to judge. We sometimes know the size of the electorate but nothing of their demography or typicality. It is possible that quite significant numbers of 'non-sports' fans were drawn into these events and their presence might have impacted considerably on the final results. Again, those with an anyway powerful media presence had a major advantage – Olympic performers were particularly fortunate – as did any performer enjoying success at the time of the poll. Fans of particular sports or individuals could sometimes act in concert, as when large numbers of voters from both his home country and adopted city pushed Liverpool and Scotland footballer, Billy Liddell, into second place in the 1949 *Sporting Record* poll. [69] There was undoubtedly considerable lobbying and canvassing; in 1947, the *Record* noted one young woman who had organised over 200 votes for her favourite. The tendency of organisers to note the broad voting trends while the competition was in progress indeed encouraged this. In the same year, the paper followed news of Bruce Woodcock's early lead over Sydney Wooderson with the exhortations, 'Wooderson fans, are you standing for that? Woodcock fans, are you going to let him be caught?' [70]

Despite these numerous limitations, some accuracy within records of standing and status may be identified. In terms of the public ballots, the voters were not entirely at the whim of the media coverage and agenda. While Peter Dimmock clearly expected Roger Bannister's breaking of the four-minute mile barrier to place him at the head of the inaugural *Sportsview* poll – 'Banister is the obvious winner' he noted, even when the award was still at the planning stages – the viewers narrowly preferred the 5,0000 metres world record-holder and Bannister's pacemaker on the run, Chris Chataway. [71] The obvious point should be made that high votes for an individual, particularly over a period of time, provide at least some clear indication that that person was highly regarded. Probably the most interesting figures are those who managed to be successful across a number of different polls. Cricketer Len Hutton, *Sporting Record*'s and SWA's 'Sportsman of the Year' winner in 1952; Roger Bannister, who emulated this feat in 1954; Gordon Pirie, as already noted, a multiple winner in both 1953 and 1955; 17-year-old Scottish swimmer Ian Black, SWA's and *Daily Express*'s 'Sportsman of the Year' and BBC 'Personality of the Year' in 1958; swimmer Anita Lonsbrough and sprinter Dorothy Hyman, who both managed the hat-trick of SWA's and *Express*'s 'Sportswoman' and BBC 'Personality' in 1962 and 1963 respectively. In many cases, these successes would hardly surprise the knowledgeable sports fan or historian. However, the lists of winners (and the other highly-placed individuals, not for the most part considered here) are the only substantial record of popular and expert acclaim that we possess and they can, with caution, give a little more substance to our generalisations. Denis Compton's star status is well known, but it is perhaps given greater definition by the fact that he won the *Record* poll in both 1947 and 1948 and was in the top 12 in all of the first six ballots; no other cricketer came close to achieving that. Reg Harris's success in winning the SWA's award in 1950 and the *Record*'s trophy in 1950 and 1951, Pirie's enormous popularity in the mid-1950s and that of Black in 1958 and Lonsbrough and Hyman in the early 1960s all suggest that there can be, too, if not surprises, then useful *aide memoirs* that might help in the more accurate reconstruction of contemporary sporting pantheons and popular sporting appetites.

As this suggests, there are other avenues for exploration that cannot be considered here. Within the wider narratives offered are many nuances and shifts over time and plentiful opportunities to add to existing debates over sporting nationalism – a more overtly patriotic note perhaps emerges in the celebration of prize winners in the mid-1950s – media representation of particular sports and sports stars and the contribution made by awards to the construction of sporting memory. So often accompanied in the media by visual or textual reminders of the previous year's events, the choice and award of the sporting prize arguably helped define and refine the collective historical sense. Again, historians of the 'last flowering of the old variety of pure amateurism' might find useful material in the records of events that celebrated amateurs as much as professionals and in which middle-class tennis players and show jumpers could still secure a place in popular affection. [72] Above all, there are rich opportunities for using the sporting award in the period from 1970 onwards both as a lens through which to view modern sporting culture and as an agent in the creation of, and element within, our ever more 'sportified' society. The build up to the major awards, especially the BBC 'Sports Personality of the Year', is now in itself a major self-referential news story, albeit one that can generate considerable derision within other sections of the media. [73] Specialist journalists take their role ever more seriously. Writing in 2007, for example, the *Guardian*'s Kevin McCarra saw the fact that Wayne Rooney's failure thus far to be 'a genuine candidate' for 'Footballer of the

Year' as evidence of the only partial fulfilment of his precocious teenage promise. [74] Whether the founders of the various awards ever expected them to last for so long or to gain quite such a high profile is unknown, but they certainly established a set of institutions which have established a particular view of the sporting world that has generally been of much benefit to both elite performers and the media that report, present and interpret them.

Notes

[1] A section of this article was presented to the 2007 'Historians on Sport' conference at De Montfort University. I am grateful to participants for their comments, and especially so to Huw Richards. I am grateful to Louise North of the BBC Written Archives Centre, Caversham, for her considerable help with sources.

[2] Similar national awards were founded within Northern Ireland, Scotland and Wales but they are not considered here.

[3] *Wisden cricketers' almanack*, 144th edition (2007), p. 84. In fact, the first listing was for the *six* bowlers of the year and the second for the *nine* batsmen of 1890. It settled on five in 1891, with wicket-keepers the chosen category.

[4] I am extremely grateful to Alexander Jackson for material on *Gamages*.

[5] *Sporting Record*, 5 Feb. 1949.

[6] From http://www.footy.com.au/dags/FAQ4v1-5.html#Section5.0, accessed, 26 Apr. 2009.

[7] From http://www.abae.co.uk/International/Senior/Olympic/valbarker/index.asp, accessed, 10 June 2008.

[8] R. Osborne, *75 years of the Oscar. The official history of the academy award* (New York, 2003), p. 15.

[9] Les Hoole, *The rugby league challenge cup. An illustrated history* (Derby, 1998), p. 202; Graham Morris, *Hero. Rugby league's greatest award winners* (Skipton, 2005), p. 8.

[10] Richard Holt and Tony Mason, *Sport in Britain, 1945–2000* (Oxford, 2000), pp. 3–4, 64. More generally, David Kynaston, *Austerity Britain, 1945–51* (London, 2007).

[11] Joyce Woolridge, 'These sporting lives: Football autobiographies, 1945–1980', *Sport in History*, 28 (4) (2008), pp. 620–40; Dave Russell, ' "Interesting and instructive reading"? *The FA book for boys* and the culture of boyhood, 1945–1973', *Journal of Sport History*, 34 (1) (2007), pp. 231–52.

[12] *Sporting Record*, 7 Jan. 1947. Unfortunately, copies of the paper in which the competition was launched in late 1946 were not available for consultation at the time of research.

[13] Ibid., 5 Feb. 1947, 18 Dec. 1954, 8 Jan. 1955.

[14] Ibid., 9 Feb. 1952.

[15] Ibid., 29 Jan. 1949, 17 Dec. 1947, 15 Jan. 1949.

[16] Ibid., 10 Feb. 1950, 30 Jan. 1954, 8 Jan. 1955.

[17] Ibid., 17 Nov. 1956.

[18] *Daily Express*, 11 Dec. 1958.

[19] Steve Rider with Martyn Smith, *BBC sports personality of the year* (London, 2003), p. 8.

[20] See especially A. Briggs, *The history of broadcasting in the United Kingdom*, vol. 4: *Sound and vision* (Oxford, 1979).

[21] Memo, Fox to Dimmock, 4 Oct. 1954. See also memo from Dimmock to either Television Publicity Officer or Programme Organiser Television, 8 Oct. 1954. BBC Written Archive Centre [afterwards, BBC WAC], T14/1190/2.

[22] Rider and Smith, *BBC sports personality*, p. 11.

[23] Memo, Fox to Dimmock, 9 Nov. 1954. BBC WAC, T14/1190/2.

[24] Rider and Smith, *BBC sports personality*, p. 34. For the code, Dimmock to General Manager of *Sporting Record*, 12 Dec. 1955, BBC WAC, T14/1187/20.

[25] Undated press release, BBC WAC, T14/1799/5.

[26] Handwritten tabulation, BBC WAC, T14/1799/5.

[27] Briggs, *Sound and Vision*, p. 776. Memo, Fox to Dimmock, 8 Nov. 1954, BBC WAC, T14/1190/2; see for example, *Sportsview* scripts 2 Nov., 16 Nov. 1955, BBC WAC, T14/1187/19.

[28] Cricinfo; Graham Selkirk, 'The story behind the footballer of the year', *FA Book for Boys*, 10 (1957–8), pp. 88–93.

[29] David Hunn, *50 years of the Sports Writers' Association of Great Britain* (London, 1998), p. 2. It changed its name to the Sports Journalists' Association in 2002, following a merger with the Professional Sports Photographers' Association.

[30] Selkirk, 'Story', p. 88.

[31] Hunn, *50 years*, p. 3.

[32] Selkirk, 'Footballer of the year', p. 90.

[33] David Hunn, *50 years*, p. 5. I am extremely grateful to the SWA for making a copy of this invaluable booklet available to me.

[34] Selkirk, 'Story', p. 89.

[35] Ibid., pp. 31–3.

[36] Woolridge, 'These sporting lives', p. 626. See also her 'From local hero to national star? The changing cultural representation of the professional footballer in England, 1945–1985' (unpublished PhD thesis, University of Central Lancashire, 2007), ch. 3.

[37] *Sporting Chronicle*, 26 Apr. 1948, 1 Apr. 1949; *Daily Mail*, 3 Apr. 1951.

[38] *Daily Mail*, 3 Apr. 1951.

[39] Although he had led the unfashionable club to the FA Cup Final.

[40] Selkirk, 'Story', p. 90.

[41] Alan Rowlands, *Trautmann. The Biography* (Derby, 1990), p. 170.

[42] Rowlands, *Trautmann* pp. 155, 169; *Manchester Evening Chronicle*, 24, 26 Mar. 1956.

[43] Brian Belton, *The battle of Montevideo. Celtic under siege* (Stroud, 2008).

[44] Hunn, *50 Years*, p. 8.

[45] *Daily Express*, 2 Dec. 1970.

[46] Don Revie, *Soccer's happy wanderer* (London, 1955), p. 93.

[47] *Cycling*, 23 Dec. 1967.

[48] Nat Lofthouse, *Goals galore* (London, 1954), pp. 108–9.

[49] Bert Trautmann, *Steppes to Wembley* (London, 1956), pp. 129–30; Gordon Banks, *Banksy. My autobiography* (London, 2002). Banks was elected in 1972.

[50] *Sporting Record*, 15 Feb. 1949.
[51] *Daily Express*, 9 Nov. 1960, 25 Nov. 1969.
[52] Ibid., 12 Feb. 1947, 28 May 1949.
[53] *Sporting Record*, 8 Apr. 1950.
[54] Lofthouse, *Goals*, pp. 108–9.
[55] *Daily Express*, 10 Jan. 1957.
[56] Ibid., 8 Apr. 1950.
[57] *Daily Express*, 12 Dec. 1957.
[58] Ibid, 30 Dec. 1957. Gordon Pirie, *Running wild* (London, 1962). Pirie was gracious to the winner, athlete John Disley, and argued that boxer Don Cockell had also been unfairly ignored.
[59] Ibid., 7 Jan. 1957.
[60] *Daily Mirror*, 29 Dec. 1957.
[61] *Daily Express*, 30 Dec. 1957.
[62] *Daily Telegraph*, 13 Dec. 1978; *Daily Mirror*, 13, 14 Dec. 1978; *Guardian*, 13 Dec. 1978. Like Pirie, he found much press criticism unhelpful and clashed with journalists on a number of occasions.
[63] Gary Whannel, *Media sport stars: Masculinities and moralities* (London, 2001).
[64] For example, A. Jackson, 'The Baines Card and its place in boys' popular culture between 1887 and 1922', in Bob Snape and Helen Pusard, eds, *Recording leisure lives: Histories, archives and memories of leisure* (Brighton, 2008), pp. 47–72; Joyce Woolridge, 'Mapping the stars: Stardom in English professional football, 1890–1946', *Soccer and society*, 3 (2) (2002), pp. 51–69; Mike Huggins and Jack Williams, *Sport and the English, 1918–1939* (Abingdon, 2006), pp. 42–59.
[65] Selkirk, 'Story', p. 92.
[66] *Sporting Record*, 22 Jan. 1947. Even hurdler Maureen Gardner, fourth overall in 1949, gained less than 5%. Martin Polley, *Moving the goalposts. A history of sport and society since 1945* (London, 1998), p. 92.
[67] Hunn, *50 years*, pp. 15–16.
[68] *Sporting Record*, 8 Jan. 1955; *Daily Express*, 11 Dec. 1958, 11 Dec. 1959.
[69] *Sporting Record*, 4 Feb. 1950.
[70] Ibid., 8 Jan. 1947.
[71] Memo from Dimmock to either Television Publicity Officer or Programme Organiser Television, 8 Oct. 1954, BBC WAC, T14/1190/2.
[72] Holt and Mason, *Sport in Britain*, p. 46.
[73] For a scathing view of the BBC event, Kevin Mitchell, 'Sue and Gary the only equals in the blandest show on earth', *Observer*, 9 Nov. 2008.
[74] *Guardian*, 12 Oct. 2007.

'In a Yorkshire Like Way': Cricket and the Construction of Regional Identity in Nineteenth-century Yorkshire

Rob Light

This paper examines how by 1900 cricket had come to be seen as an important representation of Yorkshire identity. It places the start of this process in the game's popular pre-modern context, as professional-centred, competitive, commercial cricket dominated its formative development across the region. The way these values led to local rivalries which became focused on the concept of a representative team building Yorkshire's status within the national context of cricket is then explored. Finally these events are set against the formation of the 'Gentleman Amateur' controlled county club in 1863, to show how a distinctive concept of county cricket developed in Yorkshire which offers a different perspective on the English county game during its formative decade and beyond.

In his introduction to the first official history of cricket in the county, which was published in 1904, Lord Hawke declared that 'Yorkshire cricket is a thing of which not only every Yorkshireman but every Englishman must feel proud'. [1] Hawke was perhaps overstating the importance of Yorkshire cricket to people elsewhere in the country. Yet his statement captured the way that, as Dave Russell has noted, by the 1890s, 'Yorkshire County Cricket Club served as a crucial mechanism through which Yorkshire became known both objectively and perhaps more importantly,

Rob Light, University of Huddersfield.

metaphorically and symbolically, to its own inhabitants and those beyond the county boundary'. [2]

Hawke's views, however, take on an additional significance when the constituent parts that made up Yorkshire cricket at the beginning of the twentieth century are examined from within the context of the first-class game in which the county team took part during this period. The statement was made at the zenith of the 'Golden Age' when the influence of the 'Gentleman Amateur' in English cricket was arguably at its height. Like its counterparts elsewhere in the country, Yorkshire County Cricket Club was controlled by a committee of gentlemen enthusiasts at this time and throughout the rest of the century. Moreover, in both literal and metaphorical terms, Hawke himself arguably provides the strongest representation of 'Gentleman Amateur' values to have been present in Yorkshire cricket during its history.

But the concept of county cricket which became such a strong focal point of regional identity in Yorkshire was built upon many aspects of the sport that were fundamentally opposed by the amateur ethos. Yorkshire county cricket retained the sense of competition, professionalism and commercialism that had dominated the sport throughout its formative years. In this sense, cricket in the region resembled the popular professional spectator sports which grew so rapidly in urban industrial communities across the north of England at the end of the nineteenth century far more than it did the county clubs that the Yorkshire side played against.

Although Yorkshire County Cricket Club had a membership of around just 3,000 people in the early decades of the twentieth century, the team enjoyed a popular appeal which, in 1904, saw 78,792 spectators watch it play Lancashire in a three-day fixture at Headingley. [3] Unlike most of its counterparts the club had no ground of its own and matches were staged at venues run on a semi commercial basis in order to raise funds for the maintenance and development of their facilities. In 1903 Yorkshire matches were played at seven such venues and £2,330 18 shillings and 3 pence, approximately a third of the takings that year, was paid in commission charges to the clubs that staged the fixtures. [4] Many of these clubs also ran professional football teams, with Headingley, Leeds, Park Avenue, Bradford, and Fartown, Huddersfield all staging regular matches in the Northern Rugby Union at this time, whilst Sheffield United played the association code at Bramall Lane.

Perhaps most importantly, however, the Yorkshire team itself provided a compelling representation of the strength and character of the sport across the region. Out of the 17 players who appeared for the 'County

Eleven' in its 31 matches during 1903, 13 were professionals who had begun their careers with local clubs from within the county, whilst only four were amateurs. By this time the side was also arguably the most competitive in county cricket, as Yorkshire had been crowned county champions six times in the 14 years since the competition became set on a formal basis in 1890, with four titles coming in the previous five years.

Yorkshire cricket had come to represent a set of meanings that clearly contradicted many of the values which dominated the game elsewhere in England at the start of the twentieth century. But how did this process take place and what does it tell us about the development of both the sport in general and county cricket in particular during the nineteenth century?

The genesis of regional identity in Yorkshire cricket

The foundations upon which the rise of cricket in Yorkshire was built during the first half of the nineteenth century had important implications for the way in which the sport subsequently developed in the region. Cricket's formative growth in the county took place in a distinctive and particularly dynamic environment in which a wide range of meanings came to find expression through the sport. As the West Riding, in particular, experienced its own definitive period of urban industrial growth, the game developed a vigorous popular following which became focused upon a powerful sense of local and civic identity. These dynamics helped numerous rapidly changing communities to define themselves and found their fullest expression through major commercial matches between rival neighbouring towns in which professional players predominantly took part. It was within this context that teams claiming to represent the county first began to appear.

However, the informal structure and disproportionate development of cricket during the first half of the nineteenth century meant that it was some time before a cohesive expression of regional identity could be articulated through Yorkshire representative sides. Indeed, the first teams to play as Yorkshire were somewhat transient affairs that did not always even claim to represent the county as a whole. For example, when the 'Gentlemen of the Wetherby Club' played the 'Gentlemen of All Yorkshire' for one hundred guineas a side in 1809 the county side was clearly limited to members of the social elite. But more commonly, early Yorkshire sides were confined to a specific geographical location. Most were assembled by backers or promoters to take part in commercial challenge matches and consisted mainly of local professionals from the town in which the contest was staged. The first appearance of an 'All England' team in the West Riding was to play against 'Twenty-two of Yorkshire' at Darnal for 1,000 guineas in 1825. This 'Yorkshire' team was almost exclusively selected from Sheffield players. But in July 1833 the *York Courant* reported on a match between 'Twenty of Yorkshire', selected from the clubs 'within 30 miles of Ripon', and Nottingham for 50 sovereigns at Ripon. [5]

Civic and regional identities were often intertwined in the sport during this period and Yorkshire cricket first began to gain national prominence through the growing reputation of players and teams from Sheffield. Outside the region, throughout the 1820s and 1830s Sheffield cricketers were often seen as representatives of the county. For example, when William Woolhouse made his debut at Lord's, playing for 'All England' against the 'Bs' in 1828, *Bell's Life* explained he 'was a stranger from Yorkshire, and we are informed this was his first match on the ground; his playing shows that we may expect a very fine hitter after a little experience'. [6] Consequently the success of players from Sheffield saw teams claiming to represent the county also start to gain broader recognition. When a county side that mostly consisted of players from the town defeated Norfolk at Hyde Park in July 1834 *Bell's Life* proclaimed, 'the Yorkshire players in this match did more to stamp themselves first rate cricketers than perhaps any other contest in which they have been engaged'. [7]

Sheffield's contribution to the growing reputation of cricket in Yorkshire was not lost on the local press. In September 1826, when 'Twenty Two of Sheffield and Leicester' had beaten 'Eleven of All England' at Leicester for 400 sovereigns and were in a strong position in a second match between the teams at Darnall, the *Sheffield Independent* proudly proclaimed that the,

> Yorkshire players, especially during the last three years, under the unremitting attention of the proprietor of the Darnal ground, have laboured to obtain perfection in the game, and to procure a reputation for themselves and the West Riding. [8]

The success of Sheffield-based early Yorkshire teams against other county sides received similar local acclaim and after Yorkshire beat Norfolk for one hundred sovereigns at Hyde Park in 1833 the *Sheffield Independent* surmised that 'the strength of the Yorkshire party lay in the Sheffield men'. [9]

But perhaps the strongest early representations of Yorkshire cricket to be made through the sport in Sheffield came with the participation of professionals from the town in major single wicket matches. These were primarily commercial events, largely built around the distinctive structure and vigorous popular culture that characterised pre-modern sport. They centred upon challenges which, in order to raise publicity, were often issued and accepted in characteristically pugnacious manner through correspondence in the press.

Whilst broader regional associations were later invoked by Harry Sampson's nickname, the 'Star of the North', Sheffield's first single wicket champion Tom Marsden was strongly portrayed as a representative of Yorkshire cricket. In 1833 Marsden took part in arguably the most famous single wicket match involving a Sheffield player when he met Fuller Pilch for the championship of England. In the four years that lapsed before Pilch finally took up Marsden's challenge a particularly lively public discourse took place between the backers of the two men. It reached its height in 1829 when Pilch's backers attempted to negotiate alternative terms to those that had been laid down in the initial challenge. As was common during this period, the dialogue took place in the press and after negotiations eventually broke down the *Sheffield Independent* stated 'from *authority*' that 'Tom Marsden thinks the friends of Pilch have rather *blinked* his challenge .... instead of replying to it in a Yorkshire like way 'play or no play''. [10] Clearly, some characteristics of the 'broadly agreed self-image of Yorkshiremen' that Russell noted had emerged at the end of the nineteenth century were not only in place during the 1830s, but were also being expressed through cricket in the county. [11]

Yet, elsewhere in the region, the undoubted success of Sheffield cricket during the first half of the nineteenth century did surprisingly little to establish a collective identity for Yorkshire cricket. The game's disproportionately localised development during this period meant that the success of the Sheffield-based players had far less impact in other parts of the county. Matches involving Yorkshire teams that took place during the 1820s and 1830s often received little interest away from the towns in which they had been organised. The seven 11-a-side fixtures that were played by Sheffield-based Yorkshire teams in the 1830s scarcely received any attention in either the Leeds or Bradford newspapers, even when the county side was victorious. Indeed, when Sheffield was strong enough to challenge and beat a Yorkshire side in 1849, the *Leeds Mercury* was at pains to make clear that the teams represented two distinctly different cricketing identities. It explained how,

> The act of a single town presuming to challenge the whole county may seem extraordinary; but it will cease to appear when it is known that cricket is better supported in Sheffield than almost any town in the kingdom. There are no less than four cricket grounds at the service of the inhabitants. High and low, rich and poor, join together to support

> the noble game; the greater part from the love of cricket, the rest for the honour of their town. No wonder then that Sheffield may challenge Yorkshire. [12]

'Our Yorkshire team': Rivalry and the making of a collective identity

By the time this view was expressed, however, Sheffield's supremacy in Yorkshire cricket was being contested. The growing strength of the sport elsewhere in the region had begun to bring the town's right to represent the county into question. A series of challenge matches for the unofficial championship of Yorkshire had taken place between teams representing major towns in the region during the 1840s and Huddersfield was beginning to emerge as a centre for the sport of comparative strength.

Yet, somewhat paradoxically, the growth of these rivalries was integral to the subsequent development of Yorkshire county cricket as a key focal point of regional identity. As Russell has also noted, county cricket enabled a shared sense of communal interest to emerge, through which local pride became a 'building block for a wider set of associational bonds'. [13]

These changing dynamics began to be articulated through a growing discourse surrounding the make up of teams that were assembled to represent the county. According to the *Leeds Times*, when Dalton played Sheffield in a match for £100 a side at Old Trafford in 1851, the challenge resulted from discontent over the non-selection of the club's leading professionals for Yorkshire teams earlier that year. Similar sentiments were also expressed by a correspondent to *Bell's Life* who, using the pseudonym Eboracensis, complained that:

> the list of players for the late cricket match 'Yorkshire versus Surrey' [bye and by], it should properly have been entitled *Sheffield* (with three given players from the county of York) . . . of the three best bowlers in Yorkshire – Armitage of Dalton, Hall of Bradford and Joy of Knaresborough – not one is chosen . . . I can only express hope that the managers of the next Yorkshire match will not depend so exclusively on Sheffield. That town can doubtless furnish the best batters and wicketkeepers in Yorkshire; but in bowlers it is inferior to both Dalton and Knaresborough . . . The county of York is, however, very strong in cricketers; and choose any eleven you would, fourteen others might be named who would rest the palm of victory from them . . . [14]

So, whilst the increasing strength of cricket away from Sheffield intensified rivalries within the region, it also helped establish the concept of a truly representative county team building Yorkshire's status within the national context of the sport. [15] After only a handful of similar fixtures in the previous decade, the number of 11-a-side contests in which Yorkshire teams faced other counties increased dramatically at the start of the 1850s. In 1851 five such matches took place and a growing affinity with the Yorkshire team developed which was articulated in the region's press. For example, the *Leeds Times* referred to the county eleven as 'our Yorkshire team' after a victory over Lancashire, 'with Caesar, Caffyn and Adams' at Sheffield in early August, and 'our county eleven' following a defeat by Surrey at The Oval a week later. [16]

Indeed the *Leeds Times* report on Yorkshire's victory over Lancashire in 1851 also demonstrates how the synthesis between local and regional pride began to be expressed through the county cricket team. Trough representing the region in the broader context of the county game, the professionals who largely made up Yorkshire sides became an immense source of pride for the communities in which their careers had been developed. [17] So, when describing Yorkshire's victory over Lancashire in 1851, the *Leeds Times* explained how on the second morning of the match,

> Coates and Anderson, who brought out their bats on Monday, presently retired, and Baldwinson was the only one to make a stand. Our Harewood champion, who we are sorry to say has been unsuccessful this season, got his 14 runs in his wanted manner. [18]

But competition between communities still remained as a key dynamic in the culture of the game across the region and this too had implications for the way county cricket came to be viewed. Matches involving the Yorkshire team were increasingly seen as contests in which the reputation of the county was at stake. So, for example, in May 1851 the *Leeds Times* boasted how '"Fourteen of All Yorkshire"' had 'signally defeated "Eleven of All England"' by an innings and 53 runs on the Hyde Park ground, Sheffield. The report then called for an 11-a-side match to be played between 'our county cricketers' and the 'All England Eleven' as a 'means of seeing the true *status* of the Yorkshire cricketers'. [19]

These competitive impulses also began to stir embryonic representations of the divide between north and south. When Yorkshire met Surrey at Sheffield in July 1855 the *Leeds Times* explained 'it has long been anxiously desired that "Eleven of All Yorkshire" should try their strength against the southerns'. [20] The match ended in a comfortable victory for Surrey. But, as in broader northern conceptions of the south that Russell again has noted, the London-based team was seen as having distinct advantages that the Yorkshire side did not enjoy. [21] It was argued that,

> The Surrey team are organised-are almost daily in the habit of practising together, and have by a careful and almost incessant training, attained a greater perfection than any other eleven in England ... The Yorkshire eleven on the contrary seldom or ever, except in matches, play together and again their practice (which is much inferior) is not so constant ... What we have urged in Yorkshire's behalf is quite obvious, and shows that we are 'not so bad as we seem'. A defeat-although perhaps not so complete as the present one, was reasonably to be expected. Yorkshire was decidedly over-matched, yet in coming seasons if a similar contest should be repeated, we certainly expect our players will run a closer game. [22]

Perhaps most importantly, however, although various different organisations assembled the sides that played in these matches, the concept of a singular Yorkshire team was developing into a recognisable entity in its own right. Even though 14 players took part in the fixture against the 'All England Eleven', only 16 different men appeared in the five matches that were staged in 1851, and 10 of them played four times or more. Despite the debate over selection, the side was also becoming more representative of the county as a whole. Because of the town's strength, Sheffield players still made up the bulk of the eleven. But players from clubs elsewhere in Yorkshire also had a significant presence. Out of the 10 men who appeared in all but one of the matches, George Anderson was from Bedale, Joe Berry and George Armitage from Dalton and Sam Baldwinson from Bradford.

The make-up of the team also had a distinctively professional complexion. Indeed of the 16 men who represented the county during 1851 only three were amateurs, with R.F. Skelton, taking part in four matches, Bernard Wake in two and Benjamin Huntsman in one. Consequently, the lack of an amateur presence was already beginning to stand out and after Yorkshire had convincingly beaten Lancashire at the Botanical Gardens ground, Manchester in August, *Bell's Life* noted that the match,

> ... terminated in favour of Yorkshire by five wickets, a result even more favourable to Lancashire than might have been expected, when the numerical strength of Yorkshire is considered. So anxious were the Yorkshire Gentlemen to give the Lancashire a thorough beating, and so bashful were they of their own abilities to assist in that object, that the Yorkshire train arrived in Manchester [without one gentleman in it!]. [23]

Although there were few opportunities for Yorkshire county cricket to develop further during the 1850s, circumstances changed significantly at the start of the next decade. The 1860s saw the circuit of regular county cricket that had previously revolved mainly around Sussex, Surrey and Kent first become established away from the southeast of England. Frequent competition with other counties brought the first successes by Yorkshire against leading teams from the southern counties and they were received with great enthusiasm. Local and regional prides were again intertwined in 1861 when the *Bradford Observer* described how Yorkshire beat Surrey for the first time. With just five runs needed and two wickets to fall, it was explained how,

> Our townsman, Hodgson, next stepped forth to the rescue and from the second ball he received made a splendid cut for three. This put the Yorkshire men in ecstasies... and after a few more balls had been given, Hodgson had the honour of contributing the run which was required to secure the victory for his county. [24]

Indeed, when Surrey was defeated again in the following year, the *Bradford Observer* turned to a more distinctive representation of regional identity and celebrated the victory by using local dialect to mock the southern side. Surrey had defeated Yorkshire earlier in the season and the opportunity to gain revenge had been so eagerly anticipated that, after the home side's victory, the report contended,

> It no longer 'remains to be seen what Yorkshire will do when Surrey cooms doon yam to them at the return match'. Surrey has now been 'doon yam' for the purpose, and has been sent home again, divested of that laurel wreath which was placed on her brow at the Oval on the 28th of May. [25]

Yorkshire identity and the genesis of county cricket

Clearly Yorkshire teams were coming to be looked upon as an important representation of regional identity well before the formalised county club was established in 1863. But more importantly, the distinctive concept of county cricket that began to develop was built around the cultural dynamics that had shaped cricket in the region over the previous sixty years. Middle- and upper-class involvement undoubtedly played an integral role in the formative growth of county cricket in Yorkshire. But the region's social elite never seriously attempted to exert any influence over the way the sport was played at this level or the meanings that it came to represent. Consequently, although club committees took over from the entrepreneur promoters in setting up fixtures, Yorkshire county cricket continued to grow around the structure of major commercial matches that had provided a compelling popular focal point for the sport since the 1820s.

So when significant changes in the context of county cricket began to take place in the 1860s, they had little impact upon the structure of representative cricket in Yorkshire. By the start of that decade the middle-class-led county club was becoming a powerful concept in English cricket. Its increasing influence led to calls for the Yorkshire gentry to follow the lead of their counterparts elsewhere the country and set its role in the sport at elite level on a more formal footing by establishing a county club. In 1861 a London journalist wrote,

> Yorkshire you are wanted that is the leading men and cricketers of Yorkshire are wanted, to bestir themselves, beat up the wealth, rank and influential men of their shire, and establish a County Cricket Club. Good cricket grounds you have already in various parts of the county. Cricketers are ready at hand of that mental and ability that even under the present disorganised – or rather, NO – state of things were found an eleven that could beat Surrey ... It is our opinion that if Yorkshiremen would but establish on a proper basis a county cricket club, they would in a year or two be enabled to bring such an eleven into the field as would make Yorkshire a cricketing county second to none in England, and Yorkshire-trained cricketers as famous as Yorkshire-trained racehorses. [26]

When members of regions social elite acceded to this demand two years later, however, it did little to establish the 'Gentleman Amateur' concept of the county club. Indeed the Sheffield-based organisation did more to revive local rivalries that surrounded the selection of teams claiming to represent the region in the 1850s. Away from Sheffield, the new county club was not viewed as an organisation that represented the whole region and in May 1863 the *Leeds Times* noted its establishment by commenting,

> What is termed a 'Yorkshire Cricket Club' has been formed in Sheffield, but as the officers (President, Secretary, Committee &c) are all Sheffield men, the project is not likely to meet with much encouragement out of that town. [27]

Independent Yorkshire county matches continued to be organised in the fashion of the unofficial professional-centred commercial fixtures of the itinerant elevens. A committee in Bradford also began arranging Yorkshire matches in 1863 whilst another county club was formed in York during the same year and over the following four seasons a pattern of regular fixtures emerged. The Bradford-based organisation arranged home and away matches with Nottinghamshire and Cambridgeshire, whilst the Sheffield-based county club was responsible for fixtures against Surrey and Kent or Lancashire. However, the York club decided to forgo fully representative county fixtures in order to concentrate solely on providing a high level of amateur cricket for the region's social elite.

As this structure suggests, the eventual decline of commercially-centred elite cricket and its replacement by the 'Gentleman Amateur' led first-class game was far from inevitable when these events are viewed in the context of the sport in the 1850s and 1860s. The *Leeds Times* gave the following endorsement of the current system of arranging independent fixtures in its preview of the 1864 season,

> The newly inaugurated county club, stated to have its headquarters in the cathedral city, has issued no programme that we are aware of; but the Sheffield and Bradford committees – who appear to hold aloof, and whose previous excellent arrangements in carrying out the matches which they have negotiated we are bound to speak in terms of commendation – appear as the promoters of two home-and-home contests with celebrated elevens of Surrey and Notts. [28]

Moreover, three years later 'Cover Point' in the *Leeds Intelligencer* could still tell a correspondent,

> I am not aware of any special committee for the arranging of Yorkshire matches. The only county committee that I know, which is not connected with a town club, is the one in Sheffield which is called ' the Sheffield County Club' but it is only for arranging county matches on its own ground. [29]

The organisation of county cricket in Yorkshire during this period continued to revolve around the dynamics of civic status that drove the development of leading venues across the West Riding. Major sporting fixtures had been coveted in the region's growing urban centres since the 1820s and the growth of such events provided new opportunities for ambitious clubs and towns. The changing urban landscape meant that most of the early proprietor-owned commercial venues, such as the Victoria Ground in Leeds and Darnal in Sheffield had disappeared by 1850. But during the second half of the nineteenth century principal clubs in leading towns across the region began to develop their facilities in order to stage major matches. Although Horton Lane in Bradford and Bramall Lane in Sheffield had become the premier venues for cricket in Yorkshire by 1860, a number of clubs in other towns across the region were also able to attract first-class matches over the course of the next decade. Non-county club fixtures continued to take place in Yorkshire until 1874 and in all, 26 were played at venues that included Middlesbrough, Hunslet, Holbeck, Dewsbury, Huddersfield and Scarborough.

Consequently, some southern commentators found difficulty accepting the structure of county matches that continued to prevail in the region. According to Holmes, the secretary of Kent wrote to the Sheffield-based county club in 1864 enquiring 'as to who were the proper parties to get up Yorkshire county matches'. [30] The situation had changed little two years later and the 1866 *Cricketer's Companion* commented that

> at present it is difficult to define which is the County Club, as York, Bradford and Sheffield aspire to that honour. That at York is more properly a gentleman's club, and includes most of the amateur talent from the county. At Bradford there is a most energetic committee and a liberal subscription list and for several seasons the matches with Nottinghamshire and Cambridgeshire have been played there. The ground, though good and advantageously situated (in Horton Lane) is too confined for first-class matches; indeed, only square hits can be run out. An enlargement is contemplated, and this done, Bradford will enjoy, as it deserves, a fair share of county cricket. Bramall Lane is a splendid area, with ample accommodation of every kind. Except Nottingham, there is no town in England where the spectators are so numerous, or enter so thoroughly into the spirit of the game. [31]

Most importantly, however, unlike its counterparts elsewhere in the country, the formation of the gentleman amateur-led county club had no real effect upon the character of the Yorkshire team and the meanings it had come to represent. Although county matches were still arranged by separate organisations during this period the concept of a single predominantly professional Yorkshire team representing the region continued to gain strength. With the exception of occasional appearances by outstanding amateurs such as Brian Wilkes Waud who played six matches in 1863 and 1864, the sides for all Yorkshire fixtures were still assembled from a select group of professional players. The mainstays of the team throughout the 1860s were Roger Iddison, who played in 37 of the 43 matches that took place between 1863 and 1870, Joe Rowbotham, who played in 36 matches, Edwin Stephenson 34 and John Thewlis 30. Other regulars in all Yorkshire matches during the early years of the county club's existence include John Berry, George Anderson, George Atkinson and Issac Hodgson. They played in 19, 15, 15 and 21 of the 24 matches that took place between 1863 and 1867 respectively, whilst of the 19 fixtures which were played from 1867 to 1870, George Freeman played in 19, Tom Emmett 18, E.B. Rawlinson 14, and Luke Greenwood 13.

The team's successes also continued to be coveted in the same belligerent manner by the region's press. When Yorkshire beat Nottinghamshire in a match that was arranged by the Bradford committee which took place at Horton Road in June 1863, the *Leeds Times* explained that:

> some few years ago a leading member of the Surrey eleven observed, if we remember rightly, that Yorkshire, as a county, was weak at cricket. Now, although our team has not the advantage of practising together, we think their recent performances entitle them to the distinction of being called the champion eleven. [32]

Professional-centred commercial cricket clearly retained its predominant position in the region during the 1860s and this was most effectively demonstrated by one of the sport's definitive events of that decade, a temporary withdrawal of labour by five leading Yorkshire players. It followed a number of incidents which saw the relationship between northern- and southern-based professionals break down, before leading members of the 'All England' and 'United All England' elevens from the south established a third itinerant team. Away from county cricket, this period arguably marked the high point of the professional players' ascendancy in cricket. The itinerant elevens had cemented their position at the head of the sport and continued to tour the country playing a full programme of fixtures against local eighteens and twenties. Indeed, similarly professional-led international tours had also taken place in North America and Australia. Consequently, the northern professionals viewed the formation of the new organisation, the 'United South of England Eleven', as a direct threat to their livelihood. So, Roger Iddison, George Atkinson, George Anderson, Edwin Stephenson and Joe Rowbotham refused to take part in the county club's fixtures against the Surrey eleven, which included a number of the players who had led the breakaway.

In response to the boycott, the county club committee attempted to exert its authority and decreed that 'every professional player is bound to play for his county when called upon to do so'. [33] But, as Holmes later recounted, the players refused to back down and the committee

> finding that every effort they made to effect any arrangement totally failed, became convinced that they must either bow to the will of the players, or play the matches with such talent as they could bring together at the risk of almost certain failure and pecuniary loss. They accepted the latter. [34]

The dispute brought the county club committee into direct conflict with the meanings that Yorkshire county cricket had come to represent. By proceeding to play fixtures with a drastically under strength team the county club was viewed to have compromised the standing of Yorkshire cricket, and widespread popular support across the county lay firmly behind the players. Consequently, when Surrey visited Bramall Lane in June the *Bradford Observer* noted that the 'match excited little or no interest throughout the county, as it was pretty well known beforehand that neither Anderson, Atkinson, Iddison, Rowbotham nor Stephenson would take part in it'. [35] The region's press was equally critical of the decision to put the reputation of the county at stake in such circumstances and when the return match with Surrey took place at The Oval in August the *Leeds Times* exclaimed,

> We designate the contest a farce because, in the first place, the Yorkshire team consisted of only 10 men – Luke Greenwood being 'absent', and in the second place, because it is simply absurd to speak of a 'Yorkshire eleven' in which neither Anderson, Atkinson, Iddison, E. Stephenson, nor Rowbotham, is included. [36]

This lack of support for the county club's ideological stance also had serious economic consequences. In July the 'All England Eleven', which was now led by George Parr, agreed to go ahead with a match against the Sheffield-based Yorkshire side at Bramall Lane without any of the five Yorkshire players who were in dispute with the county. A fee of £65 was guaranteed for Parr's men. But, without these leading local players, the fixture once again failed to capture any significant popular interest and poor attendances led to a deficit of £75, as Yorkshire lost the match by an innings and 255 runs. [37] Facing financial disaster, the county club then decided to suspend its matches for the 1866 season. So the organisation of Yorkshire county cricket was left in the hands of the Bradford club, which continued to select the five dissident players in its regular programme of fixtures throughout the dispute.

The gentleman amateur-led county club clearly had little control over county cricket in the region or the professionals who represented Yorkshire during the 1860s and this was demonstrated further in its attempts to resolve the issue. With county club's future in serious doubt, at the start of 1867 it was decided that the

> choice of players in the coming season be left in the hands of the committee, and they are empowered (if they think well) to play those cricketers who refused to play in the past season, on their expressing regret for what has occurred. [38]

Iddison and Rowbotham were prepared to make the much-compromised concession. The other three players, however, still refused to take the field against Surrey, and Atkinson and Stephenson did not play for the county club again until 1868, whilst none of Anderson's remaining four appearances in first-class cricket were for the Sheffield-based organisation. The stance of these players was also supported by the Cambridge professionals who refused to take part in any fixture staged by an organisation that had dealings with Surrey and their match with the Yorkshire county club was cancelled.

But, as we have seen, there were other clubs eager to stage prestigious major matches during this period and the 1867 fixture between Yorkshire and Cambridgeshire was still able to take place. The rearranged match was the inaugural first-class fixture at the recently developed Savile ground and represented a major success for the club. A report in the *Leeds Times* explained,

> Probably never before has such an interesting match been played in the county as that which began at Dewsbury on Thursday between the two county elevens of Yorkshire and Cambridgeshire. It has been the principal match in the lengthy calendar of the Savile club and right earnestly have its members busied themselves to ensure its successful issue. Their efforts have not been in vain. [39]

The Saville Ground subsequently became a regular venue for first-class cricket and continued to stage Yorkshire County matches until 1933.

Despite the dispute, the 1867 season provided a ringing endorsement of the values that still dominated the organisation of county cricket in Yorkshire cricket during this period. It was the county side's most successful to date. All of the seven matches which were arranged by the various enterprises that were responsible for staging fixtures that year ended in victory and the Yorkshire team was crowned unofficial county champions by the press. [40] So in June, after gaining a second success that month over Surrey, the *Bradford Observer* could boast

> Time was, in the recollection of children not yet breached, when the Surrey eleven was thought by many, and certainly thought themselves, to be perfectly invincible. The difficulty now appears to be to find a county eleven not able to whip them into fits. [41]

Conclusion

The 1870s, however, saw the predominance of professional players in elite cricket decline rapidly as the first-class game was placed firmly under the control of 'Gentleman Amateur'-led county clubs. The growing popularity of county cricket during this period enabled these organisations to underscore their ascendancy by establishing a set of qualification regulations in 1873 that compromised the economic and social position of professional players for most of the next 100 years. These events finally enabled the Sheffield-based Yorkshire club to assume full control of county cricket in Yorkshire.

But as we have seen, many of the definitive meanings that had come to dominate the sport within the region continued to find expression through Yorkshire county cricket. Despite the new formation of the first-lass game, matches in the region retained their semi-commercial character and the venues that hosted Yorkshire fixtures remained as a source of great pride for the towns in which they had been developed. The county team also continued to be assembled primarily from Yorkshire-based professionals upon whom a compelling combination of local and regional pride was invested by the sport's considerable popular following throughout the region.

The popular concept of the Yorkshire team representing the county in the national context of the sport still provided the foundations upon which the distinctive model of regional identity that was built around Yorkshire county cricket came to find expression. Indeed in the light of these observations it is necessary to question Dave Russell's assertion, in an otherwise exceptionally perceptive analysis, that

> Yorkshire county cricket perhaps had the most intense meanings for the class that watched it the most and got the closest to its centre of power: the middle and upper-middle-classes. [42]

It was clearly the way in which the Yorkshire team 'engaged the attention and affection of a wide section of the county's population' that describes most closely the distinctive relationship that county cricket developed with the region. [43]

Consequently, towards the end of the nineteenth-century, employees in the Sheffield metalworking industries could still express their distinctive cultural identity during Yorkshire matches in the same way the cutlers had done when the Darnal ground first opened in the 1820s. As part of the formalised County Championship, these fixtures were now commonly held on weekdays which, due to the new rationalised working week, prevented regular popular attendance. They were also staged at the town's modern multi-sports stadium. But the survival of St Monday in Sheffield meant that the first day of the match between Yorkshire and Lancashire in 1898 attracted a crowd of around 30,000 spectators. The *Manchester Times* sent a reporter to Bramall Lane to record his observations of the event and he produced the following enthralling description of the crowd that attended the match on that day,

> Monday was 'grinders' day. They turned up together to cheer Lord Hawke and his colleagues with utter recklessness of appearance. Judging whole groups of them by their attire, they had very few of this world's possessions. Without being in rags, they were distinctly shabby. But they were very jovial and very good-humoured. Crushing they did not mind a bit. Elbowing one another seemed to be a favourite pastime. An occasional sparring match, without serious intent, they regarded as a pleasure and a lucid interval. There was very little horse-play, however. For the most part they were content to watch the game and relieve their minds with caustic comments on the performances of the players. [44]

But perhaps more importantly the report also provides an illuminating picture of the great sense of regional pride and identity that was invested in the Yorkshire professionals, and the team that they formed, by its popular following.

> On the first day's play things were going very well with Yorkshire. Brown, the famous Brown from Driffield, 't'mon who beat Orstralia three year ago, and wold ha' done it again if they'd taken him, was playing a great innings for his side. Briggs and Cuttell were using all their arts to puzzle him, and hardly one of their devices passed unrecognised. I cannot reproduce the remarks verbatim. The sentences would have to be mainly made up of dashes if I did. The effect of the comment was that Cuttell should have been playing for Yorkshire, as he was a 'reight good mon,' who learned his cricket in Sheffield.

A burning shame

'Most of the good'uns they have are Yorkshire,' said one perspiring old gentleman, who had all the appearance of a beerhouse keeper, and was regarded as an oracle. Bowdlerised his remarks were something like this; Call this Lancashire. It's a burning (only the word was not burning) shame. I'm told they have spies picking 'em up from everywhere. There's not only Cuttell, but there's Ward and Baker, both born in Yorkshire.

Their captain's not Lancashire, nor Mold, nor Briggs in fact, there's hardly a Lancashire man among them. [45]

Notes

[1] R.S. Holmes, *The history of Yorkshire county cricket 1833–1903*, (London, 1904), p. 1.
[2] Dave Russell, 'Sport and identity: The case of Yorkshire county cricket club, 1890–1939', *Twentieth Century British History*, 7 (2) (1996), pp. 206–30.
[3] John Woodcock, ed., *Wisden cricketers almanack 1981* (London, 1981), p. 291.
[4] A.W. Pullin ('Old Ebor'), *History of Yorkshire county cricket 1903–1923* (Leeds, 1924), p. 11.
[5] *York Courant*, 21 Aug. 1833.
[6] *Bells Life*, 29 June 1828.
[7] *Bells Life*, 27 July 1834.
[8] *Sheffield Independent*, 2 and 9 Sept. 1826.
[9] *Sheffield Independent*, 7 Sept. 1833.
[10] *Sheffield Independent*, 30 May 1829.
[11] Russell, 'Sport and identity', p. 214.
[12] *Leeds Mercury*, 14 July 1849.
[13] Russell, 'Sport and identity', p. 216.
[14] *Bell's Life*, 31 Aug. 1851
[15] Russell, 'Sport and identity', pp. 215–17
[16] *Leeds Times*, 2, 9 Aug. 1851.
[17] Russell, 'Sport and identity', p. 215.
[18] *Leeds Times*, 2 Aug. 1851.
[19] *Leeds Times*, 17 May 1851.
[20] *Leeds Times*, 26 July 1851.
[21] Russell, 'Sport and identity', pp. 207–8.
[22] *Leeds Times*, 9 Aug. 1851.
[23] *Bell's Life*, 7 Sept. 1851.
[24] *Bradford Observer*, 1 Aug. 1861.
[25] *Bradford Observer*, 10 July 1862.
[26] Holmes, *Yorkshire county cricket*, p. 40.
[27] *Leeds Times*, 2 May 1863.
[28] *Leeds Times*, 14 May 1864.
[29] *Leeds Intelligencer*, 21 Aug. 1867.
[30] Holmes, *Yorkshire county cricket*, p. 42.
[31] Holmes, *Yorkshire county cricket*, p. 43.
[32] *Leeds Times*, 27 June 1863.
[33] Holmes, *Yorkshire county cricket*, p. 44.
[34] Holmes, ibid.
[35] *Bradford Observer*, 22 June 1865.
[36] *Leeds Times*, 19 Aug. 1865.
[37] Holmes, *Yorkshire county cricket*, p. 44.
[38] Holmes, ibid.
[39] *Leeds Times*, 17 June 1867.

[40] See Woodcock, *Wisden cricketers almanack 1981*, p. 294.
[41] *Bradford Observer*, 13 June 1867.
[42] Russell, 'Sport and identity', p. 229.
[43] Russell, 'Sport and identity', p. 213.
[44] *Manchester Times*, 15 July 1898.
[45] Ibid.

Egg and Chips with the Connellys: Remembering 1966

Dilwyn Porter

More than 40 years have passed since England beat West Germany to win FIFA's World Cup in 1966 yet this singular historical event remains with us, securely embedded in English popular culture and revisited by the media whenever occasion justifies. References to it are so frequent and so ubiquitous that they have become banal yet powerful signifiers of English national identity. It is argued here that the folk memory of 1966 is also shaped by the way in which the story of England's triumph dovetails with other narratives through which the English try to make sense of the world they live in and the history they have lived through.

Tony Benn, recently appointed Minister of Technology in Harold Wilson's second government, spent the weekend of 29–31 July 1966 with his family at their country home. 'All day doing nothing on Saturday', he noted in his diary. At some point he moved an old pillar box, a gift from the Post Office, into his garden; he was 'very proud of it'. [1] Not for the first or last time, Benn was out of step with the majority of his countrymen. 'Almost anyone over age 50', as Tony Mason has observed of the English, 'can tell you where they were on July 30, 1966'. [2] This was the day of England's exciting and controversial 4–2 victory over West Germany at Wembley Stadium, the only time that the nation that claims to have given football to the rest of the world has won FIFA's World Cup. If you were English, as James Walvin has noted, the 1966 final was 'impossible to forget, not least because the media recycled the whole affair whenever it seemed appropriate – that is, as often as possible'. [3]

Dilwyn Porter, De Montfort University.

For the 11 England players who wore their country's colours on what Sir Bobby Charlton has called 'the diamond of my days' the experience was both unforgettable and life-changing. 'Well what about that, kiddo?', his brother Jack exclaimed as they took their lap of honour. 'Our lives will never be the same, I don't suppose', Bobby replied, perhaps a little nervously, and he was right. [4] Years later Nobby Stiles, who had celebrated victory with an impromptu jig, was advised that he was assured of success as an 'after-dinner' speaker on account of 'memories of the greatest day in English sport, a day on which I had danced my way into the ken of a large part of the nation'. [5] For those who had the good fortune to be among the 93,000 spectators there was a sense of being present while history was being made. Football journalist Arthur Hopcraft, in the stands for once rather than in his customary seat in the press box, 'gulped and shouted like everyone else, and congratulated myself on being English with all the acclamation at my command'. [6]

What most English people alive in 1966 would actually remember, however, was a match that they watched on television. It was television, as Mason notes, 'and especially coverage by the BBC that made the 1966 World Cup the sizable shared national experience that it became'. [7] The total audience of 30.5 million exceeded by five million the number of viewers who had watched coverage of Sir Winston Churchill's state funeral two years earlier. A further two million listened to the match commentary on radio. 'Well over half the population of the UK aged five and over', it was reported at the time, 'watched the World Cup Final on television last Saturday'. [8] Perhaps this is why recollections of the final so often convey a sense of participating in an extraordinary event that occurred within the everyday context of family and home. 'I threw myself behind Dad's back on the old blue sofa in the living room, peeping out a few seconds later, just in time to be inconsolable when Weber scored Germany's equaliser', is how David Winner remembers the goal that sent the match into extra time. [9]

It is important to remember how most people experienced England's World Cup triumph because television coverage shaped – and continues to shape – their memories of the occasion. The words with which BBC match commentator Kenneth Wolstenholme greeted England's fourth goal, scored in the last minute of extra time – 'Some people are on the pitch. They think it's all over ... it is now!' – have resonated powerfully over the years. By 1970, according to Richard Weight, they had become 'a patriotic mantra for all seasons, as well known as Churchill's most famous speeches'. [10] That an overwhelming majority of viewers (26 million) tuned into the BBC for the live match coverage was no doubt an important factor here. That it was 'a line any commentator would die for', as Brian Moore was to observe, was also critical. [11] When Lee Honeyball chose his 10 'greatest bits of commentary ever' for the *Observer* in 2002, he omitted this 'bit' from his list, justifying his decision by arguing that it had become 'a tired cliché'. [12] The point about clichés, however, is that people rarely tire of using them. It was through hearing Wolstenholme's words repeated time and again that the British public were to become so familiar with them in the years that followed.

The British media has been largely responsible for this phenomenon. Wolstenholme's commentary has proved a reliable standby for headline writers. 'They thought it was all Rovers . . .' (on Doncaster Rovers versus Arsenal); 'They think it's all over . . . of course it isn't' (on England's prospects without Wayne Rooney); and 'They think it's all over. I wish it was' (a female columnist in the *Times* complaining about the media's obsession with the 2006 World Cup) are indicative. Its use, moreover, was not confined to the sports pages. The *Sun*, in 2006, greeted the news of Saddam Hussein's impending execution with a front-page story headed grotesquely, 'They think it's all OGRE! Saddam to hang in hours'. [13] It had by then been adopted as the title of a BBC television sports quiz – a repository of over-the-top laddishness – which enjoyed a successful run from 1995 to 2006. *They Think It's All Over*, had suggested itself to Des Lynam, who hosted an earlier radio version of the show, because the phrase 'was already in the public's consciousness'. [14]

Lynam's judgement was sound. Wherever one looked Wolstenholme's words – and the reminder of 1966 that went with them – were easy to come by and difficult to avoid. They often surfaced in the most unlikely places. Eric Hall, more concerned about the date he had arranged than with the outcome of the match, was waiting in Debden for a 20A bus only to find that its departure was delayed because driver and conductor were following the match on a television in a nearby shop window. 'They think it's all over! ', recalled the show business and football agent with some feeling in his memoirs. 'It was certainly all over for me with that young lady because I was too late for the date and she hadn't waited'. [15] In 2005, the Vicar of Elstow, Bedfordshire, opened a letter to parishioners with a reference to 1966 and the words 'They think it's all over', before observing that the disciples, when they saw Jesus nailed to the cross, 'thought that it was all over too'. [16] It was possible before the 2006 World Cup to buy a set of cufflinks engraved with the shorter version of Wolstenholme's benediction on England's achievement, those 'eight little words that have entered the national consciousness'. [17]

What this suggests is that the collective memory of the English is constantly being jogged by reminders of 1966. A personal appearance in

2005 by Sir Geoff Hurst, scorer of three goals in the final, prompted the headline 'Girls get on the ball with 1966 legend', along with an invitation to 'tell us your 1966 World Cup memories'. [18] Like the poor, 1966 is always with us. 'I was only three years old when England won the World Cup', Simon Hattenstone has recently observed, 'but I grew up with their victory. It seemed to be part of the national curriculum'. [19] The failure of the national side since 1966 to match the achievement of Sir Alf Ramsey's team has helped to preserve its iconic cultural status. It has become something of a national obsession that can mystify even the English, so powerfully entrenched that it invites and defies parody simultaneously. 'This was the last time in history when every player in the England team was called Bobby', explained Craig Brown in *1966 and All That* (2005). 'Their average age was 53'. [20] *They Think It's All Shite*, an 'alternative guide' to the World Cup, published a year later, was rather less gentle. Referring to England's disputed third goal it concludes: 'the historic victory was, to say the least, dubious. On the other hand, it was against the Germans, so who cares?' [21]

Banal nationalism?

Since the mid-1990s *Three Lions*, the football song composed by Ian Broudie of the Lightning Seeds, with words by David Baddiel and Frank Skinner, has supplied the most significant popular invocation of 1966. First issued in 1996 to coincide with the finals of the European nations championship (Euro 96), which were staged in England, it quickly reached number one in the UK pop charts, remaining there for several weeks, and was adopted by England supporters as their unofficial anthem. It enjoyed comparable success in 1998, when it was re-issued to coincide with England's appearance in the final stages of the World Cup in France, and new versions were recorded and released in both 2002 and 2006. Introduced by a sample of Wolstenholme's commentary and underscored throughout by the hypnotic mantra – 'It's coming home, it's coming home, it's coming, football's coming home' – the song uses the folk memory of 1966 to cast aside the demons of doubt and uncertainty arising from the 'thirty years of hurt' that followed.

> Everyone seems to know the score
> They've seen it all before
> They just know
> They're so sure
> That England's gonna throw it away
> Gonna blow it away

But I know they can play
'Cause I remember . . .
Three lions on a shirt
Jules Rimet still gleaming
30 years of hurt
Never stopped me dreaming. [22]

The success of *Three Lions*, it has been noted, owes much to nostalgia for 1966 and 'a lost era of football triumph and national self-certainty'. [23] Christopher Young, however, has recently suggested a more complex reading. The song's plaintive tone, he argues, acknowledges past disappointments while simultaneously allowing England supporters to dream once more of success. [24] *Three Lions* thus served a therapeutic purpose. It pulled off the trick of celebrating one of England's remembered glories while hinting subtly that the time had come to put past disappointments in their place, to 'draw a line' (as a therapist might say) and 'move on'.

This suggests that the 1966 phenomenon could be characterised as one of the 'sleeping memories' that comprise the English national *habitus*, a kind of 'second nature' that is activated from time to time. [25] Yet it has to be recognised that this particular memory rarely sleeps for long. World and European championships, any England–Germany match, the untimely deaths of Bobby Moore in 1993 and Alan Ball in 2007 – events of this kind have provided the media with ample opportunities to breathe new life into the old story. In addition, the daily reiteration of well-worn clichés associated with England's moment of World Cup glory ensures that reminders of the event are both ubiquitous and ever-present. Perhaps, the phenomenon might best be understood as an example of what Michael Billig calls 'banal nationalism', a feature of the political landscape in relatively stable western democracies. 'The reproduction of nation-states', he has argued, 'depends upon a dialectic of collective remembering and forgetting, and of imagination and unimaginative repetition'. It is not always necessary to wave the flag aloft to remind people of their national identity because they are made aware of it every day in so many different ways. Nowhere is this process more evident than in media coverage of sport which generates endless points of reference that help to shape the collective consciousness in such a way that the nation's imagined community coheres. [26]

England's World Cup triumph, achieved on home soil in 1966, has an important place in the nation's cultural history but it also belongs to the present. It can, in effect, be 'remembered' by those who were not there when it happened, and even by those who had yet to be born. Wembley

1966 is, in effect, a powerful self-sustaining myth that has been wired into the nation's collective consciousness. As such it demands the serious attention of historians, not least so that past and present might be productively disentangled. There are ways, for example, in which the relatively low-key, low-budget tournament of 1966 was different from the over-hyped, multi-million pound extravaganza that has come to characterise the World Cup in recent years. It is thus important to grasp that it was, as Tony Mason has argued, 'a traditional as much as a modern sporting event'. [27] Too often in the past it has been referred to only in passing, as part of the backdrop to events that were considered the conventional province of the historian. 'At a time when Britain seemed at its most "swinging", joyously celebrating England's victory in the World Cup final at Wembley', noted Kenneth Morgan in 1997 with an old-fashioned sense of priorities, 'its Labour government appeared beleaguered even with years in office still to run'. [28] More recently, as historians have warmed to the task of writing what might be called the cultural history of British politics, analysing the significance of the 1966 final has seemed more important.

For Richard Weight, England's victory 'showed the extent to which cultural achievements had come to act as a compensation for Britain's political decline since the war'; it also 'speeded up the process by which football became the focus of national identity'. [29] Dominic Sandbrook's *White Heat* has located English football's 'finest hour' within a cool reassessment of 'the sixties'. It did not represent, it seems, 'the dawn of a new era'; it was merely 'the last day of a long, lazy summer about to be swept away by the winds of autumn'. [30] This trend also reflects a growing interest in the phenomenon of Englishness. Introducing his volume in the *Oxford History of England* series, first published in 1965, A.J.P. Taylor observed that, twenty or thirty years previously, the word 'England' had been 'all-embracing'. It had been used indiscriminately when referring to England and Wales, the United Kingdom, even the British Empire. To use it in this fashion in the 1960s 'was likely to prompt protests, "especially from the Scotch"' [sic], but he continued undeterred. [31] The recognition that 'England' and 'Englishness' – not to mention 'Britain' and 'Britishness' – are no longer applicable in a generalised way to Scotland and Wales is one of the factors that historians now have to take into account. Both Weight and Sandbrook note that English fans in the stadium and elsewhere waved Union Jacks; the cross of St George had yet to be adopted. 'The English team', claims Sandbrook, 'was automatically equated with Britain as a whole even though many Welsh, Scottish and Irish observers had been praying for anything but an English victory'. [32] The World Cup final of 1966 now seems a useful starting point from which to explore the relationship between England and its Celtic neighbours in the second half of the twentieth century.

The intention from here on is to explore the ways in which memories of this momentous event have been constructed and to identify some of the processes through which they are assimilated into England's popular culture. It will be argued that the durability of the 1966 phenomenon and its capacity to validate national identity, albeit in a banal fashion, owes much to its versatility and its capacity for dovetailing with other familiar narratives. These, it is suggested, might be categorised as either personal or political, reflecting a commonsense distinction between what people regard as their private lives and a public domain in which themes such as national decline, Anglo–German relations and the unravelling union between England and Scotland are discussed. [33] This is not to say, of course, that such categories are watertight or that the personal and the political are unconnected. Indeed, as will become apparent, one of the reasons that 1966 is remembered so vividly and so often is that it provides ways of connecting them.

Personal myths: Humble heroes and pampered superstars

It is important to recognise the way in which the events of 30 July 1966 have been internalised and integrated with the stories that people tell about themselves, their families and their friends. Those who feel that they have experienced 'history in the making' are apt to recall where they were when they heard that war had been declared or that Kennedy had been assassinated. For many English people the World Cup final of 1966 prompts a similar kind of response: 'My wife and I were at Fontainblue while England's team were winning the World Cup; and at the *Folies Bergere* in the evening – a cheerful and memorable occasion indeed!' Or more typically: 'We watched the final on my parents' TV in their home, Wardo Avenue, Fulham'. [34] The rich description provided by David Thomson in his book *4–2*, published in 1996, suggests a perfect fusion of history (as we all know it) and life history (as only he knows it) as he remembers his response to England's fourth goal.

> I roar in the living-room in Isleworth in front of the black-and-white TV. Mathew [21 months] cannot quite yet know the grace that has touched Geoff Hurst. But I was crying first. His mother comes into the living room and tells me not to scare him so.

Thomson then adds: 'And I have never let him forget that moment and his [Mathew's] less than fully-witting presence'. [35] Hurst's goal was thus assimilated into the Thomson family's history. In 1993 the news that Bobby Moore, captain-hero of 1966, had died caused Jason Cowley to think fondly of his father. 'I'd grown up in a household in which Moore was a revered figure', he explained. 'To my father he was a symbol of a certain kind of English innocence, the ball-player of unusual dignity and grace'. [36]

In 1960's Britain, as Judy Giles has observed, the home and the traditional nuclear family was for most people 'the centre of their lives, the locus for personal intimacy, and the space in which leisure activities took place'. [37] This – along with the fact that most households by then had access to television – helps to explain why so many memories of Wembley 1966 are recognisably homely and familiar. 'For the final', recalls one of the contributors to Norman Shiel's *Voices of 1966*, published in 2000, 'Dad moved all the furniture and placed the television in the centre of the room and we all said what are you doing that for?' 'It's going to be worth watching. I just know it is', was Dad's reply. 'When England scored, the whole of Milton Avenue ran out into the street'. [38]

That the match happened live in people's own homes ensured that it was not an exclusively male experience. 'I have always hated football and everything about it', wrote a Liverpool woman; nevertheless 'we all sat round the television to watch the final and afterwards my brother went out with his girlfriend to celebrate'. [39] Fabio Chisari has argued that one of the most significant features of television coverage of the 1966 tournament, especially the final, was that it attracted female viewers to football in significant numbers for the first time. With few households enjoying the luxury of a second set it was for some, no doubt, an occasion to be endured while others enjoyed it . . . after a fashion. 'My mother and I found the tension of the extra time so unbearable that we had to leave the room', one London woman remembered. [40]

It is when the personal narrative relates to events experienced outside the home that it begins to connect with more general discourses in which the state of the nation, both then and now, features strongly. 'The atmosphere was very good-natured in those days, both at the games and afterwards', characterises many recollections. The idea that there was 'no trouble at all just exuberance' emerges as an important theme. [41] The rosy glow draped over the event in an illustrated history of twentieth-century Britain published by the *Reader's Digest* reinforces this impression. On arriving at Wembley with a friend Jeremy Harwood, a 16-year-old schoolboy in 1996, bought 'two tickets from a friendly tout'. Even members of that much-despised fraternity, it seems, were on their best behaviour. Once inside the stadium he found English and German fans mingling happily. [42] 'Everyone was very friendly with lots of singing and banner waving and passing round of beer', wrote another of Shiel's correspondents, who had attended the match as a 12-year-old. 'You wouldn't get any of that nowadays', he added, 'what with segregation and a ban on alcohol'. [43]

A London woman recalled joining the crowd outside the Royal Garden Hotel where the heroes of the hour were attending a post-match reception and then returning to the *Golden Lion* in Fulham. 'It was all so simple. Every person encountered that evening was happy and well behaved', she remembers. [44] The simplicity invoked here is redolent both of an uncomplicated state of innocence and a benign, well-ordered society in which people knew what was expected of them. It adds an appealing element of nostalgia to the tale as habitually related, not least because it is rooted in the assumption that standards of behaviour have deteriorated in the 30 years or so of 'hurt' that followed and taps into contemporary concerns about hooliganism and football-related disorder. Perhaps life *was* happier in some ways in 1966 but historians have to be careful when confronted by what Alistair Moffat, in his remembrance of childhood, characterises as 'youth as it is too often remembered by the old – impossibly gilded, bent out of shape by the need to console'. [45] Memory, as Giles, reminds us, 'is a process by which people shape the past into a set of meanings that makes sense to them in the present'. [46] It thus forms an intimate connection between the personal and the public spheres.

Having gained one of world sport's major prizes England's footballers of 1966 have more excuse than most to remember their youth as 'impossibly gilded'. In coming to an understanding of 1966 and what it means to English people today, however, the players and how they have chosen to remember the occasion are important, not least because the interviews that they give to journalists and the memoirs (often 'ghosted') that they publish help shape the public memory of an historic event of enduring cultural significance. Sporting autobiographies often disappoint even the keenest of sports fans; it is one of the characteristics of the *genre*. [47] For historians wrestling with the collective consciousness of the nation, however, they have their uses, not least because they tend to tell people what they think is expected of them. 'What emerges in the end', D.J. Taylor has observed, 'is a version of how the subject sees himself, and – even more important – how he wants to be seen'. [48]

What Taylor would call the 'personal myths' generated and authenticated by 'the boys of 66', aside from descriptions of the match and how it was played and their feelings when it was all over, have a modest homespun quality about them. In his autobiography, published in 1996, Jack Charlton, England's central defender, explains that he became detached from the official celebrations in the West End and eventually found himself at a party in Leytonstone where he eventually slept on the settee. The story, which he has often repeated, continues:

> The next morning, we were having breakfast in the garden when this woman pops her head over the wall and says, 'Hello, Jackie'. I couldn't believe it! It was one of our neighbours from Ashington, and she was visiting relatives who just happened to live next door. 'How are you getting on, Jackie?' she asked a little suspiciously.

On returning to the team's hotel he was confronted by his mother who demanded to know where he had spent the night. 'I had to laugh really, because we'd just won a World Cup and my mother's telling me off for going absent without leave!'[49] It is the celebration of ordinariness here – along with working-class neighbourliness – that gives this story meaning. Folk heroes of the 1960s, apart from winning world cups, were expected to rub along with ordinary folk. 'After the celebrations', Alan Ball recalled in 2004,

> . . . Lesley and I drove home with the Connellys in our red Ford Zephyr. We stopped off at the Knutsford services area on the M6 and I smiled to myself as I sat there eating egg and chips with a World Cup winners' medal in my pocket. [50]

Egg and chips seems to have been the preferred food of English heroes in 1966; Jack Charlton ordered the same meal, 'with a nice bread roll', when he stopped off on his way back to Leeds. [51]

Ball's account of his meal at Knutsford services has surfaced dozens of times in various forms. His wife Leslie recalled it slightly differently when she gave her version to Shiels, but also remembered the egg and chips. [52] Not long before he died, Ball was interviewed by Simon Hattenstone of the *Guardian.* He had recently, at the request of his wife, who had died of cancer, sold his World Cup winner's medal in order that his three children might benefit financially: 'she said you can't split that in three and I don't want any favourites'. Ball went on to compare the lifestyle he had enjoyed as a player in the 1960s and 1970s with that of current Premiership stars.

> I tell you what made us what we were. We had this wonderful feeling that we were still part of the people. Every street in England had a footballer living in it. Not any more. They're behind big barbed wire fences, they've got security, they've got blacked out windows, they hire clubs to have a

> night out. They are not part of the people any more. We were ordinary approachable people. You were welcome to walk the streets, you were patted on the back, you were touchable, reachable. [53]

To characterise this heartfelt narrative as an example of personal mythmaking seems unkind but it resonated powerfully. What is interesting is the way in which it struck a chord that chimed in 2006 with the widespread tabloid criticism of 'pampered' footballers and their 'WAGS' (wives and girlfriends), which reached one of its periodic crescendos after England returned from the 2006 World Cup finals empty-handed. It was recycled, almost without amendment, in a tribute written by Leo McKinstry for the *Daily Mail* when Ball died a year later. Elsewhere in the same edition Ball was celebrated as 'the humble hero'. 'He belonged to an era before footballers became vain multi-millionaires with the morals of alleycats'. [54] The *Daily Express* set the same agenda: Ball had been 'loved and revered'. Its third leader asked a question that needed no reply: 'Will any of our present generation of footballing superstars ever be able to claim the same?' A few days later, when Ball's son Jimmy revealed that the sale of his father's medal had left the family with a substantial inheritance tax bill, the story was integrated into a long-running *Express* campaign against 'the hated death tax'. [55] The episode illustrates the facility with which the ever-present memory of 1966 is periodically resurrected as a yardstick and used to measure the present, which is always found wanting. Martin Peters' autobiography, published in 2006, supplies another illustration. He had recently met current Chelsea and England captain, John Terry, in the VIP lounge of a London theatre. 'John was casually dressed in blue jeans, the attire of choice for most professional footballers these days. I was in my usual suit and tie, the customary attire for a footballer on a night out in my time'. Terry came across as 'a really nice boy' but a few days later was at the centre of unwelcome tabloid attention. 'I wouldn't have liked that', Peters observed. 'We weren't all angels in the sixties and seventies but, in general terms, professional footballers were more aware of their responsibilities and took greater care of their reputations'. [56]

Public discourses: English football and British history

A few months before the 1966 Wold Cup tournament *Time Magazine* had attached the 'swinging' label to London. Tina Moore, Bobby's first wife, as she recollects 1966, suggests that 'the boys' were very much 'part of the fabric of the sixties: . . . student protests, flower power, the Beatles and the

Stones, white boots and mini-skirts, Biba and Mary Quant'. [57] It is important, however, to recognise some boundaries. The sixties may have swung in London's West End but across the river in Lambeth, they did not swing at all, as John Major has observed. Neither, it might be added, were they much in evidence in Hornchurch where hat-trick hero Geoff Hurst, returned to family life after the Saturday night celebrations. He remembers cleaning the car and mowing the lawn. 'It was pretty much like any other Sunday afternoon'. [58] For many people, Sandbrook claims, Wembley 1966 seemed 'the perfect ending to a hot, contented summer, stamped with the cultural self-confidence of Swinging London'; but there was no organic connection between them. [59] It seems significant that so many descriptions of the post-match euphoria alluded to VE night, marking the end of the war in Europe in 1945, though, as was noted at the time, given that England had beaten Germany, 'this was not the most tactful analogy'. [60] However, it does suggest that there may be a more important connection to pursue here than with the gadfly 1960s where a much-vaunted cultural revolution came unstuck in mid groove. References to VE night in the context of 1966 imply that many English people were more comfortable when they were allowed to walk backwards into the future. One of the reasons that the 1966 phenomenon endures is that it was assimilated from the start into public discourses of long standing through which the British – and the English in particular – had come to understand the country they lived in and the times they were living through.

One of the contributors to *Voices of 1966* remembered 'standing next to two drunken Liverpool fans . . . who gave the Nazi salute during the German national anthem'. At the time, he admits, 'it seemed amusing'; 'now I would be embarrassed'. Another recalled England fans singing 'We won the war'. [61] Though such incidents, if the reports are reliable, appear to have been few and far between on 30 July 1966 it is possible that the excesses of English tabloid coverage of the Anglo–German football relationship at the end of the century and, in particular, the *Daily Mirror's* notorious 'Achtung! Surrender' campaign at the time of Euro 96 – have desensitised historians to the impact of less blatant transgressions in 1966. 'The newspapers', Young has noted, 'although letting through the odd war reference remained largely free of militaristic rhetoric'. [62] It appears that Germans were generally made welcome in 1966; the local newspaper in Derbyshire, where the squad stayed during the group stage, bade them farewell with the headline 'Ashbourne has taken German team to its heart'. [63] Yet, as John Ramsden has indicated, 'the odd war reference' found its intended target and was much resented. The *Daily Mail* was one of several papers to beat the drum: 'If Germany beat us at Wembley this afternoon at our national sport, we can always point out to them that we have beaten them twice at theirs'. This led Werner Schneider, West Germany's leading football commentator, to criticise Fleet Street's 'tin soldiers' and to complain that in England 'winning at football is treated like victory in a battle'. [64]

No doubt, much was left unspoken in 1966. Martin Peters, whose wife's family had suffered grievous losses when east London was blitzed during the war, remembers that he was aware of 'an added responsibility'. 'References to the war might have been considered tasteless in some quarters', he has observed, 'but the fact is they were inevitable in some homes'. His West Ham colleague, Geoff Hurst, also remembered 'a residue of lingering bitterness towards the Germans'. [65] Perhaps it was especially intense in east London, where Peters had grown up and he and Hurst both earned their living. It could not be denied in 1966 that football was embedded in a longer and more troubled course of Anglo–German relations stretching back to 1939–1945 and 1914–1918 and that it remains so. When England and Germany met at the semi-final stage of the 1990 World Cup the *Sun's* headline was able to make what to its readers was probably an obvious connection': 'We beat them in '45, we beat them in '66, now the battle of '90'. [66] Football, it seemed, was war by other means. 'I enjoy watching football', observed a Leicester housewife just before the 2006 World Cup finals, 'but I do think that with games involving Germany and England people like to gloat about the war'. [67]

One England supporter remembered leaving the stadium in the company of German fans and admiring 'their up-to-date buses with compartments at the side for luggage as opposed to the sort we had with the big boot at the back'. [68] By the mid-1960s, the British in general were becoming acutely aware of the progress made by the West German economy since 1945 and of Britain's relatively disappointing performance. 'Anyone who can rest content with Britain's economic performance in the 1950s', wrote one leading economist in 1961, 'compared with those of other leading industrial nations must have set his sights desperately low in the late 1940s'. [69] By 1966, when their respective teams met at Wembley, West Germany's post-war 'economic miracle' was well established whereas the British were struggling desperately to shore up sterling on the foreign exchange markets, a battle that was finally lost in 1967. Thereafter the British began to envisage their nation-state's decline primarily in terms of its economic performance. One side-effect of this development, as Maguire *et al.* have argued was that the tabloid press, whenever it was necessary to get metaphorically behind 'our boys', tended to focus on historic occasions when Britain had triumphed over Germany at war and on the football field. This was especially evident in the mid-1990s when the so-called 'Beef War' (British exports to European Union countries had been banned on account of the health threat posed by BSE) coincided with Euro 96. With little else to boast about the tabloids turned gratefully to 1966, 'the last time that Britain/England could claim any form of superiority over Germany – on or off the sports field'. [70]

It has been suggested that to live in England during the second half of the twentieth century 'was to take part in a sort of a wake'. [71] It was an era when, despite the comforts of greater personal affluence, the ideology of 'declinism' prevailed. England's 1966 World Cup victory became intrinsically linked to the idea that the country was going to the dogs. 'It was post-1966, too', Jimmy Greaves observed as he reflected nearly 40 years later, 'that we began to see the first trouble on the terraces'. [72] It probably seemed a natural connection to make at the time. 'The game', as Walvin has observed, 'quickly entered popular memory as a peak of England's footballing achievement, and a talisman against which all subsequent English teams have been compared – unfavourably'. [73] Whatever magic Ramsey had worked in 1966 eventually lost its potency as England teams were found wanting, failing even to qualify for the final stages of the World Cup in 1974, 1978 and again in 1994. In these circumstances the prevailing discourse of decline was impossible to avoid. It could be encountered as often on the sports page as anywhere else in a newspaper.

Having raised public expectations – and these remained high until at least 1970 – what Ramsey's teams and those of his successors delivered was something of an anti-climax. '1966 and all that' remained at the heart of much writing about English football but it has increasingly come to be seen as a part of a problem rather than a part of a solution. 'Let me just say', reflected David Thomson in 1996, 'that there are ways in which England's victory in 1966 made later defeats a little more likely'. [74] David Downing, in his popular history of England–Germany matches, published four years later, was prepared to go further. Characterising England's 1966 win as 'the fatal victory', he claimed that 'the real loser in 1966 was English football'. [75] The reassessment continues. Ramsey's management style and tactical thinking, once deemed scientific, is now seen as rooted in a more compromised tradition of English pragmatism. [76]

This tracked much of the literature on British decline that had appeared in the 1980s. Football writers seemed as inclined as economic historians to round up the usual suspects. The deeply conservative culture of the English game and the sclerotic tendencies of its governing institutions paralleled much of the analysis regarding Britain's underperforming economy. Correlli Barnett's explanation for the relative decline of British industry after the Second World War, for example, argued that victory over Germany in 1945 and the methods by which it was achieved were partly responsible for the years of underachievement that followed. 'Behind the deceptive facade of victory and the propaganda about the scale of the national effort, the symptoms of the "British disease" of the 1960s and 1970s were already present'. His *Audit of War*, published in 1986, was followed by *The Lost Victory* in 1995. Barnett's characterisation of 1945 as 'the lost victory' matches Downing's depiction of 1966 as 'the fatal victory'. In both instances victory achieved over Germany is seen as flawed in that it generated unrealistic 'dreams and illusions' which, in turn, helped to make underperformance in international competition more rather than less likely. [77] England, as Baddiel and Skinner put it later, was 'gonna throw it away'.

'Jules Rimet' does not gleam quite so brightly now that modern readings of 'the fatal victory' have brought it into alignment with the story of Britain's relative decline. It is placing 1966 in the unfolding narrative of the 'the break-up of Britain', however, that now preoccupies cultural historians. Since 1997, Scottish devolution, the establishment of a Welsh Assembly and the political arrangements associated with the peace agreement in Northern Ireland marked the start of a new era. The old British state, essentially the institution devised by the English to rule an empire, may be fading away; it is certainly not what it was. Weight has observed: 'With their world mission at an end and their post-imperial economy failing to live up to expectations the English, Scots and Welsh returned to their core nationalities, once more defining themselves against rather than with each other'. [78] It seems likely that England's World Cup victory of 1966 has played its part, especially as a source of media representations that remind Scots of something that separates them from 'the auld enemy' south of the border. It is not unknown for people in Scotland viewing a televised England match to bet on the number of minutes that will pass before a BBC commentator mentions '1966'. They rarely have to wait long. [79] They remember 1966 in a different way to the English. 'As a Scotsman', recalled someone who attended the match at Wembley, 'I had mixed feelings when England won'. For Manchester United and Scotland footballer Denis Law, who chose to play golf rather than watch the final, there was no ambivalence. His reaction to England's victory is on record: 'I thought it was the end of the world'. [80]

The English, it now seems clear, were inclined to overestimate the extent to which their joy was shared by others. Though the Scottish Football Association congratulated its counterpart in England on a great

British achievement, 'most Scots did not see it as such'. [81] Roger Hutchinson's catalogue of complaints, published almost thirty years after the event was probably indicative, though it was something of a rant. 'Bobby Moore's annoyingly hitched-up shorts' apparently suggested insufferable English arrogance. [82] England's controversial third goal – whether or not the ball actually crossed the line remains in doubt – provided an obvious pretext for anyone disposed to deny the legitimacy of England's victory. Geoff Hurst complained that Scotsmen would approach him years after the event to whisper, 'It never went in, wee man'. [83] England, so Scottish friends tell me from time to time, is the only side ever to win the World Cup 2–2. Not only did the third 'goal' not cross the line; the fourth should have been disallowed because spectators were on the pitch. Diego Maradona, in Glasgow in 2008 with the Argentinian national side, endeared himself to his hosts when he brushed off questions from English journalists about his infamous 'hand of God' goal in the 1986 World Cup. 'He asked how the English could keep lecturing him when they celebrated a goal in the 1966 final that was the wrong side of the line'. Meanwhile a group of fans in kilts sang 'You put your left hand in, you put England out', to the tune of the hokey-cokey. [84]

Conclusion

'At the end', one Wembley spectator remembered, 'there was the overwhelming feeling that you had really seen history being made'. He went on to recall 'feeling a supreme pride in being English and all that is best about that'. [85] Such feelings were instantaneously validated by the media. 'What they will tell their grandchildren in the years to come', declared the *Sunday Express* on the day after the final, 'is that it was English nerve and English heart and English stamina which finally overcame the tenacious resistance of the Germans'. [86] The discourse employed to describe the success enjoyed by Ramsey's team was derived from a set of assumptions about what it meant to be English. [87] Victory achieved in what was said to be instantly recognisable as the English national style was thus experienced as a positive affirmation of Englishness. It was later to prove problematic when these 'traditional' strengths failed to achieve success in that each defeat cast not only England but also Englishness in an unfavourable light.

Memory, through which we link the past with the present, is subject to a process of continuous readjustment. As far as the English are concerned this means abandoning some of the illusions that have attached themselves to Wembley 1966 and its place in the nation's collective consciousness. Memories of England's controversial third goal as recalled by those who were on the field at the time are a significant indicator here. Some, like goalkeeper Gordon Banks, remain adamant that the ball crossed the line. 'True', he concedes, 'I was standing at the other end of the pitch', but he had been convinced by Roger Hunt, the nearest English player to the ball as it bounced off the crossbar, who had appealed for a goal. Banks aimed a hefty sideswipe at 'boffins from the Academy of Rear-End Speech' – he had Oxford University in mind here – who had 'wasted countless hours of computer time trying to show that the ball had never crossed the line'. 'What's the point?', he asked, and, more to the point, 'Where's their patriotism?' [88] But most of his team-mates have grown more circumspect over the years. 'At the time', Bobby Moore is reported to have said, 'I had no doubt but on reflection I've got to say that I wouldn't like a goal like that given against England'. [89] This line has recently been endorsed by George Cohen. 'The relatively infant TV technology wasn't really conclusive but when all the emotions had drained away I had to concede that the most beautiful goal I have ever seen was also one of the most dubious'. [90]

In 2000, a National Archives education project aimed at schools even dared to pose the question: 'Did England rig the result?', pointing out that the performance of European referees in matches played by South American teams had been much criticised. It supplied evidence in the form of Foreign Office correspondence that leaves the reader in no doubt as to the ill-feeling that greeted England's victory elsewhere. 'The net result', wrote A.S. Blackwood, Information Officer at the British Embassy in Montevideo, Uruguay, 'has been to raise doubts in the minds of many normally friendly people as to whether the traditional British "fair play" really exists now'. Two weeks after the final, the Foreign Office acknowledged 'that we have had an extremely bad press in some countries over the World Cup, mainly, we believe, in Latin America but also in other parts of the world including Italy'. [91] In addition, sports journalist Ken Jones has recently reminded readers that the behind-the-scenes influence exerted in 1966 by Sir Stanley Rous, English President of FIFA, especially in relation to the appointment of referees and the switching of England's semi-final against Portugal from Liverpool to Wembley, had prompted South American countries 'to mutter darkly . . . although the suggestion that they would withdraw from FIFA to form their own championship was more rumour than threat'. [92] It is as well that these things should be acknowledged.

The English, as they reformulate their national identity in the twenty-first century, will no doubt continue to draw on Wembley 1966 and the positive endorsement of Englishness that it seemed to embody even if the story of England's afternoon in the sun is more complex than it once seemed. It was an occasion that seemed to put the nation in touch with itself and 40 or so years on it retains some of that magical capacity. 'I was not at any of the games', explained one of Shiel's correspondents, 'but my father who died some years ago went to all the England games including the final and I have his ticket stub from that game with me'. He continued: 'One of my last memories of him was sitting together and watching a black and white re-run of the final, with him pointing out where he stood and so on'. [93] You don't need to have lived through it to remember it, but it helps if you are English.

Notes

[1] Tony Benn, *Out of the wilderness: Diaries 1963–67* (London, 1988), pp. 462–3.

[2] Tony Mason, 'England 1966: Traditional and modern?', in Alan Tomlinson and Christopher Young, eds, *National identity and global sports events: Future, politics and spectacle at the Olympics and the football World Cup* (Albany, NY, 2006), p. 94.

[3] James Walvin, *The only game: Football in our times* (London, 2001), pp. 256–7.

[4] Sir Bobby Charlton with James Lawton, *My England years: The autobiography* (London, 2008), pp. 2, 287–8.

[5] Nobby Stiles with James Lawton, *After the ball: My autobiography* (London, 2003), p. 295.

[6] Arthur Hopcraft, *The football man: People and passions in soccer* (London, 2006), p. 222; first published in 1968.

[7] Mason, 'England 1966', p. 84.

[8] For television coverage of the tournament see Fabio Chisari, '"Shouting housewives": The 1966 World Cup and British television', *Sport in History*, 24 (1) (2004), pp. 94–108.

[9] David Winner, *Those feet: A sensual history of English football* (London, 2005), p. 2.

[10] Richard Weight, *Patriots: National identity in Britain, 1940–2000* (London, 2002), p. 461.

[11] Brian Moore, *The final score: An autobiography* (London, 1999), p. 66. See also Simon Briggs, *Don't mention the score: A masochist's history of the England football team* (London, 2008), p. 204.

[12] Lee Honeyball, 'The ten best bits of sports commentary ever', *Observer Sports Magazine*, 6 Oct. 2002, available at http://www.guardian.co.uk/sport/2002/oct/06/sixnations2008.features, accessed 15 June 2009.

[13] *Daily Express*, 22 Dec. 2005; *Leicester Mercury*, 3 May 2006; *Times*, 6 May 2006; *The Sun*, 30 Dec. 2006.

[14] Des Lynam, *I should have been at work! My autobiography* (London, 2005), pp. 162–4. See also Kenneth Wolstenholme, *50 sporting years... and it's still not all over* (London, 1999), pp. 151–3.

[15] Eric Hall, *Monster! True tales from a showbiz life* (London, 1998), pp. 117–18.

[16] *Elstow Parish Magazine*, (Mar. 2005), p. 1, available at http://elstow-abbey.org.uk/magazine, accessed 15 June 2009.

[17] Menkind original gifts and accessories for men; http://menkind.co.uk?Productdetails Hori.asp?ProductID = 10867, accessed 3 May 2005.

[18] *Evening Mail* (Birmingham), 7 Feb. 2005.

[19] Simon Hattenstone, *The best of times. What became of the heroes of 1966?* (London, 2006), p. 4.

[20] Craig Brown, *1966 and all that: A history of modern Britain comprising all the parts you can almost remember* (London, 2005), pp. 95–6.

[21] A. Parody, *They think it's all shite... it is now!* (London, 2006), pp. 20–1.

[22] *Three Lions*, words by David Baddiel and Frank Skinner, music by Ian Broudie. For the lyrics see http://www.risa.co.uk/sla/song.php?songid=20127, accessed 15 June 2009.

[23] Jon Garland and Mike Rowe, 'War minus the shooting? Jingoism, the English press and Euro 96', *Journal of Sport and Social Issues*, 23 (1) (1999), p. 82.

[24] Christopher Young, 'Two world wars and one world cup: Humour, trauma and the asymmetric relationship in Anglo–German football', *Sport in History*, 27 (1) (2007), pp. 14–16.

[25] Joseph Maguire, Emma Poulton and Catherine Possamai, 'Weltkreig III? Media coverage of England versus Germany in Euro 96', *Journal of Sport and Social Issues*, 23 (4) (1999), pp. 439–41.

[26] Michael Billig, *Banal nationalism* (London, 1995), pp. 10, 119–26.

[27] Mason, 'England 1966', p. 95.

[28] Kenneth Morgan, 'The Wilson years: 1964–1970', in Nick Tiratsoo, ed., *From blitz to Blair: A new history of Britain since 1939* (London, 1997), p. 140.

[29] Weight, *Patriots*, pp. 458–64.

[30] Dominic Sandbrook, *White heat: A history of Britain in the swinging sixties* (London, 2007), pp. 305–25.

[31] A.J.P. Taylor, *English history, 1914–1945* (Oxford, 1965), p. v.

[32] Sandbrook, *White heat*, p. 317.

[33] For a succinct account of football's links with these major themes see Matthew Taylor, *The association game: A history of British football* (Harlow, 2008), pp. 284–306.

[34] Norman Shiel, ed., *Voices of 1966: Memories of England's World Cup* (Stroud, 2000), pp. 100, 106.

[35] David Thomson, *4–2* (London, 1996), p. 201.

[36] Jason Cowley, *The last game: Love, death and football* (London, 2009), p. 225.

[37] Judy Giles, *The parlour and the suburb: Domestic identities, class, femininity and modernity* (Oxford, 2004), p. 22.

[38] See Shiel, *Voices of 1966*, pp. 87–8.

[39] Ibid., p. 106.

[40] Chisari, 'Shouting housewives', pp.105–7; Sheil, *Voices of 1966*, pp. 111–12.

[41] Sheil, *Voices of 1966*, pp. 71, 115.

[42] *Reader's digest yesterday's Britain: The illustrated story of how we lived, worked and played* (London, 1998), p. 270.

[43] Shiel, *Voices of 1966*, pp. 116–17.

[44] Ibid., pp. 100–1.

[45] Alistair Moffat, *Homing* (London, 2004), p. 3.

[46] Giles, *Parlour and suburb*, p. 25.

[47] David Foster Wallace's essay explaining how Tracy Austin's autobiography broke his heart brilliantly deconstructs the *genre*. See David Foster Wallace, *Consider the lobster: And other essays* (New York, 2005), pp. 141–55. See also Joyce Woolridge, 'These sporting lives: Football autobiographies 1945–1980', *Sport in History*, 28 (4) (2008), pp. 620–40.

[48] D.J. Taylor, *On the Corinthian spirit: The decline of amateurism in sport* (London, 2006), p. 113.

[49] Jack Charlton with Peter Byrne, *The autobiography* (London, 1997), p. 122.

[50] Alan Ball with James Mossop, *Playing extra time* (London, 2004), p. 204.

[51] Jack Charlton, *Autobiography*, p. 123.

[52] Leslie Ball in Shiels, *Voices of 1966*, p. 25. Alan Ball recalled that they were with Mr and Mrs Connelly; his wife thought they had been with Mr and Mrs Stiles. The evidence is not entirely conclusive but on balance it seems more likely that they were with the Connellys. See Stiles, *After the ball*, pp. 207–8.

[53] See Hattenstone, *The best of times*, pp. 113–20. Gordon Banks has also made this point: 'When I played there was an intimacy between players and fans that is absent today'. Gordon Banks, *Banksy: My autobiography* (London, 2002), p. 231.

[54] *Daily Mail*, 26 Apr. 2007.

[55] *Daily Express*, 4, 9 May 2007.

[56] Martin Peters with Michael Hart, *The ghost of '66: The autobiography* (London, 2006), p. 123.

[57] Tina Moore, *Bobby Moore by the person who knew him best* (London, 2005), p. 4.

[58] John Major, *The autobiography* (London, 1999), p. 41; Geoff Hurst with Michael Hart, *1966 and all that: My autobiography* (London, 2001), p. 13.

[59] Sandbrook, *White heat*, pp. 322–3.

[60] McIlvanney, *McIlvanney on football* (Edinburgh, 1997), p. 175; see also Weight, *Patriots*, p. 461.

[61] Shiel, *Voices of 1966*, pp. 104, 122.

[62] Young, 'Two world wars', pp. 7–9.

[63] Football World Cup 1966 – when the Germans invaded Derbyshire, available at http://bygonederbyshire.co.uk/articles/FOOTBALL_WORLD_CUP_1966, accessed 10 May 2009. I am grateful to James Panter for this reference.

[64] John Ramsden, *Don't mention the war: The British and the Germans since 1890* (London, 2006), pp. 353–4; Weight, *Patriots*, pp. 459–60.

[65] Peters, *Ghost of '66*, p. 100; Hurst, *1966 and all that*, p. 10.

[66] Cited in Maguire *et al.*, 'Weltkreig III?', p. 441.

[67] *Leicester Mercury*, 12 Apr. 2006.

[68] Shiel, *Voices of 1966*, p. 109.

[69] Graham Hutton, 'The UK economy 1951–61: Performance and retrospect', *Lloyds Bank Review*, 61 (1961), p. 1.

[70] Maguire *et al*, 'Weltkreig III?', p. 451. For football and national decline generally see Dilwyn Porter, ' "Your boys took one hell of a beating": English football and British decline *c.*1950–80', in Adrian Smith and Dilwyn Porter, eds. *Sport and national identity in the post-war world* (London, 2004), pp. 31–51.

[71] Jeremy Paxman, *The English: A portrait of a people* (London, 1999), pp. 233–4.

[72] Jimmy Greaves. *The heart of the game* (London, 2005), pp. 256–7.

[73] Walvin, *The only game*, p. 143.
[74] Thomson, *4–2*, p. 221.
[75] David Downing, *The best of enemies: England v Germany, a century of football rivalry* (London, 2000), p. 118.
[76] Jonathan Wilson, *Inverting the pyramid: A history of football tactics* (London, 2008), pp. 142–52.
[77] Correlli Barnett, *The lost victory: British dreams, British realities, 1945–50* (London, 1996), pp. xii–xiv, for a succinct summary of his main arguments.
[78] Weight, *Patriots*, p. 727.
[79] Steve Brocklehurst, 'England's coming home', available at http://news.bbc.co.uk/1/hi/Scotland/2057595.stm, accessed 15 June 2009.
[80] Shiel, *Voices of 1966*, p. 107; Denis Law with Bob Harris, *The king: The autobiography* (London, 2003), pp. 171–2.
[81] Weight, *Patriots*, p. 464.
[82] Roger Hutchinson ... *It is now! The real story of England's 1966 World Cup triumph* (Edinburgh, 1995), p. 207
[83] Hurst, *1966 and all that*, pp. 2–3.
[84] *Times*, 19 Nov. 2008.
[85] Shiel, *Voices of 1966*, p. 84.
[86] *Sunday Express*, 31 July 1966.
[87] See Liz Crolley and David Hand, *Football, Europe and the press* (London, 2002), pp. 19–32.
[88] Banks, *Banksy*, p. 138. For the tests of which Banks was so critical, undertaken at Oxford University in 1995, see Briggs, *Don't mention the score*, pp. 204–6. Computer analysis of available footage had suggested that the whole of the ball did not cross the line.
[89] See Jeff Powell, *Bobby Moore: The life and times of a sporting hero* (London, 1993), pp. 106–7; see also James Corbett, *England expects: A history of the England football team* (London, 2006), p. 231.
[90] George Cohen, *My autobiography* (London, 2005), p. 251.
[91] 'World Cup 1966. Did England rig the result?', available at http:// learningcurve.gov.uk/snapshots/snapshot28/htm, accessed 15 June 2009.
[92] Ken Jones, *Jules Rimet still gleaming? England at the World Cup* (London, 2003), p. 124.
[93] Shiel, *Voices of 1966*, p. 127.

Wray Vamplew: A Bibliography 1969–2008

Richard W. Cox

1969

'The railways and the iron industry: A study of their relationship in Scotland', in M.C. Reed, ed., *Railways in the Victorian economy* (Newton Abbot, 1969), pp. 33–57.

1970

'Railway investment in Scottish highlands', *Transport History*, (1970), pp. 141–53.
'Sources of Scottish railway share capital before 1860', *Scottish Journal of Political Economy*, (1970), pp. 425–40.
'The paraffin factory at Mandal: A study in business enterprise', *Scandinavian Economic History Review*, (1970), pp. 143–58.

1971

'Nihilistic impressions of British railway history', in D.N. McCloskey, ed., *Essays on a mature economy* (London, 1971).
'Railways and the transformation of the Scottish economy', *Economic History*, 24 (1) (1971), pp. 37–54.
'The financing of Scottish railways before 1860: A reply', *Scottish Journal of Political Economy*, (1971), pp. 221–23.
'Banks and railway finance', *Transport History*, (1971), pp. 166–72.

Richard W. Cox.

1972

'Railways and the Scottish transport system in the 19th century', *Journal of Transport History*, 1 (3) (1972), pp. 133–45.
'Scottish railways and the development of Scottish locomotive building in the nineteenth century', *Business History Review*, 46 (3) (1972), pp. 320–38.
'The evolution of international whaling controls', *Maritime History*, 2 (2) (1972), pp. 123–39.

1974

'A careful and most ingenious fabrication of accounts: Scottish Railway Company accounts before 1868', *The Accountants Magazine*, (1974), pp. 307–12.

1975

Salvesen of Leith (Edinburgh, 1975), 311 pp.
'The sport of kings and commoners: The commercialization of horse racing in the nineteenth century', Proceedings of the conference *The Working Class and Leisure – Class Expression and/or Social Control*, University of Sussex, 29 Nov. 1975.

1976

The turf: A social and economic history of horse-racing (London, 1976), 231 pp.

1977

'Years of paradox: Consumption in the 1930s', in I.R.H. Hirst and W.D. Reekie, eds, *The consumer society* (London, 1977).

'The sport of kings and commoners: The commercialization of British horse-racing in the nineteenth century', in R. Cashman and M. Mckernan, eds, *Sport in history: The making of modern sporting history* (St. Lucia, Queensland, 1977), pp. 307–25.

1978

'The north British railway enquiry of 1866', in R.H. Campbell, ed., *Scottish industrial history* (Edinburgh, 1978).
'The nineteenth century gazette *Corn Returns*, a word of warning', *Journal of Historical Geography*, 4 (3) (1978), pp. 291–93.
'The sport of kings and commoners: The commercialisation of British horseracing in the nineteenth century', in Richard Cashman and Ian McKernan, eds, *Sport in History* (Brisbane, 1978).
'Ungentlemanly conduct: The control of soccer-crowd behaviour in England, 1888–1914', in T.C. Smouth, ed., *The search for wealth and stability* (London, 1978).

1979

'The progress of agricultural mechanics: The cost of best practice in the mid-nineteenth century', *Tools and Tillage*, (1979), pp. 204–14.
'The sport of kings and commoners: The commercialization of British horse-racing in the late 19th century', in R. Cashman and M. Mckernan, eds, *Sport in history: The making of modern sporting history* (St Lucia, 1979), pp. 307–25.

1980

'A grain of truth: The nineteenth-century corn averages', *Agricultural History Review*, 28 (1) (1980), pp. 1–17.
The protection of English cereal producers: The Corn Laws reassessed', *Economic History Review*, 33 (3) (1980), pp. 382–95.
'Ungentlemanly conduct: The control of soccer-crowd behaviour in England, 1888–1914' in T.C. Smout, ed., *The search for wealth and stability: Essays in economic and social history presented* to M.W. Flinn (London, 1979), pp. 139–54.
'Sports crowd disorder in Britain, 1870–1914: Causes and controls', *Journal of Sport History*, 7 (1) (1980), pp. 5–20.
'A history of horse racing in south Australia: A statistical approach', *Australian Historical Statistics Bulletin*, 1 (1980), pp. 14–53.
'The influence of economic change on popular sport in Britain, 1600–1900', in R. Crawford, ed., Proceedings of the *1st Australian Symposium on the History and Philosophy of Physical Education and Sport*, Melbourne, 1980, pp. 126–51.

'Counting the bawbees: An economic analysis of Scottish gate money football, 1890–1914', *Flinders Working Paper in Economic History*, 2 (1980).

1981

'Tithes and agriculture, some comments on commutation', *Economic History Review*, 34 (1) (1981), pp. 115–19.
'Australian historical statistics: Policy and progress', *Australian Historical Statistics Bulletin*, 3 (1981), pp. 3–10.
'Playing for pay: The earnings of professional sportsmen in England, 1870–1914', in R. Cashman and M. Mckernan, eds, *Sport: Money, morality and the media* (Kensington, New South Wales, 1981), pp. 104–30.
'Ownership and control in gate money sport: Scottish football before 1915', *Canadian Journal of History of Sport and Physical Education*, 12 (1981), pp. 56–83.
'Sports crowd attendance in south Australia 1919–39: An economic interpretation', *Australian Historical Statistics Bulletin*, 2 (1981), pp. 20–40.

1982

'Profit or utility maximisation?: An analysis of English county cricket before 1914', in W. Vamplew, ed., *The economic history of leisure* (Budapest, 1982), pp. 38–60.
The economic history of leisure (Budapest, 1982), 193 pp.
'The economics of a sports industry: Scottish gate money football, 1890–1914', *Economic History Review*, 35 (1982), pp. 549–67.

1983

'Unsporting behaviour: The control of football and horse-racing crowds in England, 1875–1914', in J.H. Goldstein, ed., *Sports violence* (New York, 1983), pp. 21–31.
'From sport to business: The first seventy-five years of horseracing in south Australia', *Journal of the Historical Society of South Australia*, (1983), pp. 15–33.
'Industrial Revolution or economic evolution? Was there really a 'take-off' in the British economy in the late eighteenth century?' *Tradition*, (1983), pp. 4–7.

1984

'Close of play: Career termination in English professional sport, 1870–1914', *Canadian Journal of History of Sport and Physical Education*, 10 (1984), pp. 64–79.
'Borderline differences? A comparative analysis of shareholders and directors in English and Scottish football before 1914', *Flinders University Occasional Publications in Economic History*, 2 (1984).
'Australian sports review 1983 – A personal view', *Sporting Traditions*, 1, (1983) pp. 56–60.
'Close of play: Career termination in English professional sport, 1870–1914', *Canadian Journal of History of Sport*, 15 (1983), pp. 64–79.
'Sport and recreation', in W. Vamplew, ed., *South Australian historical statistics* (Sydney, 1983), 351 pp.
with W. Hancock and J. Griffiths, eds, *South Australian historical statistics* (Sydney, Kensington, N.S.W., 1983).

1985

The turf: A social and economic history of horse-racing (Tokyo, 1985), 231 pp. (Japanese edition).
'Sport and industrialisation: An economic interpretation of the changes in popular sport in nineteenth century England', *Flinders Paper in Economic History*, 9 (1985).
'Sport and the Industrial Revolution: An economic interpretation of the development of popular sport in nineteenth century Britain', Proceedings of the *XI HISPA Congress*, Glasgow, 1985, pp. 104–6.
'Not playing the game: Unionism in British professional sport, 1870–1914', *British Journal of Sports History*, 2, (1985), pp. 232–47.
'Time to get a Guernsey: Sport in local history', in B. Dickey, ed., *Ideas for local history* (Adelaide, 1985).

1986

with K.A.P. Sandiford, 'The peculiar economics of English cricket before 1914', *British Journal of Sports History*, 3 (1986), pp. 311–26.
'Sport', in R.J. Morris and J. Langton, eds, *Atlas of industrialising Britain, 1780–1914* (London, 1986), pp. 198–201.
Sport and colonialism in nineteenth century Australia (Adelaide, 1986), 80 pp.

'Sport: More than fun and games', in E. Richards, ed., *The Flinders history of south Australia* (Adelaide, 1986), pp. 433–64.
'Malthus and the Corn Laws', in M. Tuner, ed., *Malthus and his time* (London, 1986), pp. 129–42.
'A careful and most ingenious fabrication of imaginary accounts', in T.A. Lee, ed., *Scottish Accounting History* (Edinburgh, 1986), pp. 91–6.
'Match delayed: Business historians and Australian sports history', *Australian Corporate History Bulletin*, (1986), pp. 3–4.
'Sport and the Industrial Revolution', in J.A. Mangan, ed., Proceedings of the *IXth HISPA Congress*, pp. 104–7.

1987

Sport, nationalism and internationalism (Adelaide, 1987), 96 pp.
Australians: Historical statistics (Sydney, 1987), 470 pp.
'Transport and communications', in Wray Vamplew, ed., *Australians: Historical statistics* (Sydney, 1987), pp. 166–82.
'Violence in Australian sport some possible strategies in violence in sport', NPRU Review, 3 (1) (1987), pp. 1–10.
'Transport and travel statistics', in N.G. Butlin, ed., *Clio: A computer based data set of economic time series* (Canberra, 1987).

1988

'Sport and industrialisation: An economic interpretation of the development of popular sport in nineteenth century England', in J.A. Mangan, ed., *Pleasure, profit and proselytism* (London, 1988), pp. 7–20.
Pay up and play the game: Professional sport in Britain, 1875–1914 (Cambridge, 1988), 394 pp.
'Odds against: The punter's lot is not a happy one', *Sporting Traditions*, 5 (1988), pp. 51–60.
'Tales we win: Some recent histories of gambling in Australia', *Sporting Traditions*, (1988), pp. 51–60.
'Violence in Australian sport: Some possible strategies', *National Police Research Unit Review*, (1988), pp. 26–34.

1989

'Horse-racing', in T. Mason, ed., *Sport in Britain: A social history* (Cambridge, 1989), pp. 215–44.

'Australian sports history: A research agenda', *International Journal of the History of Sport*, 6 (1989), pp. 252–55.
A healthy body: The Australian Sports Medicine Federation, 1963–1988 (Canberra, 1989), 98 pp.

1990

with D. Adair, 'Not so far from the madding crowd: Spectator violence in Britain and Australia – A review article', *Sporting Traditions*, 7 (1990), pp. 95–103.
'Who is at fault? Understanding sports violence in Australia', *Sportsnetwork*, 5 (4) (1990), pp. 19–24.
'Salve Christian Fredericke Salvesen', in S.G. Checkland and S.A. Slaven, eds, *Dictionary of Scottish business biography* (Aberdeen, 1990).
'Jubilee International Exhibition Adelaide, 1887–1988', in J.E. Findling, ed., *Historical dictionary of the world's fairs and expositions, 1851-1988* (Westport, Ct., 1990), pp. 98–9.
'Alfred and Louis Von Doussa', in J. Ritchie, ed., *Australian dictionary of biography* (Melbourne, 1990).

1991

Sports violence in Australia: Its extent and control (Canberra, 1991), 79 pp.
A view from the bench: Coaches and sports violence in Australia, a report for the National Sports Research Program (Canberra, April 1991), 6 p; also published in *Sports Coach*, 15 (3) (July/Sept. 1992) pp. 39–43.
with L.D. Parker and R.F. Fleishman, 'New cost counting perspectives on technological change in British Industrial Revolution', in O.F. Graves, ed., *The costing heritage* (1991), pp. 11–24.

1992

with Katherine Moore, John O'Hara, Richard Cashman and Ian Jobling, *The Oxford companion to Australian sport* (Melbourne, 1992), 575 pp.
'Sports medicine', in Wray Vamplew, Katherine Moore, John O'Hara, Richard Cashman and Ian Jobling, eds, *The Oxford companion to Australian sport* (Melbourne, 1992), 575 pp.
'A view from the bench: Coaches and sports violence in Australia', *Sports Coach*, 15 (3) (1992), pp. 39–43.

'Sports crowd disorder: An Australian survey', in J. O'Hara, ed., *Crowd violence at Australian sport* (Campbelltown, NSW, 1992), pp. 79–111.

1993

'Australian sports history: Past, present and future', *Journal of the Historical Society of South Australia,* (1993).
'The making of the *Oxford companion*', *International Journal of the History of Sport,* 10 (1993), pp. 101–3.
with Katherine Moore, John O'Hara, Richard Cashman and Ian Jobling, *The Oxford companion to Australian sport* (Melbourne, 1993, 2nd edition), 575 pp.

1994

with Brian Stoddart, eds, *Sport in Australia: A social history* (Melbourne, 1994), 346 pp.
'The Australian way of sport', in W. Vamplew and B. Stoddart, eds, *Sport in Australia* (Cambridge, 1994), pp. 1–18.
'Boxing', in W. Vamplew and B. Stoddart, eds, *Sport in Australia* (Cambridge, 1994), pp. 40–57.
'Violence in Australian soccer: The ethnic contribution', in J. O'Hara, ed., *Ethnicity and soccer in Australia, (ASSH Studies in Sports History* series) 10 (Sydney, 1994).
'It's not cricket and perhaps it never was: Australian crowd and player behaviour', *The Sports Historian,* 14 (1994), pp. 3–12.
" Wogball' : Ethnicity and violence in Australian soccer', in R. Giulianotti and J. Williams, eds, *Games without frontiers: Football, identity and modernity* (London, 1994), pp. 207–24.
'Not playing the game but perhaps they never did: A historian's view of the behaviour of Australian cricketers', *The Journal of the Cricket Society,* (1994), pp. 5–10.

1995

'Sports violence in Australia: An attitude problem', *Sports Law Journal* (1995).
'Ethnicity and soccer in Australia', Working papers of University of Warwick Centre for the Study of Sport and Society.

1996

'Artifacts, archives and analysis, sports, museums and sports historians', Paper presented at the *First European Seminar of Sports History*, Rome, 29 Nov.–3 Dec., 1996. Published in A. Kruger and A. Teja, eds, *La comune eredita dello sport in Europa*, (1996), pp. 43–8.
'Wogball': Ethnicity and violence in Australian soccer since the 'forties', *Australian Studies*, (1996), pp. 119–29.
'History', in D. Levinson and K. Christensen, eds, *Encyclopedia of world sport* (Santa Barbara, 1996), pp. 414–18.
'Horseracing', in D. Levinson and K. Christensen, eds, *Encyclopedia of world sport* (Santa Barbara, 1996), pp. 441–50.

1997

'Les sportifs professionnels: Les jockeys', in C. Louveau and A. Waser, eds, *Sport et cite: Pratiques urbaines, spectacles* (Rouen, 1997), pp. 113–32.

1998

'A history of horse racing in south Australia: A statistical approach', *Australian Historical Statistics Bulletin*, 1 (1998), pp. 14–53.
with John Tolson 'Derailed: Railways and horse-racing revisited', *The Sports Historian*, 18 (1998), pp. 34–49.
'Facts and artifacts: Sports historians and sports museums', *Journal of Sport History*, 25 (2) (1998), pp. 268–82.
with Daryl Adair, 'Sport and Leisure', in G. Davidson, J. Hirst and S. Macintyre, eds, *The Oxford companion to Australian history* (Melbourne, 1998).
with John Coyle, J. Heath and Brian Naysmyth, 'Sweet FA: Fans' rights and club relocations', *Occasional Papers in Football Studies*, 1 (2) (1998), pp. 55–68.

1999

with S. Bailey *100 years of physical education* (Reading, 1999), 119 pp.
with Keith A.P. Sandiford, 'County cricketers benefit and testimonials, 1946–85', *International Journal of the History of Sport*, 16 (1999), pp. 87–116.

'Riding for a fall: The health hazards of professional jockeys in nineteenth and twentieth century British horseracing', in T. Terret, ed., *Sport and health in history* (Berlin, 1999), pp. 118–26.
'More than beer and skittles: Alcohol and sports in Britain', in A. Capanni and M. Marchioni, eds, Proceedings of the 4th *European Congress on Sports History*, pp. 66–77.

2000

'Still crazy after all those years: Continuity in a changing labour market for professional jockeys', *Contemporary British History*, (2000), pp. 115–45.
'Still crazy after all those years: Continuity in a changing labour market for professional jockeys', in D. Porter and A. Smith, eds, *For the love of the games: Amateurs and professionals in British sport since 1945* (London, 2000), pp. 115–45.
with Joyce Kay, 'Horse racing', in G. Jarvie and J. Burnett, eds, *Sport, Scotland and the Scots* (East Lothian, 2000), pp. 159–73
with Tony Collins, 'The pub, the drinks trade and the early years of modern football', *The Sports Historian*, 20 (2000), pp. 1–17.
with Richard W. Cox and Grant Jarvie, *Encyclopedia of British sport* (Oxford, 2000), 463 pp.
with Iris Middleton, 'Sport and the English leisure calendar', *Ludica*, (2000), pp. 65–82.
'The American invasion of the English turf: A study in sporting technological transfer', in J. Toleneer and R. Renson, eds, *Old borders, new borders, no borders* (Leuven, 2000), pp. 219–26.

2001

'Sports history', in K. Boyd, ed., *Encyclopedia of historians and activity* (London, 2001), pp. 1136–9.
'Gentlemen versus players', in F. Galligan, ed., *Sports history for 'A' level physical education* (Manchester, 2001).
'The sport of kings', in F. Galligan, ed., *Sports history for 'A' level physical education* (Manchester, 2001).
'Boxing', in C. Blakemore and S. Jennet, eds, *Oxford companion to the body* (Oxford, 2001), pp. 107–8.
'Horseracing', in K. Christensen, A. Guttmann and G. Pfister, eds, *International encyclopedia of women and sports* (New York, 2001), pp. 537–44.

2002

with Tim J.L. Chandler and Mike Cronin, *Sport and physical education: The key concepts* (London, 2002), 288 pp.
with Richard Holt and Peter N. Lewis, *The Professional Golfers' Association, 1901–2001: One hundred years of service to golf* (Droitwich, 2002), 252 pp.
with Tony Collins, *Mud, sweat and beers: A cultural history of sport and alcohol* (Oxford, 2002), 151 pp.
with Joyce Kay, *Weatherbeaten: Sport in the British climate* (Edinburgh, 2002), 219 pp.
with Richard W. Cox and Dave Russell, *Encyclopedia of British football* (London, 2002), 372 pp.

2003

with Iris Middleton, 'Horse racing and the *Yorkshire Racing Calendar* in the early eighteenth century', *Northern History*, 40 (2) (2003), pp. 259–76.
with John Tolson, 'Facilitation not revolution: Railways and British flat racing, 1830–1914', *Sport in History*, (2003), pp. 89–106.
'Reduced horsepower: The Jockey Club and the regulation of British horseracing', *Journal of Entertainment Law*, (2003), pp. 94–111.
'A modern sport? ' From ritual to record' in British horseracing', *Ludica*, (2003), pp. 125–39.

2004

'Sporting innovation: The American invasion of the British turf and links, 1895–1905', *Sport History Review*, 35 (2) (2004), pp. 122–36.
'Taking a Gamble or a racing certainty: Sports museums and public sports history', *Journal of Sports History*, 31 (2) (2004), pp. 176–91.
'70+ entries', in B. Harrison, ed., *Oxford dictionary of national biography* (Oxford, 2004).
'From histories to histories: An investigation of the development of the golf club as a British social institution', in T. Gonzolez Aja, ed., Proceedings of the 5th *European Congress on Sports History*, pp. 269–77.

2005

'Alcohol and the sportsperson: An anomalous alliance', *Sport in History*, 25 (3) (2005), pp. 390–411.

with Joyce Kay, 'Captains courageous: Gentlemen riders in British horse racing, 1866–1914', *Sport in History*, 26 (3) (2005), pp. 370–8.
'The beginnings of a commercial sporting culture in Britain, 1793–1850', *Sport History Review*, 36 (1) (2005), pp. 80–3.
with Tony Collins and John Martin, *Encyclopedia of British traditional rural sports* (London, 2005), 301 pp.
with Joyce Kay, *Encyclopedia of British horseracing* (London, 2005), 384 pp.

2006

with Joyce Kay, 'Under the weather: Combating the climate in British sport', *Sport in Society*, 1 (2006), pp. 94–108.
with Joyce Kay, 'Captains courageous gentlemen riders in British horse-racing, 1966–1914', *Sport in History*, 26 (3) (2006), pp. 37–385.
with Joyce Kay, 'Horseracing', in D. Levinson and K. Christensen, eds, *Berkshire encyclopedia of world sport* (Berkshire, 2006), pp. 758–66.
'Major Dick Hern' and 'Sir Arthur Gold', entries in L. Goldman, ed., *Oxford dictionary of national biography* (online).
'The economics of British horseracing' and the 'Evolution of major team sports', in W. Andreff and S. Szymanski, eds, *Handbook of economics of sport* (London, 2006), pp. 374–78 and 435–39.

2007

'Empiricist versus sociological history: Some comments on the "Civilizing Process" ', *Sport in History*, 27 (2) (2007), pp. 161–72.
'Playing with the rules: Influences on the development of regulation in sport', *International Journal of the History of Sport*, 24 (7) (2007), pp. 843–72.
with Joyce Kay, 'The rough and the fairway: Processes and problems in Ryder Cup team selection 1927–2006', *Studies in Physical Culture & Tourism*, 14 (1) (2007), pp. 27–36.
with Joyce Kay and J. George, 'Women to the fore: Gender accommodation and resistance at the British Golf Club before 1914', *Sporting Traditions*, 23 (2) (2007), pp. 79–98.
'Success for all: Australian's (un)sporting record', in A. Hassan, ed., *Australia studies now* (New Dehli, 2007), pp. 361–74.
'Horses, history and heritage: A comment on the state of the going', in C. McConville, ed., *Historians and racing* (Melbourne, 2007).

2008

'Ethics, money and sport this sporting Mammon', *Sporting Traditions*, 25 (1) (2008), pp. 114– 17.

'Successful workers or exploited labour?: Golf professionals and professional golfers in Britain, 1888–1914', *Economic History Review*, (2008), pp. 54–79.

Index